A Different Kind of War Story

A Different Kind of War Story

Carolyn Nordstrom

PENN

University of Pennsylvania Press

Philadelphia

Published by
University of Pennsylvania Press
Philadelphia, Pennsylvania 19104-6097

Library of Congress Cataloging-in-Publication Data

Time passes by and it never comes back
Too much violence
The unstoppable cannon
Stunned people running aimlessly
The moment has come
Kidnaps without days, hours, minutes
Helpless children
Who do not know where they came from, or where they will go
Who will justify this moment?
The regions of Coloa, Muaquia
Without people
because of these [war] criminals
My uncles and aunts killed without thought
How can one forget this moment?
How can we call peace?
Where is peace?
How can I return to my homeland?
Taking up arms?
Talking?
Nothing is impossible in this world
Everything depends on us
And it is we who will conquer
with Peace
—Santos

Contents

Acknowledgments

I remember one day in 1991, standing on a patch of level ground that served as a makeshift runway watching the cargo plane that was coming in to drop off its last load of the day fly off without landing. It had circled several times, and from my vantage point it appeared as if the pilots could not get the landing gear down. Night was rapidly approaching, and that was the last chance of a ride out that day, for there was a strictly enforced no night flying regulation. I was in the middle of Mozambique, and because of the frequency of night attacks in the area there was a no-overnight security rule for anyone who was not local to the area. The town I was visiting that day had seen the worst of war: it had been attacked, looted, and burned out any number of times by passing troops of both sides. People had few resources of any kind, and food was at a premium. I had few resources of my own at that moment. Expecting to be home by nightfall, I carried the anthropologist's tools: pens, paper, dictionary, mostly empty canteen, and two stale crackers.

I might have had to worry about the war, but I certainly did not have to worry about being taken care of that night. Within minutes of seeing the plane fly off, several people came up and clapped me on the back and said it looked like we could continue our conversations into the night. I was taken to a little mud hut and made at home. After dinner, the ten or twelve people sharing the hut and I sat around on the floor sharing stories. At one point the conversation turned to how little I carried with me. They shook their heads in mirthful disbelief as they looked at my pens and papers and notes: "Could I eat these if I had to run into the bush for a week to escape attack? Could I wrap up in them at night for warmth and protection from mosquitos?" War, they, explained, is a traveling companion, and one has to be prepared for it. It was a lesson I took to heart from that time on.

It is people such as these to whom I own a debt of gratitude; the people who made this book and all I learned about surviving war possible. They are people whose last names I don't even know, never writing their true names down in my notes for fear they might be confiscated. They are people I am unlikely, for the most part, ever to meet again: many were refugees who have returned to their homelands with peace.

* * *

Each chapter of this book begins with a poem. They are all written by Mozambican teenagers. I collected them one day when I asked a secondary school teacher in Zambezia if it might be all right if I invited his students in the 10th class to write a poem about their experiences of war and peace. He decided to put the request to the students, and they agreed. It was March 1991, the height of the war, and education had been seriously disrupted country-wide. In the best of circumstances, I would find the quality of the poems impressive.

I have chosen not to include the youth's surnames and the name of the school here. At the time I collected these poems, I explained to the students I would like to use their poetry in my work, and they readily agreed. But in the changing landscapes of politics, I am hesitant to assign names to these very powerful analyses. As this book demonstrates, poetry is politics.

I want to extend my gratitude to Professor Gregorio Firmino for helping me translate these poems from Portuguese into English while retaining their original style and phrasing.

* * *

A number of people made this work possible in Mozambique, though I hasten to say this work represents only my own views: Dr. Leonardo Simão, Ambassador Melissa Wells, the Election sponsors who hosted me in 1994 (particularly CCM, AWEPA, and Africa Fund), Julius Schlotthauer, and Mary Pat Selvaggio, to whom I will always be grateful for feeding me when I came down to Maputo from my research sites during the war years. My special thanks to the pilots of Interocean and Air Serve who gave me rides on cargo planes country-wide; to my Campo Base neighbors; and to the health care staff at the 4 Dezembro clinic in Quelimane, who adopted me. Closer to home, I would like to thank the Institute for International Studies at the University of California, Berkeley for hosting me and the MIGISS (MacArthur) grant; and the the United States Institute of Peace for their research and writing grant. I extend my thanks also to the Peace Research Centre and the Department of International Relations at Australian National University who hosted me as a visiting fellow during the writing of several of these chapters. I greatly appreciate the colleagueship of Gregorio Firmino,

Joel Chiziane, Chip Oliver, Humberto Cossa, Anna Loforte, Isabel Casimiro, Gil Lauriciano, Allen Isaacman, Micalena Martins, Jorge Tinga,
Jose Basilio, Katia Airola, and Tamara Jane, who all added something to
this book. And my mother, Patricia Clark, who actually flew out to visit
me in the midst of the war. My special thanks to my editors: Patricia
Smith and Professor Cynthia Mahmood for showing me that publishing
can be both dignified and fun.

And most of all I thank Keith, who journeyed with me from the thick
of fighting in Mozambique to the thick of writing in academia.

Prologue

Why
Mothers crying
Instead of smiling
Brides, sisters full of despair
Instead of hope

Why
Tears on the faces
Abandoned children

Why in the earth
The seed dies
Before it germinates

But don't ask me
Don't ask me
Who was
His race and age
It was the blood of humanity

Don't ask me
The color of the dream
That used to be dazzling
                —Arminda

Doorway to war, 1996. Photo by Carolyn Nordstrom.

Behind the printed word and the theories in a book is a more profound reality. It might be called the heart of a discipline: that which motivates an author to seek out a particular study, and the principles that guide that author in her or his quest. This study is about violence, it is about creativity, and, in a curious way, it is about hope. It has not always been so.

I inadvertently began studying political violence in July 1983 on the streets of Sri Lanka, when I was caught in the middle of the seven-day rioting that took more than one thousand lives and destroyed one-sixth of the country's infrastructure. I remember my first thought upon watching a mob surge toward me. I knew I had to decide how to act, and I racked my memory for everything I had heard or read on mobs and riots to help me. I realized that nothing I had read or seen in the literature or media presentations on mobs and political violence resembled what I was observing. I felt momentarily angry that people produced "truths" about subjects from the safety of their offices, and that I might get into serious trouble because these "truths" did not match the realities at hand and thus provided no workable blueprint for analysis and action. At that time I was conducting medical anthropology research and had not specialized in issues of socio-political violence. Looking back now, after years of teaching and researching political violence, I know the excellent analyses that exist on the topic, and that they exist side-by-side with tomes whose theoretical conclusions concerning field realities are grounded in personal politics and supposition, not in fieldwork.

In trying to comprehend what I had seen during the riots, I strove to understand the larger dynamics fueling socio-political violence and its impact on people and their societies. As the ethnic tensions in Sri Lanka crystallized into escalating guerrilla war and counterinsurgency following the riots, in the north with the Tamil separatist movement and then in the south with the Sinhalese leftist insurgency, my research expanded along these lines.

Because there was little information available on how to conduct ethnography in violent areas, I did not have preconceptions of what was or was not possible. In 1985, becoming increasingly frustrated over the lack of representative information on the Tamil situation, I went alone to the Jaffna Peninsula and then to Trincomalee, both of which were undergoing severe fighting at the time. I point out the concept of the "possible" as, when I arrived in Jaffna, I was taken to the headquarters of several local Tamil leaders who wanted to know how I had gotten into Jaffna. I was told that, except for one BBC correspondent, I was the only researcher to have entered Jaffna in well over a year. When I told them I had simply boarded a train unchallenged and taken it to the final destination, Jaffna, they shook their heads in amazement. Apparently I had not "learned" the prevailing conceptions that it was impossible to go from the Sinhalese south to the Tamil north. This conception was so pervasive that no military checkpoints stopped people from traveling to the north. I also did not really understand the dangers possible—both to me and to people with me. I encountered several situations where luck, quick reflexes, and the foresight of those around me protected me from physical violence I had not anticipated. While the data I collected were invaluable, hindsight has led me to conclude that our discipline would be well advised to provide its researchers with a more realistic and critical methodology than I first took with me to the field.

Like the riots, the stories I collected and the massacres and ruins I saw in the north of Sri Lanka showed how the field reality is often quite different from the pictures conveyed in the literature and the media. I was quite optimistic during this time, convinced that if ethnography could show the true dynamics of violence, then the dangerous processes fomenting domination, repression, and dirty war atrocities would begin to be undermined.

I became interested in exploring the differences and similarities in regional responses to socio-political violence and those characteristics of war shared across geography and culture in the contemporary world. In 1988 I began a comparative study of warfare in Mozambique (Nordstrom 1997). Mozambique is in many ways an opposite case scenario from Sri Lanka: through the 1980s the Mozambican government was Marxist-Leninist, and the primary human rights violators, the right-wing rebels, enjoyed little internal popular support. The war in Mozambique did not follow strict ethnic lines, nor was it confined to certain contested areas. The entire country suffered the ravages of war, and little ethnography had been conducted on either Mozambique or the war there. Yet in certain vital ways Sri Lanka and Mozambique did not appear so different. The sheer numbers of civilians wounded, maimed, terrorized, and murdered and the devastating impact such terror-warfare has on people, societies, and cultures at the frontlines of war are shared across the two nations.

The year 1988 was the most difficult period of my research and the period during which I was most filled with a sense of hopelessness. In that year, I traveled to both Mozambique and Sri Lanka to conduct research. On the way from Mozambique to Sri Lanka, I decided to stop in Somalia as an ethnographic respite between two demanding warzones. By sheer coincidence, I arrived as the civil war broke out. Through a bureaucratic mistake, I was given an entry visa when foreigners were expelled en masse from the country. When I returned home I had seen three wars in one year. I had seen friends killed, strangers massacred, and villages obliterated. The words and emotions of the survivors flowed through me like a river that never seemed to end, flooding with new violences upon old. I had repeatedly seen the sheer nihilation wrought by terror-warfare: its ability to tear apart lives, dismantle societies, deconstruct culture. I learned that, at least in the short run, ethnography did not readily stem the flow of violence. I also learned that studying violence can take a considerable toll on a person.

I returned to Mozambique in 1989, 1990–1991, 1994, and 1996. I avoided the capital city as much as possible in favor of collecting first-hand experience and second-hand accounts of the processes of war in the villages and towns directly affected by violence. And as I listened to people talk about how they worked to reconstruct their world in the face of a war intent on destroying it, I realized that, in the midst of terror-warfare, ordinary citizens were undertaking a remarkable process of revitalization: mourning and healing wounds both physical and emotional, combating the insidious hegemony of violence in their daily lives, and repairing ruptures in cultural viability maimed by the atrocities of lethal conflict. It was these observations of the creativity people employ in rebuilding their worlds destroyed by warfare that renewed my optimism that violence is not "always already" in our societies, but can be stemmed. The picture was not all rosy. There were those who sold out their loved ones for power and privilege, who capitalized on violence for their own personal gain, who internalized and reproduced the violence to which they had been exposed. But the truth is that most did not. Indigenous civil traditions operated quietly in all this chaos to dismantle systems of violence. These traditions are deeply entrenched in everyday culture, and average people worked to solve daily realities while the overarching peace negotiations of the power brokers bogged down in rhetoric, vested interests, and bureaucratese. I do not mean to denigrate formal peace accords, for the resolution of war on an institutional level is critical, but to point out that they do little to reach into the everyday life of the people living the harsh reality of frontline warfare. People on the frontlines generate their own solutions.

Chapter 1
Creativity, Violence, and the Scholar

The Last Assault

It was in a beautiful afternoon
when the sun was just
beyond the horizon
Life was totally calm
One and other people
were wandering in the sandy
streets of that beautiful and calm village
lined with pretty houses
shops, restaurants
simple residences
Suddenly
A feminine cry
broke the silence
that was in the village
Then
a rainstorm of bullets
fell on the village
villagers started to run around
disoriented
in the large streets
looking for refuge
Some hours later, everything stopped
the village was deserted
in the streets
were the bodies of old people, children
and women, lifeless
It was the last assault.

—Aldirro

"Let the Children Dance." Dancing in Zambezia province, 1987. Photo by Joel Chiziane.

This is a book about war, and about the remarkable creativity average people bring to the fore in surviving violence and rebuilding humane worlds. More than anything else, the book is an exploration of the human condition. When I began to study war, I could not predict where investigations would take me. Generations of traditional political studies have mapped the terrain of war through the offices and institutions of (predominately elite) political and military officials. Yet when I began to follow the threads of war they took me to the center of civilian societies, where the vast majority of wars today are fought. The threads wound through stories of jackals who sold information and people to the highest bidder as well as to soldiers. They wound through average civilians who risked their lives for others in the middle of battlezones as well as to formal governmental and nongovernmental organizations working with emergency relief. Most important, the investigation into war led me to people on the frontlines who insisted that I understand the nature and culture of violence, not as it was fictionally portrayed in media and literary accounts but as they experienced it. Because the encounter with violence is a profoundly personal event, it is fundamentally linked to processes of self-identity and the politics of personhood—for ultimately, war victims have taught me, violence is about the destruction of culture and identity in a bid to control (or crush) political will. People at the epicenters of violence demonstrated to me that resistance emerges at the first sign of oppression, and is most powerfully coded in re-creating culture and identity against the vicissitudes of violence and oppression. It is in creativity, in the fashioning of self and world, that people find their most potent weapon against war.

When I first began writing about war, I found it surprising that it spoke so clearly to contemporary issues of core cultural processes and personal identity. I found it equally surprising that wars in what many consider more remote parts of the world's power grid illuminated key dynamics of contemporary warfare in the world as a whole. In fact, I first began writing notes for this book with the paragraph: There is a fundamental irony in the observation that war can illuminate some of the most profound questions of personal endeavor and cultural creation. It is often in what we relegate to the margins of life process and theory— violence and the unspeakable—that speaks most fundamentally about core aspects of human existence. "Truth," Michael Jackson (1989:187) writes, "is on the margins. . . . It makes its appearance fleetingly, when systems collapse and dogmas are exploded."

I have since come to view the assumption that there are centers and margins of politics and power as dangerously misleading. Either naiveté or arrogance leads people to assume that what takes place in Europe, Moscow, or Beijing is more relevant, world-setting, and important than what takes place in Sri Lanka, Mozambique, Guatemala, or Georgia. Having conducted on-site research at the epicenters of wars over three continents and a decade and a half, I have learned that the whole concept of local wars, whether central or peripheral, is largely a fiction.

Massive interlinked and very international war-related industries make war possible in any location in the world. I have seen the same weapons vendors, mercenaries, military advisors, supplies, and military training manuals—both illicit and formal—circle the globe, moving from one war to the next. Politicians, military and paramilitary troops, and diplomats meet and talk across virtually all boundaries of nation and state. Business salespeople and blackmarketeers sell the items necessary to outfit troops and launch a battle. Media specialists create a cultural diaspora of every war-related ethos from the Rambo figure to BBC broadcasts reaching the farthest regions of the globe. Propagandists the world over exchange information on how to make casualties palatable to noncombatants and human rights organizations. Everything from development dollars to human rights organizations, from covert operations specialists to illegal industries that gain from conflict, builds on the linkages of these networks that shape war and peace as we know it today.

And in all this a powerful set of cultural prescriptions develops around the concept and conduct of war. It is at once international and localized: as people and goods move from war to war, through multinational industries and negotiating centers in "peace-locales" to the frontlines, an ethos of war is continuously being forged and refashioned to meet the most current worldwide conditions. Cultures of militarization, violence, resistance, humanitarian aid, and peacebuilding move fluidly around the globe, dipping deep into the most central and remote corners of war and politics alike. This global flux of information, tactics, weapons, money, and personnel brokers tremendous power throughout the warzones of the world. The examples supporting this are legion. To give but one, when a new torture technique is introduced into a country, that same technique can be found throughout the world in several days' time. Obviously transmitted with the physical techniques of harming bodies is a complex culture that specifies who can and should be targeted for torture, how and for what reasons, and to what end. The culture extends to such considerations as how such torture is politically justified, and justified to international bodies concerned with human rights abuses. Kevin Clements writes that there are over 70,000 treaties insuring human rights (1992: 10). Considering the fact that in the world today 90 percent of war's casualties are civilians, and that more children than soldiers are killed in war, getting around Geneva Conventions is a significant part of the modern war enterprise.

I have also come to question traditional assumptions that people experience life in uniquely cultural-specific ways, that what happens to individuals in World War II Europe, in Bosnia, in Mozambique, or in the Amazon Basin is fundamentally different and that these experiences are ultimately incommensurable, incomparable, unique. There *is* something unique about being Mozambican, Bosnian, or of the Amazon region, but there is as well a shared experience of coeval political violence. Contemporary theory, moving away from static notions of identity and culture, is recognizing the importance of seeing people and cultures as coessentially both unique and resonating with the human condition in myriad complex ways. To give a concrete example: if military strategists share torture tactics throughout the world, then there is something victims share in the experience of torture in the most profound ways. Cultures of militarization and the ontological experiences of being victimized by militarized actions span cultural divisions based on national and ethnic identities to link people in warzones throughout the world.

If dirty-war tactics can be forged and shared internationally, so too can resistances to oppressive violence. I am convinced that the ways Mozambican civilians creatively redefined violence as acts of resistance and peacebuilding can stand as models for other noncombatant communities suffering the ravages of war with few resources to fight back. In fact, Mozambicans' sophisticated understandings of the processes of non/violence can help experts rethink the very notions underlying current conflict resolution theories and practices. Survivors of violence have long recognized this fluid cultural construction of violence and its resolution. Like Native Americans and Aborigines from the United States and Australia who meet with Africans to work on the problem of dismantling cultures of violences and like the Madres of Latin America and Gabriella in the Philippines who go to meet with women's groups in former Yugoslavia to forge solutions to both political and gender violence, researchers like ourselves can also recognize the fluid international constructions of peace and conflict, that the experiences of one can resonate with the experiences of many others.

*   *   *

Writing about violence is not a simple matter. The subject is fraught with assumptions, presuppositions, and contradictions. Like power, violence is essentially contested: everyone knows it exists, but no one agrees on what actually constitutes the phenomenon. Vested interests, personal history, ideological loyalties, propaganda, and a dearth of firsthand experience or information ensure that many published definitions of frontline violence are powerful fictions and negotiated half-truths. One of the more entrenched debates surrounding violence concerns the question whether it is an intrinsic aspect of human nature and society. During the years I have researched socio-political violence, I have spent half a decade conducting on-site ethnographic work in warzones, and I am convinced that violence is not "always already" in people or in their communities. Like all cultural products, it is a potential that is socially and culturally constructed by specific people within the context of particular histories toward certain ends. Warfare is, as Margaret Mead (1964) says, "only an invention." Yet where, exactly, should researchers enter into the study of this "invention"? War is a manifold phenomenon representing heterogeneous cultures. Many realities define the cultural construction of war. There is the political reality: the doctrines, deeds, and behind-the-scenes machinations of power brokers. There is the military reality: the strategies and loyalties of commanders and the actions and opinions of soldiers. There is the intellectual reality, bantered about in the coffeeshops and halls of academia. There are the front-line vignettes of journalists.

And there is the reality of life on the frontlines. This reality represents the most profound aspect of war, and the most silenced. The truth of war for those who live in its midst is a far more encompassing reality than one of battles, casualties, and survival skills. It shapes the very context of being. These enduring realities of war resonate through the words of a Mozambican woman who, in the middle of a conversation on helping the recent victims of an attack in her town, told me:

> I don't know if anyone really knows war until it lives inside of them. A person can come in and see the war, fear the war, be scared of the violence—but their life, their very being, is not determined by the war. This is my country, the country of my parents, my family, my friends, my future. And the war has gotten into all of these. I know everyone has suffered a loss in this war: a family member killed, a loved one captured and never heard of again. But it goes much deeper than this, to the very heart of the country, to my very heart. When I walk on the road, I carry nervousness with me as a habit, as a way of being. When I hear a sharp noise, I do not stop and ask "what is that?" like a normal person. I start and fear my life is in jeopardy. And I do this for my family as well. Whenever I am parted from them I have this gnawing worry: will I ever see them again, is something terrible happening to them at this moment? I cringe for my very land, soaked in blood so it can't produce healthily. This lives in me—it is a part of my being, a constant companion, a thing no one can understand if they only enter here and worry about their own safety from one day to the next. I want to leave Mozambique, to go away and work or study—I want to get away from all this, to run from it for a little while. But the

even stronger feeling is that I can't stand to leave my country, for I can never leave the war. I will carry the war with me, and that inflames within me a passion to be here, to be a part of my country and help even in its worst moments. For if I leave, when I come home my most cherished things may be ashes, what is a part of me may have died, and I wouldn't have been here to know, to have tried to do something. The passion that makes me want to flee my country's problems binds me to my country so that I can't bear to leave.

Frontline realities are as nuanced as the international associations that make war possible. I have already pointed out that, contrary to popular assumptions, war is not primarily about adult male soldiers doing battle. Combatants and noncombatants cannot be cast in generic categories, nor can the lines between them be clearly demarcated. Children and adults, women and men, fight and die, some in uniforms and some as civilians in wars they neither started nor support. The battlefields are home to rogues and thieves as well as to the honorable, to old and young, rich and poor, political and apolitical. Together, they forge the reality of war and peace. All their stories are woven together in daily life on the frontlines. In this book I will try to do justice to representing war by weaving these stories in prose. I do so with the recognition that no one voice is more important than another. The experiences of the village woman who has just suffered an attack is as crucial to understanding war as is the voice of the soldiers that carried out the attack. The ordeals of a five-year-old child in a battlezone are as meaningful as the policy proclamations of a political elite. The jackal who sells accurate information to grieving family members on the whereabouts of kidnapped kin for profit and the soldier who protects a village from attack and then loots it himself are contradictions as painful to people in warzones as are the opposing military factions. To understand the processes of war and peacemaking is to give voice to all of these interconnected experiences.

Ethnography can be conducted at any of these levels of warfare, from the broad systems of international militarization that stoke specific conflicts to the experiences of people in the midst of fighting. But in order to be representative, ethnographic analyses should be conducted at the centers, and not just the sidelines, of conflicts. For ultimately the doctrines of the politico-military elite, the exposés of journalists, and the critical theories of scholars are wor(l)ds apart from the experiences of those living and dying at the centers of war. To include research at the epicenters of violence involves a number of responsibilities above and beyond those associated with more traditional ethnography: responsibilities to the fieldworker's safety, to that of her or his informants, and to the theories that help forge attitudes toward the reality of violence both expressed and experienced.

This research has prompted me to rethink questions concerning fundamental definitions of what constitutes violence, terror, knowledge, culture, and survival as both ethnographic realities and theoretical issues. It has led me to delve into questions concerning a responsible and responsive ethnography of warfare and to explore the relationships of self, identity, socio-cultural process, and power as they are highlighted in the deconstructive environment of war. And it has challenged me to understand the presence of self and creativity that average people exhibit in both surviving military violence and forging new worlds to replace those shattered by war.

*   *   *

Writing people's experiences of violence is even more difficult than "writing about violence" per se. Unlike some topics, violence cannot be separated from its action. Political violence is done to someone, by someone. When we speak of this, we are entrusted with telling someone's personal experiences of violence. We can do yet further violence in the telling. Every time a bullet is made, there is a chance it will be fired at a person. Every time someone pulls a trigger, there is a chance that bullet (or grenade, or landmine, or mortar, or bomb, or chemical weapon) will tear into a person's flesh, and, more than 90 percent of the time in the world today, that person will be an unarmed civilian. With each casualty there is a world of loved ones, enemies, and associates who will feel this bullet in their lives as well, sometimes in devastating ways.

Treating a person's experiences of violence with dignity is arguably the most important part of studying and writing about violence, and it is certainly the most complicated. This question weaves through the entire book. But let me introduce it here. Sixteen million people lived in Mozambique at the time I was there. A full half had been directly affected by the war. The people I met, spoke with, or read about in all my time there are an exceedingly small fraction of that group. The people directly quoted in this book may number little more than a hundred. Each met violence in a profoundly personal way. How responsible, how representative, can any generalization be?

It is not enough to say that Mozambique has more than a dozen major language and cultural groupings. Nor is it sufficient to say that women, men, children, farmers, politicians, refugees, soldiers, the wounded, and the dying all "lived" the war differently. Clearly a woman who has been shot by soldiers feels the war differently from a man who has seen his village burned. But in truth, violence and the creativity necessary to withstand it successfully are ultimately, and intensely, personal. I will not experience being shot or tortured the same way you or anyone else would. My history, my personality, my circumstances, my physical and social environment of family, friends, and enemies make it a uniquely individual reality.

To bridge these disparate but equally powerful realities—the pervasive fact of war in a country and the profoundly personal experience of violence—I follow individuals' encounters of war with an ear and eye to understanding what cultures of violence, survival, and creative resistance were shared by people throughout the warzone(s) of Mozambique. In order to do this, as I explain in detail in Chapter 3, I introduce an "ethnography of a warzone." This is an experimental methodology based on studying a process (political violence and creative resistance) rather than a study based in a circumscribed locale (the war as it occurred in the town of Quelimane, or the province of Zambezia). To study "war" and "peacebuilding" is not the same as studying war and peacebuilding in a particular place among a set community. Thus this study is grounded in a *topic* and a *process* rather than a *place*. War is about flux, and this approach works to report on that flux as realistically as possible.

Whether in Mozambique or the world, soldiers enter new battlefields, refugees flee, healers tend broken bodies, and teachers try to continue teaching children. Mothers and fathers seek the best possible means to protect their families from the latest terror tactics and rogue troops, soldiers share rations and strategies, politicians bend ideologies to fit battlefield realities. Looters follow troops, traders follow looters, and arms merchants make sure the cycle of attack and defeat can continue yet again. And through all this, each person talks with the next, and together they forge a means of thinking about and acting within a warzone. These conversations cross borders of gender, age, language, social, cultural, and politico-military associations. Some people agree with others, some disagree, but a vast interrelated compendium of information is gathered, shared, and learned.

This shared information on war and surviving war linking people war-wide constitutes shared culture(s). Every piece of information is encoded with values, orientations, ethics, strategies for survival, and basic concepts of humanity or inhumanity. Each person experiencing the war in any of its guises and then relating that experience—in word, action, or reaction— tells a war story, one as individual and personal as that of the protagonist. But the telling always has listeners, who then incorporate what they have heard into their own experiences. These *contes* of war and peace are carried through spoken words and prose, poetry and song, dance and fighting, fleeing and protecting; through parable, myth, and ideology; through life and death. All, taken together, begin to form cultures of violence and survival that shape Mozambicans' lives—not as institutions that can be interacted with or avoided but as facts of life and daily realities. These cultures contain the information necessary to sustain life in life-threatening conditions. They are reaffirmed and revitalized in every conversation, every action, people share in war and peace. War is fought, resisted, survived, and defeated by these cultures.

It is this shared culture across all the many differences defining life and living that interests me in this book. The citizens in Mozambique demonstrated the most sophisticated country-wide conflict resolution practices and ideologies I have observed anywhere in the world. This shared culture, this cross-fertilization of ideas extending beyond local and regional communities, in Allen Isaacman's words to me, "created the conditions for new ways of coping and knowing" (personal communication). To say this is not to say that every Mozambican helped forge the cultures of peace that finally brokered the war's end. Nor is it to say everyone in society participated in or upheld shared principles or had the same set of experiences. But it is to say that a culture of peacebuilding can exist across remarkable differences throughout a nation to broker the end of a war.

The differences among people are as vital to understanding cultural processes as are the shared cultures. People on the frontlines of fighting applied available cultural wisdom on surviving the war in a far more immediate and practiced fashion than those living in relative zones of peace. Various communities prepared for violence differently. It was not unusual to see the inhabitants of one town avoid the ravages of war due to careful escape planning while those of a neighboring town suffered numerous casualties by running directly into the soldiers' paths without forethought. Equally, people in the matrilineal north of Mozambique deal with land tenure battles and children orphaned by war differently from those in the patrilineal south of the country. These differences ripple across the whole of social life. For example, Save the Children UK in Mozambique found less incidence of malnutrition in children in the matrilineal areas of the country. In the upheaval and deprivations of war, these societies channeled more scarce resources toward children.

Yet as different as the inhabitants are in a war, they are linked by the warzone cultures I describe throughout the remaining chapters. These cultures move beyond individual survival actions. These many acts coalesce into political movements in their most fundamental sense and constitute, in essence, politics in the making. My goal in this book is to explore the widely shared cultures of violence and the profound creativity that defeats, not one side or the other, but violence altogether—while attending to the very personal experience of violence and peacebuilding in people's lives. The fact that many people have expressed surprise at the truly national extent of the shared systems of creative resistance to the war among the citizens of Mozambique leads me to conclude that social scientists are just beginning to crack the codes of creative worldbuilding as they are instituted by populations at large.

Creativity

Perhaps the most surprising aspect of this research to me was the tremendous creativity average people employed in surviving and working to resolve the war in Mozambique. The legacy of Hobbes was strong in my education before I began to study political violence. According to this model the natural state of humans is a violent one, the famous "war of all against all." In the absence of government controls, people revert to a "natural state," and this is an aggressively self-serving one. For Hobbes, "people" meant exactly that: a generic and largely undifferentiated mass guided by societies' elites. I had worked in several warzones before arriving in Mozambique in 1988, but the level of destruction I encountered there was the most severe I had seen. It was certainly a rich site to test Hobbes, though at the time that was not my intention. Rarely do researchers have the chance to study societies completely bereft of all formal governmental and social institutions, of all the formal controls Hobbes and his legacy posit are crucial to a functioning society. In some of the districts of Mozambique, I encountered precisely this situation. Renamo was infamous for social and civil destruction (Minter 1995; Vines 1991; Gersony 1988): all formal institutions and their personnel—hospitals, schools, administration—and more informal necessities—trade routes, crops, emergency supplies—were heavily targeted.

I visited a number of towns and districts where no formal institutions were intact and no formal governing controls in place, where battles had stopped all trade and supplies, where crops had been razed and villages leveled. This was not unusual in wartime Mozambique: fully half of the entire population of sixteen million people were directly affected by the war, a quarter fled their homes as refugees, and one million people, the vast majority noncombatants, were killed in a decade of fighting. By Hobbes's reckoning, the countryside should have been embroiled in a "dog-eat-dog" mentality of unstructured survival. But I found quite the opposite: *most* people were actively dedicated to rebuilding their lives and societies, working with others to find solutions to the deprivations of war and instituting conflict resolution measures at the local level.

Looking at the level of destruction wrought in Mozambique, it is easy to assume that Hobbes is right, that war conditions breed cultures of violence that dictate everyday norms. But more than two years of research in Mozambique demonstrated to me that in fact a very few can wreak tremendous destruction on the many. In addition to the one million killed, one-third of all hospitals and schools were destroyed; and the damage to economic viability is incalculable. And all this by only 30,000 to 60,000 troops.

Far from finding a dog-eat-dog survival mentality in the absence of all institutional and governing supports, I found most people operating according to a strong code of humane ethics. It is a profound ethics; it is an ethics intricately linked with the constitution of self and world when both are under attack. Much has been written on the cultural construction of reality: that being human entails more than anything else creating the cultural worlds we live in and endowing them with significance. Yet that research has been conducted for the most part in societies with functioning institutions. In that context, people do not create worlds anew but fine-tune the ones they are born into. Very few empirical data exist to show how people's worlds are newly crafted. How does cultural creativity take that first step into constructing the wholly new? At the epicenters of war, this question is particularly pressing: if people rebuild their lives and worlds as they were, they will simply be open to re-attack. Survival, then, involves crafting a new universe of meaning and action.

The creativity I saw in Mozambique goes beyond a discussion of world-building. It is a core survival strategy and a profound form of resistance to political violence and oppression. In fact it is, in my experience, one of the most sophisticated mechanisms of asserting personal agency and political will in the face of intolerable repression. Interestingly, contrary to Hobbes's notion that the formation and governing of (a naturally unruly) society is in the hands of elites (and that civilian war casualties are hapless victims), I found innovative solutions to society and war were instituted largely by average citizens who found themselves on the frontlines of political violence they neither started nor supported. Society and culture were sculpted from the ground up—a process invisible to Hobbes and his proponents who write far from civilians' experiences of war on the frontlines.

This creativity, this worldbuilding in the face of violent onslaught, is not a simple thing. It involves life-threatening risks and demands courage and skill. Because examples are presented throughout the book, a single example will suffice here. When troops besieged a town, in addition to sacking buildings and destroying infrastructure, they often persecuted and killed health care workers, teachers, administrators, and other service people. I talked to scores of people who said that, as Renamo rebels approached their community, they waylaid a person of the area and asked for the names and locations of local officials, nurses, healers, and teachers. Social service facilities were often ransacked, and supplies and medicines taken back to the soldiers' bases. When troops came near a town, many service personnel fled as refugees before the soldiers arrived. Those who stayed behind did so at considerable risk. One such person sticks in my mind. She was a health care practitioner in an area under siege. The towns in the area had been heavily targeted, and most of the resources and infrastructure destroyed. During the first severe attack on her town, she ran to the clinic and grabbed as many supplies and medicines as she could easily run with, and then, with the other survivors, fled to the bush to hide until the soldiers left. The soldiers had her name and were looking for her, other townspeople warned her, and they recommended she flee the area. But she decided to stay. Because the area remained in the path of the frontlines and troops passed by continually, she lived something of a nomadic existence, fearing to stay in her family home as it would be easy for the soldiers to find her. She buried the medicines and supplies outside town and held "clinic hours" there. As in any dangerous situation, well-established communication networks transmit survival information, including where health care and medicine can be obtained. The townspeople kept her secret from troops and brought her patients ranging from children with physical illnesses to victims of gunshot wounds. She would change the spot in which she buried the medicines and held clinics every so often so that it would be harder for troops to locate her.

There was nothing forcing this woman to stay and treat patients. The town was cut off from outside help, and the Ministry of Health could neither pay her nor provide support. In fact, in these embattled times, they would not even have known whether she was in the town or had fled to a refugee camp. Even the townspeople counseled her to leave. But in her act she provided much more than medicines and health care.

It is difficult to conceptualize a society bereft of all institutions that ground social life. Without their houses and crops, without their schools and clinics and markets, people's lives simply do not progress in a known way. Terror-warfare is predicated on the assumption that if all the supports that make people's lives meaningful are taken from them, they will be incapacitated by the ensuing disorder; whether hapless victims or Hobbesian animals, they will be shorn of political agency.

But terror-warfare is defeated by the thousands of people like this health care practitioner, for this story is repeated a thousandfold across Mozambique. In the sheer act of remaining in the face of danger, they defy danger, and defying equates to a sense of control. In setting up "clinics" order is reestablished in a disordered world. Compassion and creative peacebuilding are supported over fear and warfare. Identity is asserted in creative resistance, and it is reaffirmed with each person's encounter with others, each story of people's courage and services. Hiding medicines successfully is a taunt in the face of the firepower and intelligence networks of the military. Success is a political victory. Society is reforged with a humane component. Hobbes is shown to be mistaken.

A Disclaimer on the Relationship Between Violence and Creativity

This analysis has been developed in the context of a warzone, but it is important to note that violence and creativity are not naturally linked. Destruction may necessitate creativity as a survival mechanism, but creativity does not in any way depend on violence. A broad epistemological current (with which I disagree), runs through western philosophical theory which posits an association between violence and creativity. In this view, like the phoenix rising from the ashes, from the realm of the deconstitutive and the destructive comes the spark of re-creation. Functional philosophies that sought to find the functions of violence have largely been discredited as supporting dangerous hegemonies, but the idea that violence can serve as the font of creative purpose remains entrenched in social theory. This notion draws on any number of philosophical traditions. From Heidegger's claim that in the shattering moments of angst Dasein finds its "ownmost" potential to the existential notion that in nothingness and in the meaninglessness of the absurd the self reconstitutes self-ness, the meeting with the specter of death is cast as the most powerful force of self-enlightenment. When philosophical theory accepts this tenet, a contentious set of factors comes into play. Whereas most authors would deny a functionalist view of violence, the function of violence is nonetheless asserted. To make violence the font of creativity essentializes and naturalizes violence.

This question is surrounded with a series of ironic entanglements. My research on people's encounters with severe violence in warzones clearly demonstrates that, to survive, people are forced to create. Those who do not, do not survive. But it is a long step to conclude that it is in violence and the encounter with death that people become their most creative. As people in warzones frequently told me: yes, to survive violence we must be creative, but these are not the best conditions under which to be creative. To create in the face of violence is to end up where you started: a world destroyed and a world rebuilt. Truly to create is to bring in a wholly new world—to add something that has not been before. It is not the space of death, but the will to create, that is utmost. And that will to create, not to destroy, is what most people in warzones consider fundamental to the human condition.

Against the Theoretical Taming of Violence

When I was a kid, I went to the state fair with my brother and wandered into a so-called freak show, where one of the performers was a profoundly deformed young man who was billed as "Lobster Boy." Before removing a cloak to display his twisted limbs to the crowd, he said in a plaintive voice, "Please don't laugh at me." There was a silent pause while he removed his wrap. Almost before it dropped to the ground, my brother began to shake uncontrollably, struggling to stifle a guffaw. He sputtered for a moment, and before he could cover his mouth he let out a loud, explosive hoot. Everyone gasped, and I quickly looked to the performer to assess the damage caused by my brother's indiscretion. To my surprise, his face was strangely calm, and it seemed to me that it was briefly crossed by a flicker of satisfaction—as if he knew full well the response his plea for pity was destined to provoke. I realized then that Lobster Boy understood us completely. By showing us his pathetic state, he revealed far more about his audience than about himself. (McKusick and Tronnes 1992:97–98)

The story of Lobster Boy reminds me of the story of violence writ large. Not the actual experience of violence, but how we approach violence in western theory and conception. It is my experience that much of how we perceive violence, write about violence, and respond to others' presentations on violence has less to do with the actual violence than it does with our own personality and idiosyncratic worldview. There is a curious irony in the popular epistemologies that surround violence in the west. Violence is presented as something both integral to the human condition and as antithetical to it. This portrayal has led to a tendency to fetishize violence, fueling a fascination with the topic while banishing it to the outer margins of human life and everyday reality. It is cast as the excessive, the abnormal, the other, and yet as intrinsic. We are taught to ascribe tremendous power to violence, and then to fear that power to the extent that we seek to remove it from "our worlds," from those places where we live our lives. We seek to tame it. Such theorizing, of course, has nothing to do with the actuality of violence. As Allen Feldman points out:

Violence and culture were conceived as external to each other, as alters, and not as historically complicit. To write about violence and culture one had to create an insulated space protecting the latter from the former. It was preferable to practice a kind of invisible ink writing, to do away with violence, erasing it in the very course of accounting for it. (1994:5)

This conception can most clearly be seen in the curious fact that most writing about violence in western theory never deals with actual violence. People write about writing about violence; they write about second-hand historical narratives of violence; they write about what people say about violence—all as if this represented the *actual experience* of violence. But in most of these cases people are writing from the safety of a nonviolent situation. The irony is not that people write about writing about violence—for this is as viable a technique as any—but that this is unquestioningly accepted as representing violence, real violence. As Feldman notes, we have erased the actual fact of violence in the very act of accounting for it. What results is not a true discussion of violence, but a taming of it into something we can manage. It is no longer violence per se, but it is safe.

When the raw fact of violence is silenced in discussion, what emerges is not theory but worldview. Perhaps in employing this style of analysis people try to make the world a livable place for themselves by controlling what they fear is uncontrollable, speaking what they have been taught is unspeakable. Of course, there is no reason to believe that violence is either uncontrollable or unspeakable. But in banishing real violence from theory people ensure that it remains uncontrollable and unspeakable—for how can we control that which we do not address directly; how can we speak of that which we have banished from our analyses?

There is a powerful yet often unstated cultural perception that hearing about violence is, in some curious existential inversion, worse than enduring it. Consider, for example, the book *Requiem for a Woman's Soul*, the story of a young woman suffering the most despicable torture under the hands of the military during Argentina's dirty war. The story revolves around the fact that a woman, Susanna, documents her experience of torture on scraps of paper which a friend smuggles out of prison. A box of these scraps is left with her priest, who decides to sort and transcribe all the bits of text into a diary. As the priest reads of the horrors to which Susanna is subjected, he descends into stark depression and finally madness. Susanna, however, keeps her wits, her integrity, and her will to survive until the bitter end.

Gertrude Himmelfarb begins *On Looking into the Abyss* with a quote from Lionel Trilling's classic essay, "On the Teaching of Modern Literature":

I asked them to look into the Abyss, and both dutifully and gladly, they have looked into the Abyss, and the Abyss has greeted them with the grave courtesy of all objects of serious study, saying "Interesting, am I not? And *exciting*, if you consider how deep I am and what dread beasts lie at my bottom. Have it well in mind that a knowledge of me contributes materially to your being whole, or well-rounded, men." (1994:3)

Himmelfarb continues by explaining:

Trilling's point was that such a course, the teaching of such books, was self-defeating, for it transformed what should have been a profound spiritual and emotional experience into an academic exercise. Instead of hearing the writer's "wild cry" of terror, passion, mystery, rage, rapture, despair, the students heard themselves (and perhaps their professor) discoursing, seriously and sophisticatedly, about *Angst*, alienation, authenticity, sensibility. The result was to vitiate the works themselves and bring about precisely the opposite of their intended effect: "the socialization of the anti-social, or the acculturation of the anti-cultural, or the legitimization of the subversive . . ." And since then, generations of intelligent students under the guidance of their enlightened professors have looked into the abyss, have contemplated those beasts, and have said, "How interesting, how exciting." (1994:4–6)

Theory has all too often been a zoo in which we cage the wild beasts of violence that inhabit our worlds. We then gaze at these beasts from a safe distance, we contemplate them, we theorize how they would act in their own environments—and we never go to those environments where the beasts roam freely to actually check our theories. To do so would be disastrous. It would point out the absurdity of our analyses and the illusion of safety so carefully crafted.

Like Lobster Boy, a spectacle is created far from where we live our lives, a place we can go to gaze on the unsettling mysteries of our world without letting them unsettle our world. And, like those of the audience of Lobster Boy, our reactions are often inappropriate. In all this, the reality of Lobster Boy, the beasts, violence, has been left far behind. A dialogue with theory creates a circuit that deletes that being spoken of: "How interesting, how exciting, this Abyss."

Anthropology has been at the forefront of generating ethnographic studies that seek to grapple with the pressing realities of violence, yet even this discipline struggles with the conundrum of silencing the hard truths of violence. I have found that if I describe a body tortured by illness in my work in medical anthropology, it is accepted as an ethnographic fact. But when I describe a body tortured by fellow humans, it becomes a field for cautionary tales of "pornography of violence"; of "reproducing violence in speaking of it"; of "the politics of the politics of speaking." There is no question that serious abuse can result from irresponsible representations of violence, but these cautions strike me as having a different focus. I do not know anyone who is cautioned against sensationalizing kinship studies, creating a pornography of market systems, or reproducing illness or art in talking about them. What concerns me is that in these discussions the "ethnographic fact"—the reality—of the body, the person, and the experience of violence is left far behind.

Allen Feldman, writing on the reception of his work on political violence in Northern Ireland, captures the control our discipline wields over such troubling topics:

I was instructed that I could not speak correctly on violence, if my speech was not moral enough, or prescriptive enough since condemnation and cure were invariably presented as two sides of the same ethical currency. I could not write violence if I was devoid of emotion or if I displayed too much emotion (one had to flag these psychic states with explicit pointers in the text, it was not enough to embed sensibility within the flesh of the writing); I must not give in to voyeurism and other practices of distantiation, but if I became too involved I would be stigmatized as morbid and violent myself; the type of person who was capable of writing a sad book. It was not coincidence that a rumor was spread that I had fought alongside the IRA while a review falsely accused me of rapid "parachute ethnography." I was repeatedly told never to make violence pleasurable to read about—to never "aestheticize" it—though how literary pleasure was being defined and what manners of depiction made things pleasurable or non pleasureable were never explicitly delineated: it had something to do with fancy writing and Mick Taussig's name was frequently invoked as a bogey man. (1994:5–6)

One question I encounter from western audiences I find particularly offensive. Phrased both delicately and not so delicately, people want to know why I do this research. Do I get some kind of thrill from it? Is there some kind of adrenaline rush to studying violence? Have I become addicted to the excitement of the frontlines? Is there some kind of inescapable perverse fascination in horror? I can only shake my head and assume the person has grown up on John Wayne, Arnold Schwarzenegger, and B-grade literature—far from any warzone—for no one who has studied a war up close asks those questions.

I respond: Do you get some kind of thrill from studying market systems? Is there some kind of rush to investigating kinship? Is there an inescapable albeit perverse fascination in narrative? When I present and publish my work on medical anthropology or cultural theory, no one asks me why I study these things, or whether I get an adrenaline rush from it. I think it is a sad reflection of our society that violence and thrill are all too often conjoined, and I emphasize the words "our society" to point out that this is not an innate human characteristic—no Mozambican villager (or any other person I have spoken with) who has been subjected to war ever conjoins these two very different modes of experience.

The parable of Lobster Boy holds a strong message for those of us who seek to understand the human condition by looking out on it. As the narrator of Lobster Boy writes: "I realized then that Lobster Boy understood us completely . . . he revealed far more about his audience than about himself."

My stand against the theoretical taming of violence is not a plea to unleash violence. Just the opposite. In trying to tame violence in theory, violence in reality is left unchecked. From the frontlines of violence in Mozambique to the parable of Lobster Boy, it is time we begin to understand those whom we write about at least as well as they understand us.

Against Taming Experience; Or the Problem of Narrative

Such an all encompassing conception of experience avoids narrowing down the field of experience to *either* the subject *or* the object, theory *or* practice, the social *or* the individual, thought *or* feeling, form *or* flux. . . .
    Lived experience overflows the boundaries of any one concept, any one person, or any one society. (Jackson 1989:2)

While all narrative is experience, not all experience is narrative. This sounds like a simple truism, but too often the two terms are relegated to a single process: the event which occurs, and which we recognize in thought, speech, and action. A strong philosophical tradition justifies the fusion of the two processes. Researchers need to believe that when they ask an informant what her or his experiences are, the ensuing narrative will convey the nature of that experience. Narrative *is* experience. But it *is not* the experience of that which it narrates.

Many contemporary schools of thought, from postmodernism to quantum cultural studies, challenge rationalist models of the logic of experience by stressing that experience is a cacophony as well as a chorus of sounds, actions, and representations.[1] Yet virtually all Mozambicans can tell you that their world is inchoate and full of dangerous contradictions and arbitrary signs and significations. They explain how identity and cultural process, as related phenomena, can come under siege in the alienation and chaos of war, and how order or disorder is a momentary construct that changes on the vagaries of time, place, person, and happenstance. The people who survive frontline atrocities stress the critical nature of self-reflexivity. The only thing they do not stress is the jargon of postmodernism. The realities ascribed to the postmodern condition were no different in modern and premodern times. As Xenophanes wrote in the sixth century B.C. speaking about the lack of certainty in the world, "all is but a woven web of guesses" (Calvin 1988:133).

An example will help to explain the relationship of narrative to experience. In 1989 I arrived in a village in central Zambezia, Mozambique, unaware that an attack was going on and that Mozambican emergency relief workers had left to avoid danger before I arrived. When I introduced myself to the village administrator, he immediately assigned me a task: he asked me to talk with the children who were distraught about the attack. (His experience was that talking about what was going on seemed to help calm and orient the children.) I went to sit in a quiet spot under some shade trees with a group of children ranging in age from about three to ten.

Mindful of Veena Das's (1985) observation on the Punjab riots that children who have been exposed to severe episodes of violence have sophisticated perceptions concerning their experiences and want to talk about them (but find most adults disinclined to do so), I decided to be straightforward with the children. I simply asked them, "What is war?" They responded immediately: "War is when there is a lot of shooting and bombs falling and noise and confusion and you run around here and there and you don't know where to go." At this point, the children's concerns were immediate—the ruptures of daily process and reasonableness that come with sudden and life-threatening attacks.

Their comments then began to change a bit, expanding to include more general and wide-ranging observations of the town: "War is when there are big holes in the streets from bombs, and the buildings are ruined. War is when people die and there are bodies in the streets." As the children settled into talking, their stories became more personal: "War is when your loved ones die, when you lose your mother and father, when you see your friends lost and die. War is running, leaving your home and trying to find safe places [most of the children had fled their birthplaces due to the war]. War is always being scared and hungry." Here the children began to tell me about their war experiences in general, tying that day's episode into a larger portrait of "living war" as a reality of life. Then, expanding into the impact of war on their lives: "We can't go to school, we can't go visit our grandparents and cousins, we can't grow up like we want to." Finally, the conversation turned to surviving the war: "You can tell a soldier by the kinds of things he wears on his feet. They always seem to come into the village at certain times and in certain ways."

Do these words, either as I wrote them down at the time or as the reader encounters them on a page, really convey what these children *felt* and *experienced* war to be? And which war: the one when soldiers are attacking; the one where the children try to make sense of the violence after the fact; the one where they await another attack? And which narrative? These conversations took place over the space of hours. Were someone to gather the children's impressions at the beginning of the conversation, or at the end, they would have very different impressions of how these people experienced and thought about war. The narrative of the attack was not the actual experience of that violence, it was trying to find a meaningful way to deal with it. And this meaning, which changes over time, circumstance, and speaker, is a cultural production.

While I had numerous experiences like this one, I mention this one in particular for a reason. Several days later I was back in the provincial capital and ran into a person who worked with emergency relief services. He said he had heard I had been to this town in central Zambezia and asked whether an attack had taken place the day I was there. I said no, in what I thought was all honesty. He grumbled about the fact that his crew of emergency relief workers there had left the town that day because of an attack, and that they must have been wrangling some vacation time. It was a few moments before I "remembered" the attack and told the man he did not, after all, have a reason to be angry with his colleagues. Perhaps I "knew" on one level that an attack had taken place, but had momentarily (conveniently?) ignored it as an immediate reality on a personal level so I would not be hesitant about traveling to embattled zones in the future. And my life was not as endangered as the lives of those living at the center of these attacks. What do people's narratives contain or delete that makes living in danger bearable? How do their narratives change over time and circumstance, by age, gender, or war experience?

I tell this story to demonstrate that narrative organizes experience *after the fact.* Though the narratives may reaffirm past violences, infusing old into new, they will never *be* the raw primary experience of which they speak. They can never be synchronous with that which they "tell about," for raw experience is now-to-*now*, and narrative is a now-to-*then* process.[2] Disputed, even embattled, realities and identities are the meat of experience, the conditions facing humankind. It is narrative that flows through the cracks and bridges the disjunctions to give meaning, but the narrator judges what "whole" the fragments should produce, what "reality" flows through ruptures. And, returning to the story of children, it is a process learned young:

About the age of three . . . a child begins to show the ability to put together a narrative in coherent fashion and especially the capacity to recognize narratives, to judge their well-formedness. Children quickly become virtual Aristotelians, insisting upon any storyteller's observation of the "rules," upon proper beginnings, middles, and particularly ends. (Brooks 1984:3)

Narrative domesticates experience.

The questions surrounding narrative raise the conundrum of "texts." My research has prompted three specific caveats against the indiscriminate application of textual analysis and what Richard Rorty calls "textualism"—the idea that all lived experience can be reduced to intertextuality. First, the widespread tendency in scholarly literature to focus on language, text, and narrative supports a possibly unintended presupposition that these arenas constitute the core of communication and understanding. The ineffable events—non-discursive, nonverbal, and nontranscribable actions and behaviors—are difficult to render transparent in the way reproducible texts are. But they are equally communicative. Pain, for example, may not have a "voice" (Scarry 1985), but it conveys and communicates. Researchers cannot easily write terror or hope; audiences do not experience them raw on the printed page or in the storyteller's *conte*. But people who have experienced these realities *know* them, though they may not be able to narrate them. And can someone who has never known terror say he or she understands it by reading or hearing about it? I am reminded of a conversation with a woman in central Mozambique who had recently survived an attack:

> We knew the war was out there, we heard about it, we knew of people who had lost family members to it, we saw smoke on the horizon. But the war had not come to us in a real way. Then one day a group of soldiers passed by a ways out in the bush. They found some people working their machambas [farms], and interrogated them as to how many people were in the village, if any enemy troops came through, who were the administrators and teachers, and where they lived. These people were reluctant to talk, so they took two of them and beat and mutilated them, as a warning they said. Then they left. The others brought the two back to the village, and both lived, though it took a long time for the Curandeiros [healers] to get them up and around. And that is when the war came to our village, when we became afraid. We looked at these people and we hurt their hurt, we felt their terror, and we became afraid. It was worse for the children, they feel so much and have so little wisdom to understand what they feel. You will see what this has done. One day the soldiers came back and without warning attacked our village. Unlike the stories we had heard about troops attacking at night, they came in broad daylight, and no one was prepared. That terror that we had felt upon seeing those mutilated people, that was made worse every time we saw them hobble down the street, that began to live with us day and night—that terror exploded for many when the same troops appeared. People could not think, they could not act logically, they panicked with nothing in their minds. A group of children ran to get away from the attack, and they ran toward the river without thinking. Now they know the village, the countryside, they know the dangers of the river and how to get around it. But that terror was upon them, and they just ran and jumped in the river, and they all drowned. The Bandidos made off with our goods and some of our people, but they did not stay, I think it was because there was a strong group of Frelimo soldiers in the area, and they feared to stay and fight them. So now we are trying to get our village back to normal, but it cannot be normal. Every time we look at the river, every time we see a child playing happily, we feel the pain of the death of those children, the grief of their parents, the horror of the war. Even those of us who did not lose our children, well, we cannot live here and be with those grieving parents every day and not feel the pain ourselves.

My second caveat against the indiscriminate application of textually based analysis is also evident in this woman's words. Certain aspects of human existence are not easily captured by the text, nor should they be. Pain, profound grief, and the existential horror of watching and responding first-hand to war's atrocities are examples of fundamental realities that can be only partially, and perhaps never responsibly, bound to a text. Jean Comaroff (1991) has stressed that to textualize personal tragedy and horror, such as restricting one's research "gaze" to "the inscriptions of power on the body" when one is talking about a person being tortured and dehumanized, is to risk losing the immediacy of the personal altogether.

Finally, people protect themselves through silence as well as speaking. People define themselves in narration, but they equally constitute themselves in the silent space of the unsaid. The untold story, the unnarrated tale, leaves the world unformed, or at least that piece which remains unsaid. History does not flow logically from past to present; identities and roles are not set; outcome is not determined. These truths can be used as weapons against a threat or an enemy. In the unformed world, a person has a multitude of options to create a survivable world. With this irony, meaning and nonmeaning, creativity, order, and chaos interfuse in a more accurate approximation of experience.

Taming the Scholar?

I'm forty-three years old, and a writer now, and the war has been over for a long while. Much of it is hard to remember. I sit at this typewriter and stare through my words and watch Kiowa sinking into the deep muck of a shit field, or Curt Lemon hanging in pieces from a tree, and as I write about these things, the remembering is turned into a kind of rehappening. Kiowa yells at me. Curt Lemon steps from the shade into bright sunlight, his face brown and shining, and then he soars into a tree. The bad stuff never stops happening: it lives in its own dimension, replaying itself over and over. But the war wasn't all that way. (O'Brien 1990:36)

I read these words by Tim O'Brien in the introduction to his book about life as a soldier in Vietnam, and, while I understand them, I know that they are not my story. As important as it is to situate ourselves as authors for our audiences, when I read O'Brien's words I am not sure what best answers the question, "Who am I, to be studying what I am, putting my experiences into words in the way that I do?" On one level it is obvious. Having seen the horrors of war, I want to do what I can to stop them. To me it is equally obvious that the war in Mozambique has been shaped in powerful ways by an international culture of violence, militarization, and politico-economic power that moves across borders with a frightening fluidity transported by every military advisor, arms merchant, mercenary, blackmarketeer; with every violence-glorifying movie, neocolonial practice, terror-based counterinsurgency theory. This fluidity transports a violence we all face in one way or another, a violence that harms us all.

But is it enough to "position" myself in this way? What indeed is this process of positioning? I remember walking out in the bush in Mozambique in an area of heavy fighting with two other foreigners, a man and a woman doing medical work hundreds of kilometers from the protection of a provincial capital. They, too, hated the war and were committed to assuaging its injustices. They, too, had left the relative comfort of the provincial capitals to sleep in cane huts, their sleep disturbed periodically by gunfire. But I had just learned that the man had gone to the highest authority in the area to request that he be permitted to burn refugees' huts if they did not come to his medical center. I knew from experience that he required all attendees to sit all day under designated trees in the hot sun to make sure they got their prescribed food and medical allotments and did not try to steal any. If people refused to come to his makeshift center, he harangued them about being evil parents who were killing their children. I was trying to explain to the man that, if he burned refugees' huts, he was little different from abusive troops: he was employing terror to gain consent. I added that people could not sit under trees for twelve hours a day just to obtain his medicines and food. He came to villages only when security clearances, airplanes, fuel, and fickle funding made his visits possible. He was here one week and gone the next—his food and medicines as fickle as his funding. Under serious threat of marauding troops, people were making the walk into the bush every day to try to eke out crops for their families. If people did not go to the fields to plant crops, they would starve in the upcoming months—and by their estimation, if they neglected their fields, they would be bad parents.

My words fell on deaf ears. The man was convinced of his "right" in his commitment to peace. I did go to the authority he had talked to and reported that, despite the fact that the man said he had permission from "high ups" to pursue the policy of burning huts, this was not true. The authority, fearing retribution if he did not allow this gruesome policy, was greatly relieved. As I talked to the foreigner, the third person accompanying us, his partner, shook from fear and prayed to God to deliver her from harm. She was so concerned with her prayers that she did not hear gunshots or watch her footing. I wondered whether her god, who had allowed one million Mozambicans to die in this war, would worry about one more.

Can positionality tell you about the day I held a young child who had been wounded, and understood in the mother's eyes the grief she was feeling? Can it explain the day I watched a son die of starvation and wanted, in typical American fashion, to "do something," to make it better? How a Mozambican journalist there stopped me from making a fool of myself with his respectful attitude toward the mother, something for which I will long be grateful?

The fact of being an American born of Northern European tradition is an inescapable position, and one that calls up critiques of occidental research by authors like Gayatri Spivak (1988) and Trinh Minh-ha (1989). These authors challenge western scholars to question their motives in studying non-western peoples, their witting or unwitting location in power relationships when they try to "speak" for those they have worked among, and the effects, both intended and unforeseen, that accrue from their work. Research and representation are irreducibly intertwined with politics and power.[3]

I take such critiques seriously. One need only read V. Y. Mudimbe's (1988) *The Invention of Africa* to come to the embarrassing realization of the extent to which the colonial enterprise resonated in anthropological texts. Yet organizations like Human Rights Watch and Amnesty International and scholars like Michael Taussig (1987) and Nancy Scheper-Hughes (1992) are equally right when they challenge people to speak out against the inequalities and injustices they encounter wherever they encounter them. To do anything less is tantamount to condoning these injustices. We have reached the stage of theoretical development where we can no longer throw out such uncomfortable contradictions as worrying about the abuse of privilege in speaking for another and simultaneously recognizing the need to speak against the injustices another is subjected to. I do not attempt to resolve this seeming contradiction, nor do I think it can be resolved. This dilemma is part and parcel of our scholastic world as I see it. I cannot pretend to escape the negative ramifications my presence and my culture will have on those with whom I work by virtue of my concern for them. Nor can I turn my back on pressing questions and problems because I can only paint the world from a palette whose colors have been tinted by the force of my culture(s).

This discussion throws into stark relief a question we cannot afford to leave unanswered. Does not theory create the other in its attempt to protect it? Do we not (re)create and perpetuate the very (post)colonial divisions and hierarchies we seek to dismantle in associating author with *authority*? Several metamessages are carried in the admonition made by westerners themselves that they should not presume to speak for non-westerners. One of the most powerful is the distinction that "we" are not "they." Encrypted in the message is a clear accounting of who is us and not-us, the hierarchy of relationships that characterizes these divisions, and the power that accrues to this naming, this control over classification. It implies that we *can* speak for others (and since we do not extend the warning to non-westerners not speaking for us, the added implication is that "they" *cannot*). It implies that our speaking has some meaning, some relevance. With this statement, "we" are associated with a power supraordinate to the other: "their" words may be important, but theirs are not the threat to us that ours are to them. In the final analysis, this message creates a hierarchy, imbues it with privilege, charges it with unequal power relationships, and places "us" on top. In this way, scholarship reifies the same divisions that produced the injustices being condemned; it reaffirms the divisions through which domination and subordination have been constructed.[4]

The ramifications of "privileged thinking" are considerable. I am reminded of an event that occurred soon after returning to the United States from my fieldwork in Mozambique. I found myself in an argument with a philosopher at a professional meeting, who said: "In the contingencies of war, people just try to survive first; they work single-mindedly to procure what they need to live, and only then can they turn to thinking." I rebutted by saying that everything I had learned about warfare taught me that, to survive, people must first think. This thinking involves creating viable realities from chaos, creating a future from the timelessness of destruction. Without this, survival is impossible. I was also challenging a more subtle point: the philosopher's premise that what "scholars do" is epistemology and what "informants do" is popular thought.

To relegate theory, philosophy, and epistemology to academia is to say that quests into the nature of thinking is a privileged scholarly process. The implications of this are legion: scholarly literature is replete with words like "popular knowledge," "indigenous traditions of thought," "local belief systems," and "local-level philosophies" that refer to the production of knowledge in ethnographic settings. When did we begin to distinguish theoretical from popular knowledge, garnishing the former for ourselves, the researchers, and assigning the latter to those we study? By applying such arbitrary distinctions, we imply that the locals (read "natives") do not theorize unless they are themselves academicians. We also imply that somehow epistemology is not popular knowledge about knowledge, but something "better," even though countless studies on the sociology of knowledge demonstrate the degree to which our "scientific frameworks" are rooted in personal and social process.

I suggest instead that theory, philosophy, and epistemology are part and parcel of cultural process. In Okot p'Bitek's (1983:106) words, "Culture is philosophy as lived and celebrated in a society." Just as society is culturally constructed, it is philosophically constituted—by its citizens.

Not everyone in a society conducts formal epistemology, but all societies have their philosophers. The respected member of a village who makes war "comprehensible" and strategies for thinking about it "graspable" in a reflexive and self-reflexive way is engaged in epistemology. Epistemology and worldmaking are related: both constitute creative and theoretical processes. These conjoined processes are necessary for those whose towns have been burned, whose families are scattered by war, and whose present (war-afflicted) life is unrecognizable by any previous standard. Not everyone in a community is equally adept at this process, and those who are most adept share their insights, constructions, and possibilities for a future with others. Knowledge systems are introduced, argued, revised, philosophized, and shared.

Countless are the times I sat with Mozambicans who theorized about knowledge and how to use it to explain and sustain their shattered worlds. To deny this the status of epistemology, to distinguish scholarly from popular knowledge among people respected for providing formal paradigms of thought for their communities, to deny that such people are our colleagues raises the hoary question of whether such acts are simply hierarchical recolonizations of the "less privileged." No epistemology, no knowledge system, is inherently more rigorous than another—though it may be privileged in terms of the power it holds over others. To try to privilege a knowledge orientation, as has been wont to occur in academia and in other institutions heralding formal versus popular distinctions, is to (attempt to) impose a hierarchical ordering. This attempt is always a statement about power.[5]

*   *   *

Whether we as researchers are responding to the critiques of occidental scholarship or to the profound dilemmas of our own research experience, situating ourselves in narrative is a bit like narrative: it is necessary, but it glosses over and smooths out the chaotic, timeless, and multidimensional qualities of lived experience. It provides ordering. And like narrative, situating ourselves all too often seems to be imbued with a moral component. I am reminded of Tim O'Brien's words on war:

A true war story is never moral. It does not instruct, nor encourage virtue, nor suggest models of proper human behavior, nor restrain men from doing the things men have always done. If a story seems moral, do not believe it. If at the end of a war story you feel uplifted, or if you feel that some small bit of rectitude has been salvaged from the larger waste, then you have been made the victim of a very old and terrible lie. (1990:76)

My work is not a simple act of writing. It will suggest theories of human behavior, it is inscribed in a moral context, it is intended to instruct—for I believe that in order to do something about the atrocities of war, we must first understand the realities, not as we wish to see them, not in metaphors that gloss over pain, but as close to the experience as words and a second-hand account make possible. But within all this is sympathy for O'Brien's observation: "If a story seems moral, do not believe it." Morals, like all cultural relationships, are fraught with contradictions, confusions, and the attendant imbroglios of human reality. Any pat constructions of morality, ethics, or theory are likely to be more ideological than accurate. Hans Magnus Enzensberger captures this well:

> Just the mention of civil war sooner or later turns into a kind of self-experimentation. No bones are broken; and yet every disagreement about civil war fuels the war itself. I am not neutral. . . .
> It is impossible to have a linear discussion on this theme. Merely stating your own position fans the flames of conflict. There is no Archimedean point. I have stepped into an intellectual and moral minefield. I have to move with great care. But I know that although I might, if I'm lucky, find my way through, I'll never be able to clear the field. I don't even see eye to eye with myself. (1990:49)

From considerations of experience to epistemology, from situating ourselves in the act of research and writing to challenging these very situations, it is important to craft our discipline with as much care as possible and to respect those we write about more than we respect our own love of theory and practice. This is neither a smooth nor an uncontested process. Like Enzensberger, "I don't even see eye to eye with myself" throughout much of this process. But that doesn't negate the academic endeavor. For me, it simply makes it more real.

Notes

1. Postmodernism and Jackson's radical empiricism build on a concept of experience that has been honed within several contemporary scholarly traditions. Phenomenology placed experience in the context of socially constructed realities, clearly rejecting any notion of an external objective reality that is experienced and is reflected in experiencing (Husserl 1962; Schutz 1962, 1964). As there is no fixed and given reality, people cannot "know" or share the same experience of reality in the same way. Experience cannot be separated from interpretation. Phenomenology combined being and thinking about being (Heidegger 1962). Scholars such as Dilthey (1954) posited "structures of experience" that equally combined thought, feeling, and volition or will, and sought to cast experience as comprising both the typical and the exceptional, the habitual and the fleeting. Many traditional phenomenologists, however, tended to focus on

the conscious, the cognitive, and the volitional in their analyses. Existentialism refined the concept of experience by expanding from a focus on epistemological realms concerned with thinking to include ontological considerations concerned with the nature of being. In this development, the emphasis on the volitional was refashioned so that experience included conditions of absurdity (the desired but not-known) and "négatité" (the expected but not-there) (Camus 1955; Sartre 1957). For the existentialists, discovery, both of oneself and of what is there as well as what is perceived as not there, unfolds in praxis. Inverting traditional phenomenology, authors like Sartre posited existence as preceding essence.

Contemporary feminist literature has provided perhaps the most compelling perspectives on experience in considering identity/culture/power relationships. Recognizing the contested culture of human relationships within a framework of dominant constructs, feminist critiques of modernism and postmodernism have taken this a step further to insist on gendered sensibilities, and to place these in transnational analyses of war. This has not been common: despite the fact that 90 percent of all war-related casualties today are civilians, and the majority of these women and children, traditional political science approaches continue to influence research foci on power brokers (male), soldiers (male), and battlegrounds (soldiers). Cynthia Enloe (1993) reminds us that behind these carefully crafted masculinized images of warfare are a host of enduring realities. The war enterprise relies on strategies of targeting women; it relies on systems of prostitution and the work of women; it is grounded in gendered ideals of family and state. Yet these facts are all too often obscured in the formal presentations of war. To depict the realities of war is to acknowledge and research how conflict and its resolution is engendered.

2. If I reproduce a narrative here like ones I heard in Mozambique about a chameleon (the untrustworthy), a rabbit (the quick and unaggressive), a bird (knowledge), and a dead body (the truth of violence); if I present this as a text that conveys secondary information, but let it stand, eternal, as a text that can be decoded in and of itself; if I leave it decontextualized from its telling and the motivations of the teller as these shift from speaker to speaker, telling to telling—what can this say about the experience of narrative? What can this convey about the particular circumstances in which a person finds herself or himself in relation to soldiers, rebels, collaborators, abusive and helpful power brokers in the community, blackmarketeers who profit from the war and the selling of information, illicit tax collectors and renegade troops, all of which affect a person's survival—since that is, in fact, what the narrative is about?

3. The anthropologist who claims to "give voice" to those less able to do so, warns Spivak, is often engaged in little better than postcolonial discourse refashioned for a postmodern world. Unless western academics undertake serious self-critique—not only as academics, but as westerners, as historical products, and as a nexus of privilege—Spivak warns, their sincerity and abilities must be doubted.

4. Abu-Lughod (1991) provides an excellent analysis of the power relations attendant to western scholarship and, as part of her argument, writes: "Even attempts to refigure informants as consultants and to " 'let the other speak' in dialogic (Tedlock 1987) or polyvocal texts—decolonizations on the level of the text—leave intact the basic configuration of global power on which anthropology, as linked to other institutions of the world, is based" (pp. 142–43).

5. I am reminded, in considering core themes concerning knowledge, of Francis Bacon's idols of the mind. Bacon, writing in the early seventeenth cen-

tury, was fascinated with the topic of knowledge and with those traits that stand in the way of our knowing, or understanding. (See his *Novum Organon* 1620 and *Advancement of Learning* 1605.) Bacon foreshadowed the present concern with the sociology of knowledge and highlighted the timeless nature of these problems. He identifies four idols of the mind to explain the existence of human error in understanding, and, while he labels each in what today appear to be sociological categories, he clearly intended these to refer to humankind in general. First are the idols of the tribe, obstacles to the intellect that affect all humans. These involve the tendency to ascribe more order to events and systems than actually exists, and to oversimplify explanations. Novelty is embraced. The latest explanatory model always appears the most profound until it is replaced by a newer one, which is then wholly embraced. Next are the idols of the cave, fallacies caused by personal idiosyncrasy. People have a habit of seeing the world in their own terms, and some focus on similarities while others are concerned with differences. Understanding is cast in the mold of the speaker, and it is only by comparing the versions of many that a more comprehensive understanding can be achieved. Third are the idols of the marketplace. These presage the works of scholars like Saussure and Derrida, and speak to the problems caused by language itself. Each person uses language differently, each word carries a slightly different significance for the speaker. Yet any claim to a universal language is bound to fail, for, ultimately, shared truths cannot be comprehended by everyone until they are translated into the systems of signification understood by each person. As each person understands words, concepts, and usage in a different way, distortions in understanding, in the framework of knowledge itself, invariably follow. Last are the idols of the theater. These are the philosophical systems within which each person operates that provide the tools of analysis for epistemological investigations—systems of ideas that cloud a fresh and unfettered perspective. Political ideologies, religious doctrines, cultural ideals on the nature of human existence, and philosophical assumptions about reality define "truth" and the parameters of knowledge and action for each individual, but vary considerably among people. Yet the degree to which each belief system is embraced by a person ensures that little understanding is possible between people holding different philosophies, different "truths." Bacon's ideas are not original, nor are they unrecognized today, but they point to some of the profound problems that continue to complicate understandings of experience, knowledge, and action—concerns that have been recast in the contemporary philosophies of postmodernism, feminist theory, and social science endeavor.

Chapter 2
Setting the Stage

My Land!

I cry a lot when you are unable
to provide charity to your children
because of the evildoers that are destroying
your love.
       Your borders are invaded
       by unidentified individuals
       who threaten
       undefended people.
Your forests have grown deaf
from the blasts of the guns
The animals are abandoning your garden
seeking refuge with your
people.
       It is sorrowful
       listening to the sad twitter of the birds
       that cannot return
       to their nests
       because of fear.
The rich savanna has become the granary
of victims without
hope
The tears of your people are getting
larger with each
violence done by the traitors of this land.
                  —Hilàrio

Mozambican soldiers in Gorongosa district, Sofala province, 1985. Photo by Joel
Chiziane.

Why and How Mozambique?

Toward the end of my stay in Mozambique in 1991, I read a short piece of prose by Mozambican writer and poet Mia Couto. It begins:

Suddenly, the ox exploded. It burst without so much as a moo. In the surrounding grass a rain of chunks and slices fell, as if the fruit and leaves of the ox. Its flesh turned into red butterflies. Its bones were scattered coins. Its horns were caught in some branches, swinging to and fro, imitating life in the invisibility of the wind. (1986:17)

I mention that I was at the end of my stay because, even though the young cowherd in the story "could not contain his astonishment," and variously wonders if Mabata-bata, the cow, was hit by lightning or, something more magical, *ndlati*, the bird of lightning, I knew when I read the first sentence that the cow had stepped on a landmine. And I knew that by the end of the story the young cowherd would meet the same fate. At the same time, I realized that when I first arrived in Mozambique I would not have "known" these things—I too would have wondered if it were lightning or perhaps something more magical. This realization prompted me to conduct an informal survey of responses to the story of the exploding cow. Wherever I went in Mozambique, I told the story above and asked people what happened to Mabata-bata the cow. Similarly, when I spoke with Africans from lands less war-ravished than Mozambique, I presented them with the same question. Mozambicans tended to come to the same conclusion I had. Clearly the cow had stepped on a landmine, though some unfortunate sorcery may have placed the landmine and the cow together to create such an untimely end. Most Mozambicans speculated, as I had, that the young cowherd would meet a fate similar to the cow's (and, in the story, he in fact did). The Africans from more peaceful lands, however, speculated about tragic misfortune, sorcery, envy, and human relationships, both mundane and supernatural. They did not tend to posit landmines, nor did they assume the inevitability of the young child's death.

I start out this chapter with the story of Mabata-bata to contrast it with the broad sweep of complex international linkages, discussed in Chapter 1, that make war possible. How do we understand the juxtaposition of the very local—an understanding of a particular war in a particular set of cultural icons like Mabata-bata the cow—and the international, whereby the vast networks of everyone from arms merchants to foreign military advisors and mercenaries coalesce in particular warzones ultimately to affect, and be affected by, the local? Down to Mabata-bata the cow.

This question is particularly important in my research, which is in a number of ways experimental ethnography. I arrived in Mozambique as an anthropologist who had cut my academic teeth in the South Asian region. My years of studying political violence demonstrated to me the value of cross-cultural and cross-country comparative research. An important question then became, how to do a responsible study of a war-zone in a comparative locale. Mozambique is my explorations of these questions. After more than a decade of studying wars and their resolutions in various locales in the world, I decided my field was better defined by a topic and a process than by a region. Or, perhaps it is defined by a region that cross-cuts the countries of the world. Although I have spent several years over the space of nearly a decade in Mozambique since my first trip in 1988, I still find my research experimental in that I am following a process unfolding locally-internationally rather than situating my study in a particular (town) site or geographical region.

War-Scapes

There is an increasing recognition among anthropologists today that we can no longer see our subject matter in terms of isolated, self-contained cultural communities. Even the most circumscribed of locales is set within a larger context of international influences, indelibly changing both the character of the local and the translocal. We must write to the contemporary world, and that world is a tangled web of transnational linkages.

Arjun Appadurai has introduced the term *ethnoscape*[1] in pursuing a transnational anthropology, arguing that "As groups migrate, regroup in new locations, reconstruct their histories, and reconfigure their ethnic 'projects,' the *ethno* in ethnography takes on a slippery, nonlocalized quality" (1991:191). This process affects not only group identity and dynamics, but the very notions of culture anthropology employs.

This concept is particularly useful in the analysis of war, though perhaps in ways Appadurai has not yet explored. In the present context, this concept can most conveniently be termed "war-scapes." Foreign strategists, arms, supplies, soldiers, mercenaries, power brokers, and development and interest groups move into a country. Guerrillas and soldiers travel to other countries for training and strategic planning. Refugees and displaced people flow across borders. An international cast of businesspeople and blackmarketeers provides goods and profit from the upheavals of conflict. As these many groups act and interact, local and transnational concerns are enmeshed in the cultural construction of conflict that is continually reconfigured across time and space. Each person, each group brings a history that informs action and is negotiated vis-à-vis the various other histories of those with whom they interact.

Precisely because of this sensitivity to historical trajectories, I must question the degree to which, as Appadurai states, the twentieth century is different from previous ones in its transnational character. For example, four hundred years ago villages in remote parts of the Zambezia province in north central Mozambique had developed marked cultural responses to invasions and incursions from neighboring African kingdoms, Portuguese colonists, Muslim traders, Indian and Goan settlers, British adventurers, and rapacious slavers. Clearly, at that time, transnational processes informed local response in a world both interpenetrated and cosmopolitanized.

I want to stress, too, that while many writers underscore the importance of the "cosmopolitan cultural forms of the contemporary world,"[2] this is not restricted to the cosmopolitan centers of the world. Just as we must not fall into what might be termed the "arrogance of the present," which assumes that *our* world, *our* problems are somehow fundamentally different from all preceding eras, we must be equally careful not to dichotomize rural, remote, and small-scale societies from the global sprawl of the modern cosmopolitan world, separating—colonizing—traditional from contemporary cosmopolitan studies. Rural Mozambique is as much a part of the contemporary flow and ebb of the cosmopolitan world as are larger urban crossroads.[3]

This concept of war-scapes also makes it possible to transcend individual expressions of the war in particular locales, to understand the creation of a culture of war throughout Mozambique. Everyone sees the world through a cultural prism. But as discussed in Chapter 1, war, surviving war, and creative conflict resolution are also cultural realities, and cross-cut people's differences to create new shared communities. War-scapes entail a shared dialogue about war and templates upon which to act and assess action. These link soldier and civilian, violator and peacemaker, for none make sense in isolation from the other. Thus it is true to say both that different individuals and cultural groups experience the war in distinct ways and that it is important not to essentialize these differences.

Shared sentiments about war and peacebuilding constitute a kind of culture that exists throughout the country. These did not spring up spontaneously in myriad separate locales, but were forged with conscious effort as a constant flow of people and goods moved about the country and through the battlezones. As millions of refugees fled to safer locales; as people went in search of distant or lost relatives, critical resources, or jobs; as renegade soldiers formed predatory bands and blackmarketeers plied their trade; as an endless number of people moved about the length and breadth of the country searching for safety, security, and livelihood, and others moved to prey on them, a culture of war and peace was created across tribal, language, gender, class, and combat(ant) divisions. With each interaction among those populating this massive transnational flow, stories were exchanged, strategies shared, antagonisms illuminated, survival plans forged, and cultural responses honed. The realities of the war linked people in powerful and undeniable ways.

Why Mozambique?

Mozambique presented a completely different kind of war from any I had studied before. When I first arrived in Mozambique in 1988, the government was black majority and Marxist-Leninist. The pro-democracy rebel group was formed and backed by apartheid leaders first in neighboring Rhodesia, and then in South Africa, and was credited with the majority of severe human rights violations. The war was one of the most violent and devastating of contemporary times, called by many the "killing fields of Africa."

The story of this war begins before independence, with another war. In the 1960s Frelimo (Frente de Libertação de Moçambique: Front for the Liberation of Mozambique) grew to prominence as the major force fighting against the Portuguese colonists for independence. When independence was achieved in 1975, Frelimo established a Marxist-Leninist government, with the party's top military and political leaders taking up the reins of government. Frelimo's political stance alienated some Mozambicans, but Frelimo, as a black-majority government, provided an even bigger threat to the Rhodesian government, itself now fighting against independence forces. Frelimo assisted these guerrillas by providing supplies and rear bases on Mozambican soil. The Rhodesian government decided to create and train an anti-Frelimo rebel group from disenfranchised Mozambicans to destabilize the Mozambican government and any support it might be able to give to the rebel forces in Rhodesia. In this way, Renamo (Resistência Nacional Moçambicano: Mozambican National Resistance) was born. When Zimbabwe gained independence in 1980, control of Renamo shifted to apartheid South Africa's Defense Forces, who were equally threatened by the model of government and the support Frelimo provided anti-apartheid forces in South Africa. Their goal remained the same as the Rhodesian one: to destabilize Frelimo. Renamo's war developed as a destructive one.

The South African military was able to pour far more resources into Renamo than Rhodesia could, and the war grew in scope and intensity throughout the 1980s. By the end of the 1980s, the war was at its height, and it remained at this lethal level until peace was achieved in 1992. The war was recognized worldwide as one of the worst of contemporary times. South Africa along with Renamo was censured for its role in promoting such a "dirty war," one so grounded in human rights abuses. Even in the United States Congress in the midst of the Cold War, Mozambique was called "the killing fields of Africa" (Frelick 1989). This is an important point to keep in mind when reading this book: the violence I am talking about here is of the worst kind. There is no way to romanticize or glorify what took place in Mozambique during these years, except, that is, what means many noncombatant civilians undertook on their own to stop the war. It is my opinion that average Mozambican citizens instituted a series of conflict resolution practices that are among the most refined I have seen anywhere in the world. For me, they stand as a model of resolving political violence and rebuilding battle-scarred communities that can assist other communities and countries embroiled in similar excesses of violence.

It helps to put this statement into context. The extent and depth of Mozambique's war-related suffering is staggering. Mozambique, writes Joseph Hanlon (1991:1), "is the world's poorest, hungriest, most in-debted, most aid-dependent country,"[4] a product, most agree, of the colonial legacy and two back to back wars, that for independence and then Renamo's war against the Frelimo government.[5] UNICEF (1990) estimates that 90 percent of the population is living in poverty, with 60 percent living in absolute poverty. Half the population, 7.7 million people, required food and other aid in the early 1990s.

Mozambique is twice the size of California, and in 1991 contained approximately 16 million people divided into some twelve major ethnic and language groups with scores of subgroupings, all of them affected by the conflict. The war has turned a sedentary population nomadic. Over one million Mozambican war refugees (*refugiados*) fled to neighboring countries, two million people were displaced within Mozambique (*deslocados*), and an additional two and a half million people have been directly affected by the war (*afetados*), meaning that violent conditions destroyed their ability to produce sufficient food or live a normal lifestyle. Altogether, the lives of one-half of the country's inhabitants have been seriously disrupted by the war.[6] No one yet has an accurate count of the landmines planted in Mozambique, but they continue to take lives long after the war has ended. We cannot say how many casualties accrue to this war, for they are still occurring.

Approximately one million Mozambicans died from war-related causes in the fifteen years of war since independence, generating 300,000 war-traumatized orphans (Ministry of Cooperation/UNICEF 1989). The physical harm, plus the severe psychological, socio-cultural, and interpersonal traumas provoked by the war, have prompted many Mozambicans to refer to the children born during the post-independence war years as the "lost generation."[7]

Experimental Ethnography: Runway Research

Having stated that my concern is with studying a theme and a process—war and its resolution—and not a place, as in traditional ethnographies, the question then becomes, "how?" I decided to follow all the threads of war and resistance spun across the country that I could. Actual war, actual resistance. In weaving these threads together over time and space, over hundreds of discussions and shared experiences with a wide diversity of people country-wide, I hoped to illuminate at least something of a picture of what it means to live on the frontlines of a war in the world today. I had one advantage that many did not: a travel permit from the Ministry of Health that could take me to any part of the country I could get to.

In trying to give a more representative understanding of the war in Mozambique, I also show how very limited my representations are. Much of this has to do with the sheer actualities of doing fieldwork in a country at war. I decided to make my base the north central province of Zambezia, the most war-affected province in Mozambique at the time. I sought to travel as extensively as possible throughout the province collecting, comparing, and contrasting people's experiences. Because Mozambique encompasses markedly different language and cultural groups—and war experiences—I also traveled to the two northernmost provinces of Niassa and Cabo Delgado, to the central provinces of Sofala and Manica, and to Gaza and Maputo provinces in the southern part of the country.

In many ways, the nature of this ethnography reflects the reality of many Mozambicans' lives. Conflict, starvation, deprivation, and the demands of work, family, and health have produced an extremely fluid population. As noted above, nearly one-third of the population have experienced some form of dislocation—constituting a population of *deslocados*, as they are called in Mozambique. These Mozambicans can no longer, at present, ground their "selves"—their lives, their livelihoods, their dreams—in a single place. In responding to an external threat, they carry reworked notions of home, family, community, and survival with them. *Repositioning* thus comes to define a major socio-cultural current. Ethnographer and Mozambican alike arrive in new locations and ask for the latest pertinent information in order to understand the war and not make potentially lethal mistakes.

This serves to introduce the reader to what I did, but not to what I did not do. I never carried a weapon or traveled with troops on assault missions at any time. I managed to enter and conduct interviews at only one high-security political prison. I did not spend time in secured Renamo-held areas, though I spoke with a number of Renamo soldiers and citizens from these areas. I did not travel to extremely remote no-man's-lands where few outsiders, including Frelimo and Renamo bureaucracies, knew who held what or who was there. I did, however, do research in several embattled areas hotly contested by both forces. I did not travel extensively by road in the interior of provinces, though I did walk and drive through as many areas in the country as possible.

In fact few people travel extensively by road in Mozambique. As one Mozambican summed up:

> I had to drive across the province and into the next last week—those people up there had not had outside contact since their attack, and I could not let them down. But the road was like some scene from hell: the whole way there were burned-out cars and skeletons of cars stripped by Renamo and skeletons of people sitting in the skeletons of cars.

The roads throughout Mozambique were landmined and subject to frequent attacks. No one knew how heavily the roads were targeted, or where—but the carcasses of vehicles and unlucky travelers provided a strong deterrent to others considering a journey. Except for a limited number of safe corridors in the country where vehicular travel was relatively unrestricted, overland travel generally took place by convoy (usually military guarded) if it took place at all. Two other forms of travel prevailed: those who could, flew, and those who did not have access to an airplane or were going somewhere where there was no runway (and this category included most Mozambican villagers) walked.

There were three types of air travel. The national airline company served only the major cities of the country. Several aid organizations rented small planes (capable of holding from six to ten passengers or a ton of cargo) that flew people and goods throughout the country wherever dirt or grass runways, and a modicum of security, existed. Finally, a small fleet of old DC3s, DC4s and Caribous (donated by international relief organizations and coordinated by Mozambican emergency services), capable of transporting three to four tons, flew emergency relief foods and supplies to designated disaster areas throughout the country.

The flow of administrators, aid workers, teachers, health care personnel, blackmarketeers, journalists, researchers, and (emergency) foodstuffs and supplies followed not the logic of need but the logic of runways. I remember well a conversation I heard one day as I was sitting on a runway waiting for a plane to arrive.

> We've been getting food to the towns of M. and N., and we know the conditions pretty well in the areas surrounding these towns. But

up to the northeast and west of those areas, no one has a clue. No one can get in, and no one seems to come out. We don't even know who holds the area—kind of a free for all. The airlifts to supply M. and N. were started because some twenty-five people were dying a day, what with the pressure of the deslocados [displaced people] and the inability of people to work their machambas [farms] due to the precariousness of the security situation. We get indications that these areas to the northeast and west are much harder hit, that the situation could be a real disaster, with people dying at a truly alarming rate. But no one knows for sure, and no one can get in. The troops aren't going, it is too dangerous or uncertain or unimportant, I don't know. Government [administrators] is not going, no one wants to risk their lives walking into chaos and possibly death. Blackmarketeers aren't going, no profit. And since there are no runways, no one can go do a look-over. So the people in M. and N. die, become statistics, prompt an airlift, get supplies. The people north of there, well, who knows? Maybe they have all died by now.

Like the airlifts and armed convoys, my research reflects the war in areas I could get to. The graciousness of the Mozambican government, and particularly the Ministry of Health, in allowing me travel permits, and of the pilots in giving me *boleia* (rides) permitted me to visit a fairly representative sample of "runway" locations. The tendency of old planes to break meant that even in areas with a "no-overnight rule" (areas the government deemed too dangerous for nonlocals to spend the night), I sometimes managed to spend several days before the repaired plane returned. This opportunity to travel in Mozambique proved invaluable. Every Mozambican knows that war is highly complex, and this comparative research helped to demonstrate just what that means.

"Factx"

I have written "factx" instead of "facts" to underscore the observation that, at least in the context of war, something is always wrong with the facts one is given. The facts of war emerge as "essentially contested" figures and representations everyone agrees are important, and no one agrees on. People generally *assume* that statistical facts concerning war are less biased than political declarations and tools of propaganda, but we seldom ask how basic information like internationally accepted figures concerning casualties, traumatization, and refugees come into being. We are even less likely to question more complex information concerning battlefield realities and military-civilian relations from sources we deem reliable.

In Chapter 3 I discuss communities that are "forgotten to death" in war—communities that never become part of official documentation because they are too inaccessible, too "political," too tragic to be investigated. Warzones are filled with such locations that defy competent investigation. However, even areas that are accessible present myriad problems to the compilation of accurate information. Momentarily leaving aside the question of the manipulation of "truth" for political reasons, several examples illuminate the sheer difficulty of collecting information in warzones.

In the first example, I was returning home from a visit to an inland village on an empty emergency cargo plane. The pilots had taken a circuitous route to show me something they had inadvertently noticed earlier in the day: a fairly large town that had just been destroyed. I was in the cockpit and had an excellent view—we flew low and circled the town numerous times. It was deserted and in smoldering flames. What had not been burned had been demolished. A very few people darted among the ruins, probably trying to salvage anything of their past lives. On hearing the plane's engines, they ran to hide. Thousands of people would have been affected by this attack. Yet when I returned to the provincial capital and inquired about the zone, no one knew anything of the destruction. In the months that followed, I continued to ask after the area, both in the province and when I visited the country's capital city. The question continued to be met with blank stares. No one had heard of the massacre. To the best of my knowledge, this was not a case of people hiding information. Responses to my carefully worded questions seemed to indicate people simply did not know that a city had been decimated. One can only guess how many other towns have been destroyed far from the logs of statisticians. When I asked how it could be that they had not heard of an entire town that had been destroyed, several people looked at me as if I did not comprehend the enormity of the war, saying, "Do you realize how large Mozambique is, how extensive the fighting is, how many reports of towns attacked and destroyed we receive? It is one place of hundreds suffering at any given time." They did not need to remind me that resources, humanpower, and communications were insufficient to the task at hand. As far as the "facts" of war are concerned, the only certainty is that the fate of this town and the casualties suffered there never reach public attention.

In the second example, I was in a village when a CNN television film crew arrived by private airplane to do a day's shooting on the war in Mozambique as part of a story on conflict in Africa. The village had recently changed hands from Renamo to Frelimo. People were dying at an alarming rate from starvation and other war-related causes. The film crew asked me to help with some translation. They asked me to inquire from the administrator how many people were dying per day. "Many," he replied. "It is terrible, everyday we have deaths and burials, you can see them wherever you go." "But how many exactly?" asked the crew. "I cannot say for sure," was the reply. "I have arrived here recently myself, and it is a large area. I just do not know. Many bury their dead quietly, and we cannot walk house to house throughout this entire area asking if someone has died today. These people are suffering enough. I just know it is too many." "But we need a figure," pressed the film crew. "How many do you think? Ten? Twenty? Twenty-five?" "I cannot say for sure," answered the administrator, flustered. "Maybe yes, we do not have the means to know for sure now, I just know it is too many, so many needless deaths." And twenty-five deaths a day it became, a figure arbitrarily established by a television crew for the largest international news service.[8]

Compounding the difficulty of physical documentation of information in conflict areas is the question of "politicized facts." In the context of violence and terror, whose voice(s) do we listen to and how do we get to them? Violence is essentially polysemic; it speaks with and through myriad and often contradictory voices, even if many of these are constituted through silences made meaningful and spaces made relevant. The question is further confounded by the fact that each voice, in the face of war's lethality, has a vested interest in making sure its version is the paramount one by discrediting, subverting, or silencing antagonistic ones.

Consider:

- the general who constructs strategic orientations;
- the field commanders who reinvent these in terms of their own personalities and battlefield scenarios;
- and the grunt soldiers who simply enact them according to their own ideas of war, violence, personal identity, and gain;
- the politicians who weave political ideology to justify their government and its actions;
- the opposition who tries to deconstruct these ideologies;
- and the officials who simply profiteer from the war;
- the journalists who write from political conviction;
- the journalists who write from literary conviction;
- and the journalists who write from bars and the offices of propaganda makers.

Consider the academics, the artists, the foreign experts, the aid personnel, the angry, and the charitable, all who publicly ply versions of the conflict based on their relationship to it.

And consider finally the average civilians who constitute both the backdrop and the battleground of the violence expressed, the targets of violence and the templates for terror: the victims, the informers, the jackal profiteers, the subversionists, the silenced. The last word, *silenced*, is critical, since 90 percent of all war casualties in the world today are noncombatants. Logically the most representative voices naming war are those who have experienced it, yet these voices are those least represented to the public and the world.

In fact, many of the most forceful public voices outlined above only speak *about* warfare—giving us reconstituted versions of a reality they have never fully experienced in a narrative of their own rendering, one necessarily constructed from the vantage point of the narrator. Simply, and simplistically: generals and politicians justify strategies of warfare they seldom themselves fight; media specialists rely heavily on information sanctioned by commanders and political officials because of political necessity and the difficulty of getting to the frontlines or into the prisons; researchers talk to refugees away from the battlefields for the same reasons; the public reads and reproduces these accounts; experts base policies on them; and the "factx" of war are born far from the realities of the actual violence.

"Facts" take place within socio-political and military contexts actively configured by ideology, vested interests, and undercurrents of resistance. Because they are seldom free of visa requirements, travel permits, restricted access, and second-hand information "provided" by their hosts, even the most probing researchers may not be able to pierce the full reality behind publicly sanctioned "facts." Thus the ethnography of socio-political violence is confronted with a situation where a great many reconstituted versions of the conflict exist, juxtaposed against the difficulty of getting "to the field," to the many places where force is actually manifested. There are many repercussions to this dilemma, and they speak directly to the possibilities for an accurate knowledge of violence and the processes of war. As researchers, we need not only be aware of Michael Taussig's (1987) mandate to speak against violence responsibly, but to be sure whose facts—whose definitions of violence and reality— we are perpetuating.

Learning the War from the Ground Up: The Cast of "Armed" Characters

When I hear people referring to a war in terms of two opposing forces— Frelimo and Renamo in the case of Mozambique—as if that defined the totality of the war experience, I am puzzled and want to ask, "What about the blackmarketeers, the arms merchants, the civilian collaborators, the roving predatory bands of quasi-soldiers and ex-militia, the mercenaries, the jackal profiteers who sell information to both sides, the private militias, and the foreign strategists—all of whom profoundly shape the dynamics of the war on the ground?"[9]

The Troops

Introductions to Mozambique generally begin with a dichotomization of (1) Frelimo (Frente de Libertação de Moçambique: Front for the Liberation of Mozambique) government and its forces, FAM (Armed Forces of Mozambique);[10] and (2) the opposition group Renamo (Resistência Nacional Moçambicano: Mozambican National Resistance). The discussion puts each into its proper historical perspective: the popular and largely unified revolutionary groundswell that launched Mozambique into independence and Frelimo into office; and the externally forged structure of Renamo—developed and led by neighboring apartheid governments of Rhodesia and South Africa. Such orientations follow traditional political science approaches to describing conflict: protagonist, antagonist, politico-military setting, ideological milieu. Frelimo represents the movement that fought successfully against the Portuguese colonists and established the first independent government, a government committed to black majority rule that was first grounded in Marxist-Leninist, and then socialist, principles. Renamo is characterized as developing largely from foreign-dominated interests. To western conservative analysts, Frelimo represented the threat of communism, Renamo a pro-capitalist force.

Important facts are transmitted in such discussions, but something else is transmitted as well. The idea takes root that each side is a coherent, identifiable political group with a grounded ideological foundation. Through such conversations, we begin to accept that "a Frelimo" and "a Renamo" exist.

But, realistically, what is Frelimo, Renamo? A part of these militaries are trained soldiers and commanders. But many of the troops are barely pubescent and were forcefully inscripted, youths like the one who responded to my question of "why are you fighting?" with the answer "I forgot." The soldiers who have cattle-poaching rings, who trade ivory for weapons, who harass and even kill civilians for money and goods, who run from base camps to form roving predatory bands living off the civilians, are as much a part of the war experience as troops "fighting the enemy." Even military units actively engaged in fighting show remarkable differences: region, charismatic leaders, need, and the personal biography of those involved insure that the "Frelimo" and "Renamo" in one region of Mozambique is quite a different force from the "Frelimo" and "Renamo" in a different site.

Moreover, everyone enacts multiple roles in life. A "soldier" is in fact a person standing on the horizon of a virtually limitless expanse of roles and relationships. A soldier is a member in a fighting group, and as well a member of an ethnic group, a language group, a gender group, a cultural group, a community, and a family group. All these alliances variously cross-cut the alliances of the fighting group. A soldier is also a child with parents, possibly a parent as well, a lover, a spouse, a person embedded in a network of friendships and economic pursuits. A soldier is a composite of history projected onto the present, imbued with variously negotiated meanings, myths, emotions. And all these interwoven identities come to bear on each soldier's actions.

When is someone acting as a soldier, a parent, a tribal representative, a businessperson, a profiteer? What does this say for any idea of a coherent politico-military ideology or identity? We can find such coherence in literary texts and political diatribes, but it has little significance on the way war is lived on the frontlines. The complexities of political loyalty and their relationship to military ideology are illustrated in the comment a man made to me one day as we were traveling through an area that had recently been under attack:

> It is difficult to really understand this war here—it is a very complicated thing. Like maybe a soldier sees you driving down the road with a nice new car and good looking clothes, and he is jealous of you, all he feels is envy. And that's what he fights for. Maybe that's all he fights for. It is like Renamo, when Frelimo came to power: some people got shoved aside, some got no power, some people felt they got cut out of the future. Like I know two people who support Renamo: both are professionals who want more education and a better future, but they don't have any opportunities here, they can't carry on with their education, they can't get the things they think they need in order to succeed. And some poor guy who doesn't have anything; well, he's walking down the road and he sees all that he doesn't have, and maybe can never get normally, and maybe fighting seems a pretty good option then. And who's to say what's really going on? You know those priests that were killed? Everyone says it was Renamo? Well, maybe it was really Frelimo—so some people say. Maybe lots of people who were killed were killed by other people and for other reasons than what is said. Renamo too, they shouldn't kill. Maybe people will back someone new, someone who doesn't kill. Someone who makes it equal for everyone in the country.

Mozambique's war was also shaped by forces that extended far beyond the purview of Frelimo, Renamo, Mozambique, and what we misleadingly label "internal conflict." This war and, I suggest, all the conflicts we label "internal" or "regional"—far from being particular expressions of unique conditions and specific tensions—are in fact strongly influenced by cultures of militarization operating throughout the world today. The specific circumstances surrounding the development of the Mozambican war are directly affected by larger international socio-political conflict processes and can be understood only in this light. The following examples give an idea of the international linkages shaping the war in Mozambique.

Frelimo was forged as a guerrilla force for independence in the early 1960s. Its leaders were internationally sophisticated (Eduardo Mondlane, the first leader and founding father of Frelimo—who was assassinated in February 1969—held a Ph.D. in Anthropology from Northwestern University). Frelimo was headquartered at this time in Dar es Salaam, Tanzania, and its members maintained far-reaching links with other revolutionary and independence movements, both in Africa and worldwide. Guerrillas trained in various sympathetic countries, and discussions among these paramilitary soldiers over the theories of Che Guevara, Mao, and Marx, to name a few, forged ideological orientations and commitment. When Mozambique gained independence in 1975 and Frelimo came to govern the country, it feared a direct war with South Africa and thus turned its hand to developing conventional war capacities with the assistance of African and Communist bloc countries. Frelimo benefited, for example, from Soviet, East German, and Cuban assistance and military advisors. Zimbabwean troops,[11] predominately along the Beira corridor that links Zimbabwe with the seaport of Beira in the central region of Mozambique, and, to a lesser extent, Tanzanian troops were deployed within Mozambique to assist Frelimo. The Cold War, however, did not restrict Frelimo's networks to the Communist bloc countries. When Renamo's atrocities became known in the 1980s, Britain sent military advisors to assist Frelimo and many western countries provided nonlethal aid.

Renamo's development was strongly influenced by western anti-Communist factions as well as by white minority governments in southern Africa. This assistance extended well beyond the level of the governmental. William Finnegan notes that

a frightful laundry list of right-wing American sects and organizations had become interested in Mozambique by then. From the Family Protection Scoreboard in Costa Mesa, California, to the End-Time Handmaidens of Jasper, Arkansas, every far-right fringe group and would-be mercenary in America seemed to want to send Bibles or worse to the Renamo "freedom fighters." The Reagan State Department became the unlikely target of ceaseless attack from the extreme right; and a ramshackle system of "privatized intervention" sprang up, shuttling supplies and light weapons into Mozambique, usually via Malawi. (1992:182–83)

Such alliances were clearly not restricted to the United States, but extended through Europe to the Middle East. Mercenaries from as far afield as Protestant Northern Ireland have been found on Mozambique's battlefields. Malawi provided rear bases for Renamo until adjoining African countries pressured President Banda to stop such assistance in the mid-1980s.[12]

Transnational dynamics do not act as unilateral forces in shaping conflicts. Local and translocal concepts of violence and war intersect and reconfigure each other. Soldiers and civilians alike accept certain cultural definitions of war while reinterpreting ideology, strategy, goals, and the role of violence in the most immediate and personal of ways. At the level of practice, military and paramilitary process becomes infused with local-level culture, personal biography, and individual motivation. In fact, political ideology and commitment can be lacking almost entirely among ground troops. For example, recruitment was often less than voluntary. William Minter (1989) estimated that 90 percent of Renamo's troops were kidnapped and "instrumentalized" (forcefully trained) to become soldiers. Frelimo was also noted for conscription sweeps. When I first arrived in Mozambique, I was struck by the fact that, in many areas, young adults disappeared from the streets in the late afternoon. People explained to me that if they were on the street when Frelimo troops came by, they often found themselves instantaneously "volunteering" for duty. Thus while Frelimo elites are largely drawn from southern Mozambique, and Renamo elites from the Ndau speakers populating the central regions of the country, both forces relied on ground troops that came from all parts of the country, whether by choice or by force.

From considerations of the European mercenaries on the battlefields of Mozambique to the village teenagers forcefully conscripted into the military to serve under a (foreign) commander who also runs guns, the more one follows the questions of who are the "two" sides and what are their political objectives, the less a clear-cut answer seems possible. Amid all these considerations, the following quote told to me by a Mozambican civilian helps put the question of militaries in perspective for me. The reality of war for the people on the frontlines (whose opinions are generally the most relevant and least often sought) is the sheer impossible fact of an old refugee woman looking for a glass of water causing an entire town to flee, and a population that for the most part no longer finds solace or solution in any military, no matter whose side or faction they say they uphold.

There was a woman who was kidnapped and taken up north. She escaped and walked all the way to [the town of] JM. She arrived tired and asking for water. Now the Bandidos Armados [Renamo] sometimes send women and children into a village to scout it out for an upcoming attack. So when this woman wandered into the village a shout went up that the Bandidos were attacking. The entire village went into flight. You have never seen anything like it: thousands of people, like a flood, pouring out and down the valley. Hundreds of children screaming and fleeing past me like a sea. Everything dropped where it stood—the entire population running and screaming for their lives. We got into the provincial capital in record time, and went straight to the military command to tell them that JM was being attacked. And they simply and calmly responded, "Sorry, there is nothing we can do." That old woman, what she must have thought. We laugh about it now, but there is something we don't laugh about. The Bandidos, we live in fear of them. But the government troops, well, we have had our trust broken there as well. About this time there was a real attack not far from here, in my home area. The Bandidos went in and killed and looted and burned, and then they moved on. Not too long thereafter, Frelimo troops heard of the attack and amassed transport carriers and all manner of fancy equipment and rolled into the attacked area, assuring people they were here now to protect them. Unbeknownst, the Bandidos circled back and reattacked the area, and the Frelimo troops promptly fled—leaving all the fancy equipment and the fate of the villagers in the Bandidos' hands. Well, Carolyn, say you are here to help and protect the Curandeiros, and if this is your work and your job, and when under attack you flee and leave them to be kidnapped and killed unprotected—well, they will come to blame you for this. This is what it is like with Frelimo and the villagers.

Splinter Groups

Renamo also generated splinter groups, who broke with the main force over ideological disagreements. All such groups were small and regionally located (such as Unamo in southern Zambezia), and many were short-lived. Generally, when an attack took place, the term "Renamo" was applied at most levels of politico-military and analytical authority. Renamo, like Frelimo, was presented as a cohesive group.

At the ground level, however, the picture was more complex. Villagers I spoke with sometimes told of the predicament of having to placate passing troops by providing them with food and goods so they would leave the village unharmed, an impossible situation because they found no unified Renamo or Frelimo. One military group would pass through, demanding certain goods and loyalties from villagers. Then another would come demanding more goods and different pledges of loyalty. And then yet another. If one of the groups returned, they could easily become enraged to violence if they discovered the assistance the villagers had given to another group. And no one was quite certain who was who. While these troops might (or might not) all call themselves Renamo or Frelimo, they appeared to pledge allegiance to their own immediate group and needs. Other than risking death or fleeing from their homes, the villagers had little option but to meet the demands of each passing group as best they could.

Frelimo has been remarkably resistant to giving rise to splinter factions, but it is not immune to excesses. FAM, the Mozambican army, was notoriously underpaid, underfed, and undertrained. Stories are legion of troops in the field who had not received food, supplies, or pay for months on end. Like Renamo, many of these troops came to rely on the population for food and other necessities. There developed, as Finnegan writes, an "economy of pillage" (1992:69). Unlike Renamo, reports of FAM looting entire towns and making off with everything from doors to electrical wiring were minimal, though there were numerous reports of *soldados* (soldiers) demanding tribute from villages, stealing from people at checkpoints, looting convoys, and attacking vehicles on the road.

Bandits

Simple banditry thrived under the name of "soldiering" as well. The following story was typical in Mozambique. One Sunday I visited a Mozambican friend and was surprised to find she had several more children than she had the last time I had been to her house. She explained, holding one of the newly arrived children in her lap:

> Last night a group of armed men wearing masks attacked several of the houses down the street. They went in waving guns and shouting that they were Renamo and demanding everyone's valuables. They grabbed as much as they could, and in the fray, several people were shot. My friends, these children's parents, were killed. The men then ran off into the night. But those of us around here are sure these men were not Renamo. We are right in the center of town, and Renamo does not come in to attack a few homes in the middle of a town. And why were the men wearing masks? Renamo does not wear masks. We think it was because these men were from the neighborhood, and they were afraid of being recognized. The clothes and the voices of several were familiar, and they knew where to go and what to look for. So now these twelve children are without parents. I have taken

several, and the rest are with other families in the area. We will keep them until other family arrangements can be made. Given the situation [situação: war], maybe we will keep them forever, who knows what the circumstances of the rest of the family are.

Ex-Soldiers and Predatory Bands

Possibly more disturbing is the issue of ex-soldiers. FAM had a history of discharging soldiers wherever they happened to be at the time their service was over without providing them means or money to return to their homes. The more canny left with their weapons. Penniless and far from home, the temptation to make a living by preying on the population was irresistible to some. There were reports from around the country that roving bands of predatory ex-FAM soldiers (their numbers swollen by deserters) were living "off the population." The "economy of pillage" became quasi-institutionalized. Predation was not restricted to the lowest echelon of ex-soldiers. In one area I visited, an investigation was taking place of an ex-commander who used his weapons, his contacts, and his influence to rustle cattle for considerable profit.

Militia

Private militias were organized to protect businesses and communities. They emerged when it became obvious that Frelimo forces simply were not large or well-trained enough to protect the many areas that came under Renamo attack. Generally, businesses and communities, often with the encouragement of Frelimo, elected to organize militias, and sometimes technical support and weapons were supplied by FAM.

The results were as various as the militias themselves. In some cases, militias were carefully organized and controlled, and few complaints were registered. Other militias, however, used their weapons to sequester goods and demand services from the population at large. In some instances, people said that militias were little better than roving predatory bands. Finnegan (1992) catches the irony of militias with the following example. The docks in Maputo were suffering serious pilfering problems. In an effort to stop the tide of stealing, officials decided to provide dock workers with weapons to guard the docks. Overnight, pilfering became armed robbery.[13]

Businesses, especially foreign-owned ones, were willing to put up the money to arm private militias to protect their factories from attack. But how it was that certain communities were able to maintain militias while others were not has never been clear to me. In fact, some of the most needy communities I visited were unable to get any support for the development of a militia. I spoke with one headman whose village had been attacked three times by Renamo. Houses and businesses had been burned, goods looted, and many people killed and kidnapped. He said many nights when they went to sleep, they could hear Renamo passing nearby, and they lived in perpetual fear. Worse, after being burned out three times and losing numerous community members, many towns-people had lost both the resources and the will to rebuild.

> The government says it is our duty to rebuild, but they give us nothing to rebuild with, and we have nothing, not even the heart to go on, in many cases. If we had a few guns to form a militia with, if we had a few landmines to protect our village, we would feel stronger, it would give us heart, we could protect what we are working so hard for. But we cannot get even one gun, even one mine, so we just work and sit watching it all be destroyed, looking at death every day, waiting for it to come for us.

Direct support from FAM for militias sometimes reflected a lack of organization and a comedy of errors. In one case I know of personally, a business approached Frelimo to request permission to form a militia to guard their plants. Frelimo responded favorably and had them contact the army for support. The army said they were willing to provide weapons and ammunition. Several days later, FAM showed up with a large truck full of used and damaged automatic weapons, and told the business to salvage what they could. With a crew of people, the business sorted through the hundreds of machine guns and rifles and patched together as many weapons as possible, which added up to an impressive number. FAM then said they would drop off some ammunition, and several days later deposited an entire truckload of armor-piercing bullets. The business contacted FAM to say they did not need such lethal ammunition, nor such a vast quantity of it, and could they exchange it for a lesser amount of regular automatic weapon ammunition. FAM agreed, but soon delivered another truckload of armor-piercing bullets while leaving the first as well. The business contacted FAM once again to try to sort things out, but were told, essentially, not to worry. So the business had guards armed with armor-piercing ammunition guarding not only the plants but storerooms filled with heavy weaponry and ammunition.

The need to use private armed guards often had tragic consequences. I spoke with a doctor whose premises were broken into so many times that she requested assistance from the government, and was provided with armed personnel. The first night on duty, one of the guards took his automatic weapon home with him and proceeded to get drunk and rowdy. Shortly thereafter, the same doctor was called to surgery: several

people had arrived from the guard's neighborhood who had been shot
by an automatic weapon.

The situation was in many ways an impossible one. With insufficient
troops, businesses and communities had to choose between leaving
themselves vulnerable to military attack or electing to organize potentially uncontrollable militias.

Civilian Collaborators

Because Renamo, as a rebel group, did not have formal government
structures during the war, a number of collaborators interfaced between
the soldiers and the populations they controlled. Neither Renamo nor
noncombatant, these people played an important part in the war. Frelimo focused on the role of traditional chiefs (*mambos*) and traditional
healers and spirit mediums (*curandeiros, macangueiros*) as Renamo collaborators, primarily because these groups were ostracized under Frelimo scientific socialism as obscurantists. Although such traditional authorities wield considerable local power and sometimes collaborated
with Renamo (though they resisted equally often), the true fluidity of
military-civilian boundaries was far more dependent on less prominent
individuals, individuals who could easily move between communities,
armies, responsibilities: beholden to all, beholden to none.

Renamo relied heavily on civilian authorities to collect taxes and supplies, to enforce Renamo policies, and to control the population. In
some cases, traditional chiefs and their assistants willingly provided such
services, but collaboration was as often won through coercion and terror tactics. When Renamo moved into an area, the choice given to many
traditional authorities was to help or to die, or to watch family members
die. This factor raises the issue of the relationship of threat and the rewards of power. Nowhere was this more evident than with the *majuba*,[14]
the "civilian police force" of Renamo. Civilians who enforced Renamo's
dictates might not always have volunteered for the job, but armed with
knives, clubs, and other nonautomatic weapons (this distinguished them
from Renamo soldiers, who carried automatic weapons), they policed
the population, sometimes brutally, and reaped the rewards of increased
access to the spoils of war and the potential for upward social mobility.

There was another type of collaborator, one not directly linked to
lines of authority. Both Frelimo and Renamo depended on civilians who
transmitted information on troop placement, strategy, and strength.
They identified potential Renamo supporters to Frelimo, or conversely,
Frelimo authorities (administrators, educators, health personnel, and
the like) to Renamo.

Civilian collaborators often worked to the detriment of the community and were frequently both feared and loathed by the community at large, but sometimes they worked to assist the community as well. I heard of repeated instances where villagers were informed of an attack before it took place, and managed to bury their valued possessions and flee the area before the troops arrived. In some areas, I have been told this form of double collaboration was virtually institutionalized: people knew where both Frelimo and Renamo troops were, when a foray was planned, and what its targets would be. They hid, left town, and returned home according to this information. It appeared that Frelimo and Renamo forces in the locales also depended on this information. An equanimity was reached in the war in these areas, with both casualties and disorder at a minimum.

Jackals

I have chosen to translate the various terms I have heard for this category of people as "jackal"—sometimes *majuba* is used, sometimes the term for a bush animal such as hyena is used, but always the term refers to someone or something that stealthily feeds off the kill of others. I cannot introduce the character of jackals better than with the following story told one day by a friend as we were walking down the street.

> Some time ago my husband's mother's village was overrun by Renamo, and they kidnapped a number of people to take back with them. My husband's mother was one of the people taken. For months we heard nothing of her, if she was alive, if she was well, where she was. It is a dangerous trip to my husband's birth village, no convoys go there, and the paths are infested with Bandidos Armados. It took him some time before he could get the money together and the time from his work to make the trip. In all this time, we could find nothing out about her.
>
> So not too long ago he made the trip. When he got to her village, he asked around for days and slowly it became apparent what he had to do. There is a bar one goes to where these people go—these jackals, Carolyn, do you know the meaning of this word jackal, a person we hate but must rely on. So he went there every day as he was told to do, and sat with a beer and made it known he was looking for his mother. Finally this man, this jackal, approaches him, and says he may be able to help. He has heard of such a woman, she was kidnapped in the attack and taken off to the bush, and he thinks she may still be alive. And he might be able to locate her, he might even be able to go out into the bush into the Renamo territory to arrange a transfer [bring her home]. But it would cost money.
>
> Epah, such money he asked for. My husband was terrified that he

would not be able to raise such a sum. He had been born in this village, but had not lived there for some time. He ran around for days, it may have extended into weeks, promising, begging, borrowing money from everyone he could. He even had to procure two shirts for the man as well.

Finally he got the money and the goods together and took it back to the man to give to him. The man explained he had "certain connections" whereby he could find out who was in Renamo's hands, and could travel to and fro to get their release. The man took the money and took off.

My husband was frantic: what if the man took all his money and simply disappeared? What if his mother was dead? It was a terrible wait for him. He couldn't eat, he couldn't think, all he could do was worry.

It took weeks, but finally his mother appeared in town. She was so sickly, so thin and malnourished, she had gotten so old. She was footsore and wounded from her long walk. Apparently one day one of the Bandidos simply came up to her and said, "Go on, get out of here." He pointed his gun at her and gestured toward the bush. She had seen so many people die, and she was terrified that as she walked away, he would shoot her in the back. But she could not stay, when the Bandidos told you to do something, you did it. So she walked off, and no bullet came. She walked all the way home, with no food or anything, never understanding why she had been allowed to go until she found her son. And her stories of her time with the Bandidos, epah, what a horror, but that is another story.

These people, these god-damned jackals, they are a real part of the war for us. Such people, becoming rich on the pain of others. Selling information to one side and to the other, selling people out for money. But how can you get along with hating them when you must rely on them to weather the war?

Resistance Movements: The Story of Manuel Antonio and Parama

Mozambique, like all warzones, contained numerous pockets of resistance to military oppression. Some, like Parama,[15] achieved epic proportions. Founded by Manuel Antonio, a curandeiro, Parama was a traditional army that developed in the north central regions of Mozambique during the late 1980s.

Mozambican officials, intellectuals and religious leaders, as well as Manuel Antonio himself, locate the power behind the emergence of the movement as

people's realization that only they themselves could end their suffering from Renamo's terror and war, and that they could find the means to achieve this from
their own "cultural resources." (Wilson 1992:561)

While periodic upsurges of traditional armies like Parama have been
documented in Africa, they usually chronicle tragic ends when the followers of charismatic leaders meet, and are slaughtered by, modern
weaponry. The story of Manuel Antonio may explain why such charismatic movements continue to surface. When I met Antonio in 1990, his
army had liberated approximately 150,000 people from Renamo occupation in north central Mozambique that year.

Manuel Antonio's commitment to saving his country from Renamo
began, the twenty-eight-year-old man told me, when he died of measles
at the age of fourteen and was buried. After six days he revived and
returned from his grave with an overriding concern to free his people
from the ravages of the war in Mozambique. (Resurrection from death
with special curative powers is a common theme in African medicine.)
His nemesis was Renamo. He discovered he knew how to vaccinate his
followers with traditional medicines that would make them invulnerable
to bullets and the cuts of machetes, and he knew the social prescriptions that the followers must live by in order to maintain the strength
of the medicines and the will to fight. Critical to their success was the
mandate that Parama were to fight only with "white weapons"—traditional spears and knives. The taboos surrounding fighting lent weight to
Parama's legendary warrior status: the protective medicines would only
work if the soldiers attacked without dodging bullets, turning to run
away, or hiding. Within a relatively short period of time from the inception of Parama, thousands of villagers, both women and men, rallied
to Manuel Antonio's cause. Virtually none had formal military training.
Neither had he, though some suggested he had been involved in some
way with Renamo in the past—how else could one explain his uncanny
knowledge of Renamo's bases and habits? Clad in the torn clothes and
rags of village youth and sporting a red cloth tied around some part of
their bodies or traditional weapons, Parama, Manuel Antonio was convinced, could rout the modern Renamo army equipped with automatic
weapons, mortars, and bazookas.

Every soldier underwent a strict initiation ceremony. These ceremonies, like Parama itself, are strongly tied to African medicine and
culture. As one man said to me, "Parama is traditional medicine—it is
one and the same thing." As noted above, Manuel Antonio was himself a curandeiro; in fact his title was *Commandante Curandeiro Manuel
Antonio*. When he went to an area to organize and inoculate troops, he
re-created his resurrection in a public ritual: he was buried in a pit and

covered with earth, and emerged later unscathed. After he vaccinated his troops with traditional medicines to make them immune to harm, he struck a powerful blow to each novice's naked chest and back several times with the sharp edge of a machete to show that the person's skin did not break. I have seen him perform this from no more than four feet away, and while he hit the soldiers with sufficient force to produce a resounding "thunk," no damage was sustained.

Manuel Antonio then explained the rules of comportment necessary to maintain the inoculations, and thus the soldier's invulnerability. Soldiers were to respect the population as they respected their own kindred. They were never to raise their hands against a civilian or a fellow Parama. Because they were imbued with inordinate strength, their capacity to inflict harm and social dissension was far greater than an average person, and it was a power they must never abuse. They were to adhere to the sexual mores of the society, and they were never to rob their wards—if they did, the power of the inoculations ensured that they would die. Ideally, Parama did not kill their enemy. Their goal was to force Renamo to flee in the face of their conviction and power. Their ultimate goal was not to seize power but to return their land to normal so they could return home to their families and farms in peace.

Manuel Antonio's exploits became legendary in Zambezia, and a typical story tells of his "magic" in taking a Renamo base. This base was considered impregnable; all Frelimo attempts to rout Renamo from there had been unsuccessful. When Manuel Antonio decided to take this base, people told him he was crazy, that it was impossible. Manuel Antonio just smiled and ordered a very large quantity of liquor to be brought to him. When it arrived he began to drink. He drank steadily for half an hour, finishing bottle after bottle, but he did not get drunk. He then left with his troops for the base, and when they arrived they found all the Renamo soldiers there mindlessly drunk. Manuel Antonio simply walked into the camp, disarmed the soldiers, captured the leaders to turn over to Frelimo, and told the rest of the Renamo there to flee and to give up fighting. The impregnable area was liberated within a few short hours without a shot being fired.

He explained that he was not a leader seeking military or political power. He was "the blood of the people." His troops were the *povo*, the people of the land. He represented the will of the people to free their lands and lives of Renamo troops. When the need was no longer there, he told me, he would return to his house and his healing, and tend to wounds of a more common nature. "When the war is over, Parama is over, when the need to protect our people from the threat of Renamo no longer exists, Parama will no longer exist." Ken Wilson, however, raises a point that was not lost on either Frelimo or Renamo:

It can be argued that the very fact of the peasantry taking matters into their own hands is a profound political statement in Zambezia, with challenging implications. Manuel Antonio's statements challenge the stranglehold of power that ruling elite and commercial interests with their "Portuguese" culture have retained on Zambezia, and he critiques the impossible economic situation that displaced people find themselves in because of the war and structural adjustment. (1992:566–67)

Manuel Antonio and Parama presented a thorny dilemma to the Mozambican government and military. The military, with the approval of President Chissano, ultimately joined forces with Parama, and often went out on joint raids against Renamo. The military, it was whispered, felt they had no choice: the population was clamoring for Parama, the new liberators. For a year, nearly every time I went out to small towns and villages in the interior of Zambezia, I was greeted by a contingent of Frelimo and Parama troops together. The FAM troops were often very supportive of Parama, and a number were themselves vaccinated to be resistant to bullets.

During the height of Parama's power, the civilians developed a faith in Parama they had lost with the FAM troops. Often, when I was asking about the security of a town I wanted to travel to, people would tell me: "Hey, no problem, Parama has arrived there, and they will protect you." No one ever mentioned the government troops.[16]

Parama are in the market today, they have come from my home area, they have been running off the Bandidos. The people respect Parama very much. They love Parama. They are allowing us a life like before, like in the old days. A life where people go to their fields to work, produce the foods that nourish their families, build the houses where they will raise their children—a good life, a healthy life. People just want to eat, to play with their children, to be able to buy a chair for their house if they can, to visit with their family and friends. These are things we can't do now, we suffer too much—our lives are suffering. A person should be able to come home from work and go to the market and buy dinner to prepare, to sit down and enjoy it with his family— but we come home from work and sit down and there is no dinner. How can we live like this? The life here, the life in the world, is no good now, it has been broken by war. Nothing is available now, and it costs so much no one can afford it. These tomatoes cost 600 Metacais, and next month one-fifth of this amount will cost the same price. A tin of milk costs 10,000 Metacais [one-third of a nurse's or teacher's monthly salary]. Tell me, how we can live like this? We eat suffering for dinner. We want to be able to carry on with our lives, to walk where we want, to do what we want—but we can't. We can't walk freely, we can't work freely, we can't eat freely, we can't live freely. The life of war is a spoiled life, and Parama is saving us from this, they are returning us to the days when life was life.

As Parama's fame increased, the more privileged soldiers crafted intricately honed and decorated spears and knives; a few even carried AK-47s taken from Renamo they had defeated. By 1991, just a year or two after Parama became a public force to be reckoned with, some of the elite troops had been given uniforms from a philanthropic source. Weapons and uniforms were not the only changes to mark Parama. When the movement began, Antonio was proud of the fact that Parama was a *people's* force, including men and women (as long as they were not menstruating) fighting side by side. But as Parama gained notoriety and joined forces with the FAM troops, women were increasingly put in noncombat roles: cooking, providing sex, carrying messages, supporting the troops.[17] And Parama soldiers came increasingly to surrender their belief in nonviolence. When Renamo troops elected to fight, Parama decided it was legitimate to kill them.

Another change became apparent in some locations. There were stories of forced population movement, of sequestering food and goods from communities, of violence against unarmed people. It is a curious irony that some members of Parama reproduced the very types of violence and power abuses they so abhorred in Renamo. Antonio's attempts to control Parama mavericks were not completely successful, and, in 1991 in Nampula province, government officials reported rogue Parama troops raping women, stealing property, and retaining *recuperados* (people recuperated from Renamo captivity) until their relatives could pay Parama for their release (Wilson 1992). The problem was in part compounded by the fact that Parama had no means to pay the troops. People who fought with Parama left their homes, fields, and jobs and all the resources that go with them. Parama thus had to depend on the goodwill of the populations to supply them, on their own ability to hunt and gather food, on what they could capture from Renamo, or, more directly, on levies from the population. "Levies" and "looting" were sometimes indistinguishable.

Larger problems loomed on the horizon for Parama. Renamo had not only lost ground and tactical advantage, but face as well. Confronted by untrained village youth armed only with knives and spears, Renamo troops had often turned tail and run. Renamo leaders sought to rectify the situation. Fearing they had lost a powerful bargaining chip in losing so much of their military advantage, Renamo delayed peace talks while Renamo President Dhlakama himself elected to lead an assault against Parama in the summer of 1991. Renamo spread rumors that they had discovered an antidote to Manuel Antonio's famous vaccination ensuring invulnerability in battle, and that Renamo had regained spiritual supremacy. In a well-publicized battle in a Parama stronghold, Renamo not only retook the town, but reports stated that they severed the heads of Parama soldiers and lined the shelves of looted shops with them. The message was clear: Parama are not invincible.

Manuel Antonio was killed in battle on December 6, 1991. Soldiers left no doubt as to his death: his body was full of bullet and bayonet wounds. The population was not so sure, however. Antonio was a curandeiro, and the reports of his death may have been propaganda, many said. Even if he were dead, he had resurrected once, he could do so again. At his funeral in Quelimane, other curandeiros and supplicants poured protective medicines in his grave to ensure his rebirth. Manuel Antonio did not reemerge. Yet.

And So On . . .

The cast of characters is as infinite as the number of people involved in some way with the war process. Foreign advisors cross borders to hone strategy; foreign mercenaries are found on local battlefields; media experts variously construct the war according to their perspectives. Arms merchants sell to one side, or both; blackmarketeers exploit the tragedies of war to their gain; others bring much needed nonlethal supplies into ravaged areas. Health care workers, teachers working with the war-traumatized, development officials, lawyers, politicians, and muckrakers ply their trades and professions in meeting the demands of conflict-ridden communities. Emergency crews fly essential supplies into devastated areas and fly landmines out, and illicit traders seek to garnish such goods to redistribute and sell to far-ranging communities. Traditional power brokers and healers try to rally communities to their own agendas, or to heal the many wounds of violence. Anthropologists attempt to uncover the cultural dynamics of conflict. The list goes on—all constitute part of the conflict process, and all affect the lived experience of war.

A Look at the Intersection of History and War

The horrors recorded and etched in their individual minds and collective psyche cannot be forgotten or left to a Western sense of history, as that which is only in the past. (Price, 1990:xix)

Wars are often portrayed as events that stand in and of themselves, adrift from historical trends and the reproduction of cultural habits. But if war is a cultural phenomenon, previous experiences influence current practices. Many of the strategies that informed the post-independence war in Mozambique, including cultures of resistance to violence and oppression, can be found in the conflict dynamics of the past. This section explores some of the social and political processes of the last several centuries that helped shape contemporary political and military cultures.

Possibly the most concise and telling account of the conflicts that have marked Mozambique throughout its history is given by Thomas H. Henriksen in the introduction to his book, *Mozambique*:

History placed Mozambique at least on the periphery of two of the world's important expansive movements. Bantu-speaking peoples had swept down east central Africa just before the Portuguese, the vanguard of European expansion, touched Mozambique on the way eastward. Their encounter acted to check each other's domination of this frontier land between African invader and Portuguese intruder. From prehistoric times no single African or foreign cultural, political, or economic influence ever rolled from land or sea to change suddenly or control all of Mozambique until the third decade of the twentieth century when Portugal established administrative posts in most areas. Yet the turbulence of contending groups was to make Mozambique one of the least peaceful regions of Africa and was to give it a legacy of war, slavery, misery, and turmoil that has lived on into the present. (1978:1)

With excellent ports, gold, ivory, and a barbaric though well-developed slave trade, not to mention rich soil and navigable rivers, Mozambique drew many who sought to profit from its riches. Much effort and many lives were spent trying to achieve control over these resources.

Portuguese colonists arrived in Mozambique in 1498, beginning nearly five centuries of political occupation that ended with independence in 1975. Portugal's control varied widely across Mozambique and over time, and it was not until the early 1900s that the colonial government first succeeded in bringing nearly the whole of the African country under its rule. Frequent wars, constantly changing zones of control, and an entrenched tendency toward rapaciousness rather than development marked Portugal's relations with the people of Mozambique through these centuries. Zambezia, a Portuguese stronghold, had one of the most curious systems of colonial "administration." During the seventeenth century, in an effort to create a significant settler population of direct Portuguese descent and a viable economic base in Mozambique, Portugal instituted a system of *prazos da coroa*, or crown estates.[18] For the most part, it was not the educated and landed Portuguese who were willing to carve out estates for themselves in faraway Mozambique. "Into the place of African *mambos* [chiefs] stepped Portuguese felons, ex-soldiers, female orphans and penniless officials to take up chiefly roles" (Henriksen 1978:55).

Prazo relied on the local chief to collect taxes, control the *colonos* (free African workers) who worked on the estates, and enforce *prazo* rule(s). Security and control were enforced by *achikunda* (private armies of slaves), which all strong *prazo* holders maintained. It is interesting to note that these patterns show a striking resemblance to Renamo's techniques of control during the war. Given that Renamo was more strongly linked with Portuguese ex-colonialists than Frelimo, there is a cultural logic to this reproduction of systems of control across time and political party, although, as will become evident, Frelimo was not immune to reproducing colonial Portuguese strategies of militarized governance.

As colonists, the Portuguese failed to develop a strong farming, plantation, or industrial infrastructure. First gold, ivory, and taxes imposed on Africans supported the *prazos*. When slaving became profitable, an extraordinary amount of energy went into procuring and marketing humans. While slaves could be purchased for a small price from Muslim slavers and competing African tribes, *prazo* holders were so swayed by quick profit that they began selling *colonos* from their estates as slaves, crippling the farming and industrial base of their estates but providing untold wealth. The impact of the slave trade leaving from the Zambezian port of Quelimane alone is staggering. During the peak years of the slave trade in this area—around the decade of the 1820s—12,000 to 30,000 humans were sold *every year* (Vail and White 1980). Isaacman and Isaacman (1983:17) figure that more than one million Mozambicans were forcibly removed from their homelands and sold as slave labor during the nineteenth century.[19]

The rapaciousness, cruelty, and lawlessness of the *prazo* holders; the tendency of the *prazos* to be bought, conquered, and sold outside the crown's influence; and the frequency with which *prazo* holders were embroiled in battling resistance movements and each other had a devastating effect on the people of Mozambique. The entire *prazo* system finally collapsed in the late nineteenth century, but some of the negative practices of the system lingered on. Both in the Portuguese war against independence and in Renamo's war against Frelimo, necessary infrastructure was sacrificed to war-making and people were sacrificed for political, military, and economic gain.

At the beginning of the twentieth century, Portugal brought most of Mozambique under its jurisdiction, spurred to action by other European colonial powers' encroachment into Portuguese-claimed but tenuously held areas. But formal colonial rule did not improve the Mozambicans' lives. Administrative reorganization came to Mozambique in 1907, grounded on Portuguese *administradors* (administrators) and *chefes de posto* (regional authorities). The latter were the closest Portuguese officials to the Mozambican population, and each presided over the collection of taxes, disputes, and punishment as well as village agriculture and government projects in his area (Isaacman and Isaacman 1983:27).

> His tyranny, especially in the early years, forms a bitter and violent chapter in Mozambique's colonial history. Underpaid and poorly trained, he came as a bird of passage not to create but to squeeze what he could from his lowly position and return to Portugal. Corrupt, cruel, and incompetent, he came to represent Portuguese rule to many villagers. (Henriksen 1978:100–101)

In order to maintain control, the Portuguese set into place a system of administrative alliances with local chiefs, called *regulos*, who were responsible for maintaining the peace, collecting taxes, and recruiting labor from among the villagers. If the traditionally appointed chiefs of the area were not receptive to these alliances and duties, the administrators simply replaced them with more amenable members of the royal family or with other collaborators (Isaacman and Isaacman 1983). African police (*sipais*) were recruited to control the population, and were noted for their brutality. The administration did not bring in much sought after revenues, however, and Portugal supplemented its coffers with concessions to foreign governments and businesses and with the opprobrious system of *chibalo* (forced labor) on their own plantations and enterprises. In many ways echoing the oppressive policies found under the *prazos*, the Portuguese system of *chibalo*, and the brutality with which they enforced it, is among the most oppressive in the history of colonialization in Africa. Both the reliance on *regulos* and *chibalo* again show distinct similarities to Renamo's wartime administrative strategies.

The inequalities generated under Portuguese colonialism extended throughout all levels of society. In 1955 the literacy rate of the entire population was between one and two percent. In 1963, at the only institution for higher education in Mozambique, the University of Lourenco Marques, only five of the nearly three hundred students enrolled were African. Mozambicans were not only segregated in education; health care, sanitation programs, and housing for Mozambicans were substandard, banished to the peripheries of more sophisticated Portuguese infrastructure. By law and by habit, for the colonists Mozambique was essentially a resource to be exploited.[20]

These were the conditions that launched Frelimo's war against the Portuguese for independence in the early 1960s, and it was this war for independence that launched the inception of Renamo, not in Mozambique but from another colonial front. Frelimo's successes against the Portuguese disturbed the white minority government of Ian Smith in neighboring southern Rhodesia, especially those in the Tete area that shared a border with Rhodesia, an area that could become a corridor for Zimbabwean nationalist guerrillas and their armaments (Johnson and Martin 1986). Worried that the Portuguese would not be able to contain Frelimo, Ken Flower, the director-general of Rhodesia's Central Intelligence Organization (CIO), conceived a plan to create a clandestine intelligence operation inside Mozambique. He envisioned a group comprised of disenfranchised Mozambicans and led by Rhodesia's CIO that would report on and destabilize Zimbabwe's nationalist guerrillas and their Frelimo supporters. Rhodesia recruited both black and white members of the (infamous) Portuguese secret police (PIDE) and members of the Portuguese colonial army's elite special forces who had fled the country. They "enlisted" many early Renamo recruits by raiding Frelimo reeducation camps and prisons where people convicted by the government of corruption, thievery, and other crimes were held (Isaacman and Isaacman 1983). "Recruitment" also entailed forcefully training kidnapped villagers. Minter (1989) estimates that roughly 90 percent of all Renamo soldiers were kidnapped, removed to locations distant from their homes, and instrumentalized into fighting.

In the spring of 1974 a coup d'état in Portugal brought down the regime that had stridently supported colonial control. The new Portuguese government had little interest in maintaining colonial wars and swiftly relinquished colonial authority in southern Africa. In 1975, Mozambique became independent, and Frelimo was vaulted from a guerrilla movement to a ruling party virtually overnight. Frelimo was confronted by a country in shambles. As Mozambicans point out, they were an underdeveloped country colonized by what was itself an underdeveloped country—leaving them impoverished at independence. Frelimo thus found itself suddenly in control of an essentially bankrupt colonial economy that had suddenly lost the vast majority of its skilled, managerial, and professional workforce with the fleeing of the Portuguese. At the time of independence, 93 percent of the population was illiterate, and less than a score of doctors, engineers, lawyers, and similar professionals remained in the country.

In 1980, Ian Smith's government lost its fight in the war for independence, bringing an end to Southern Rhodesia but not to Renamo. As Flowers explains: "I knew from previous approaches that the South Africans could be interested. . . . We made the arrangements in a few days between making the decision in principle to the actual handover, to effect a transfer to the South Africans."[21] In some of his last interviews, Flowers notes wryly, "I guess we created a monster."

Even with the extensive problems Frelimo inherited at independence, many party members expected that they would be able to defeat the thousand or so Renamo forces without great difficulty. No one foresaw the commitment South Africa's political and military leaders had to developing Renamo into a large-scale destabilization movement. In the 1980s Renamo grew to include 20,000 to 30,000 troops operating in all ten provinces of Mozambique. Their reputation for atrocities, particularly against unarmed civilians, grew with their numbers. Only when Frelimo was able to document these atrocities and Renamo's direct links with South Africa did international support for Renamo begin to dry up (Hanlon 1984, 1991; Johnson and Martin 1986; Minter 1994). Even the U.S. Congress, which until this time supported Renamo in its stand against a communist government, made a formal statement against the rebel forces, calling them "the Khmer Rouge of Africa," and Mozambique "the Killing Fields" (Frelick 1989). The South African government, along with many of the other formal supporters of Renamo, publicly disavowed further support of the rebel group in the mid-1980s. Yet undeclared support continued, with extensive reports of Renamo's links with foreign advisors, of sophisticated communications equipment Renamo could little afford without assistance, and of white military commanders operating with Renamo inside Mozambique.

The Reproduction of Terror and Creative Resistance Across Time

They had orders to burn and exterminate everything. They burnt all the houses and huts they found between the villages of Mahanda and Antonio. We ourselves saw more than 50 huts burned. Among them were our school in Antonio and the teacher's house. Maize, clothing, chairs, bicycles, carts, everything was destroyed. I found the victims shortly after the soldiers had left. One man's skull had been split into two parts, another man's genitals had been mutilated in such a way that I could not bring myself to photograph him, although I had my camera with me. (International Defence and Aid Fund 1973:14)

This quote, standing alone, can refer to any number of eras in Mozambique's history: *prazo* holders retaliating against indigenous resistance movements; Portuguese colonial government troops fighting during the war for independence; Renamo's recent war against Frelimo. In fact, this is a quote from a group of priests working in colonial Mozambique in 1973 who were documenting Portuguese massacres of civilians. In the same report, the official Portuguese version of the events brought to light by the priest's report states,

the Government determined to institute a rigorous inquiry. The first result of this investigation showed that the alleged incidents never happened. (International Defence and Aid Fund 1973:26)

Many of the patterns of violence evident in the most recent war were set in motion in by-gone years, such as Renamo's habit of relying on (or forcing) traditional chiefs and civilian go-betweens to collect taxes and enforce cooperation among villagers. The practice is markedly similar to the *prazo* system of the Portuguese colonialists of the nineteenth century. Similar, too, was their reliance on the forced labor of villagers and the failure to develop economic or governmental infrastructure, preferring instead to bleed profits from "slaving," taxes, and contraband.

Frelimo was not exempt from reproducing historical actions. The communal villages instituted at independence and the strategic villages enforced during the war (see Chapter 3 for details) bear a striking resemblance to the strategic hamlets of Portuguese authorities. The irony is that, in both cases, widespread dissonance and outright resistance by villagers accompanied these moves. In both cases, the forced relocation of villagers is cited as a primary factor in undermining the legitimacy and authority of the governments. Like Renamo's reliance on *prazo*-like forced labor and the extraction of resources and taxes, both groups have reproduced actions from the past that are sure to promote widespread resistance from civilians and which will therefore ultimately fail.

Specific tactics as well as large-scale strategies follow one war to the next. Certain acts of terror have become mainstays in many conflicts: burning entire villages for the suspected collusion of some of its members; massacring civilians in order to assert authority and instill acquiescence through terror; and mutilating and torturing civilians and soldiers alike, not to gain information, but as a threat against resistance. That these do not prove successful in the long run, and in fact appear to undermine a military's ultimate objectives, has not deterred the continuation of such tactics. Cultural habits die slowly.

*   *   *

Resistance, and the creativities that shape resistance, have been in place as long as have the cycles of political and military terror. The historian Allen Isaacman has delved into this topic in Mozambique, showing how traditions of resistance have accompanied all major instances of political oppression through the last several centuries. While Isaacman (1976) focuses more on the colonial era, he points out that, before the Europeans arrived in Africa, numerous examples of African expansionist forces, and resistance to them, mark precolonial history.[22] These habits of resistance, Isaacman continues, have thus been forged against forces both internal and external to Africa throughout the last millennium of African history.

Isaacman (1976; see also Isaacman and Chilundo 1995) explores multiple levels of resistance, from large-scale militarized insurrections to social banditry, from organized labor protests to daily acts among the population to reduce oppressions and misery. As in Mozambique's most recent war, these coalesced into shared patterns—cultures—of survival and a fight for independence from onerous and violent conditions. And across the various wars, while the political and military elites tried to suppress information about the strategies and successes of resistance:

> It could not control the indigenous oral communication system. Throughout the colonial period Zambezian elders defiantly transmitted accounts of African resistance which served both as a source of pride and a model for future activity. Young Mozambicans sitting around the evening fire or attending pre-puberty schools learned of the exploits of Mapondera, the Makombe and Muenemutapa Chioco as well as of the deeds of their own ancestors who had lived in their neighborhood. Spirit mediums and cult priests sanctified and enshrined these heroic efforts. As late as 1972 the legacy of resistance constituted a vital and living part of Zambezian oral traditions. (Isaacman 1976:199)

This description was published in 1976, just after independence was achieved and before anyone knew what kind of war was developing between Renamo and Frelimo. Twenty years later, in 1996, these oral traditions are equally strong.

Spirit mediums and African medicine, as Isaacman (1976) demonstrates, have also long been associated with fighting oppressive rule. Rebellions taking place over the last several centuries have been accompanied by powerful spiritual leaders and curandeiros who provide medicines that render the insurrectionists immune to the bullets of the enemy. A rich history thus supported Manuel Antonio's war against Renamo in the early 1990s. Regardless of what modern science says about this phenomenon, it is important to remember that Antonio opened up large tracts of Zambezia and Nampula in a single year of fighting only with spears and protective medicines—successes his predecessors have enjoyed in the past.

Though Manuel Antonio, like a number of previous spiritual leaders, ultimately lost his life to the war, his cause won—and the end of the war was near. Hannah Arendt (1969) has argued that a state that uses violent force to control its citizens is already in its death throes. Perhaps the drastic conditions that launch movements like Manuel Antonio's Parama also signal the impending death throes of an oppressive rule of war and the creative civilian will to deliver this death blow. The fact that Manuel Antonio was finally killed may have little to do with the ultimate success of a population's independence from oppressive conditions. Isaacman (1976:196) has summed up what perpetrators of terror-warfare around the world seem to have yet to learn: "Defeat did not deter a group from participating in subsequent insurrections."

Encoded in Manuel Antonio's death was the continuance of this culture of resistance. During his brief military life, he was considered the founder and inspired leader of Parama. He was the supreme commander of Parama to his troops and the population at large; the power of his traditional army flowed from Manuel Antonio himself.

Yet immediately upon his death a new social discourse circulated the length and breadth of the Parama areas. Manuel Antonio, it was now said, had learned his skills and his medicines from a powerful and venerated spirit leader and healer who lived in the remote bush of Nampula province. This healer was continuing to teach people these invaluable skills and medicines. Because he was a hermit, and because he did not want his teachings to be used for anything except good, he and his students did not circulate and practice this work widely in the country. Only when a great need arises do people like Manuel Antonio leave to fight for the freedoms humans have a right to. Until that time, this healer and his students practice the healing arts in the remote parts of the country where rural people far from clinics and pharmacies most need them. No one emerged to replace Manuel Antonio because peace was achieved within a year of his death. But should the peace process falter, people say, this healer and his protégés are ready to take up the fight against oppression.

This man's existence and power were taken seriously: even officials and foreign nongovernmental organization (NGO) workers from as far away as the capital city of Maputo told me they "knew for sure" the governor of Nampula province had made a trip to this healer's home. He had taken gifts and eaten dinner with this powerful visionary, and, in doing this, the governor had paid his highest respects to this man. Whether this is actually true matters less than the fact that people from the remote northern provinces to the power elite in Maputo believed it to be true. What is true is the message: resistance from oppressive violence is already in place; moreover, it has the backing not only of the people of the country, but of high-placed government officials.

In these circumstances the reproduction of creative resistance flows not from past to present, but from the present to a time of future need. It is "always already" in the cultural repertoire of the country. In this sense, Michel Foucault's observation that resistance begins at the moment oppression begins could be refined. Here, resistance is in place before the blow is struck. In a way, oppression is defeated before it even begins. That is why people say Manuel Antonio has not come back to life. Yet.

Notes

1. "By *ethnoscape*," Appadurai (1991:192) writes, "I mean the landscape of persons who make up the shifting world in which we live: tourists, immigrants,

refugees, exiles, guest-workers, and other moving groups and persons constitute an essential feature of the world and appear to affect the politics of and between nations in a hitherto unprecedented degree." This concept, he suggests, provides us with a tool more suited to addressing the complexities of identity and culture in a complex, interpenetrated, and cosmopolitanized world than one circumscribed by bounded geographies and monolithic cultures.

2. For both sides of this debate see, for example, Strathern (1995); Fardon (1995); Rabinow (1986).

3. Dumont's (1992) discussion of Marco's use of the movie *The Killing Fields* in rural Filipino villages as an implicit threat against supporting communist guerrillas is an apt reminder of this, a political example of the same process Appadurai notes in India where cinema has shaped notions of sexuality and the "art" of prostitution.

4. Hanlon cites the World Bank's *World Development Report 1990* to substantiate his figures.

5. The impact of the war has been compounded by natural disasters in the last decade, predominately drought; emergency relief supplies and measures have been impeded by fighting, decimated infrastructure, and a lack of security along transportation routes.

6. Community-sustaining infrastructures have been a primary target of Renamo campaigns, particularly health, education, and trade. Between 1980 and 1987 Renamo attacks closed or destroyed 822 of the 1,373 existing health units in the country, and an untold number of health care personnel have been murdered or kidnapped. By 1988, 30 percent of the country's health care system was nonfunctional, leaving 2,300,000 people in rural areas without any clinical care (Cliff and Noormahomed 1988; Ministerio da Saude/UNICEF 1988). Similar levels of destruction have ravaged the educational system. Of the 5,709 primary schools which existed in 1981, 32 percent have been destroyed by the rebel forces, and only 425 of those schools still in existence are capable of providing the full five years of primary education. Only 31 percent of the country's children are able to complete primary education (Mozambiquefile, March 1990, quoting Fatima Carrilho, a national director in the Ministry of Education).

7. The mortality rate for children under age five in the early 1990s in Mozambique was the second highest in the world (325–375 per 1,000 live births), primarily as a result of the war (UNICEF 1989). The rate of malnutrition escalated from 8.7 percent in 1986 to 35–40 percent in 1989 (UNICEF/Ministry of Cooperation 1990). Correspondingly, during the war, there was a high prevalence among children of wasting, stunting, and low birth weight, with 16 percent demonstrating growth faltering (World Health Organization 1990).

8. These problems do not plague Mozambicans alone. UNICEF (1989) has written that Mozambique has the second highest infant and below-five mortality rate in the world, primarily as a result of the war. The figures they give estimate that between one-fourth and one-third of all children die before the age of five. Yet numerous physicians and researchers I spoke with in the field said they could not determine how UNICEF arrived at those figures, nor could they themselves calculate an infant mortality rate for the country with any precision. Judging from the number of areas outside the capital cities I visited showing a dearth of adequate reporting techniques or trained field staff from nongovernmental organizations, I share these questions.

9. This can be expanded to ask, "What about the media representatives who forge public opinion about the war; the foreign aid organizations who work

on war-related development projects; the internal political frictions that shape policy; and the international political alliances and antagonisms that affect political, economic, and military power blocs, trade, and decision-making?"

10. Also known as FPLM, Mozambican People's Liberation Forces.

11. There have been as many as 20,000 Zimbabwean troops deployed in Mozambique, primarily to guard the Beira Corridor that affords landlocked Zimbabwe sea access without having to rely on South Africa. Estimates of Zimbabwe's expenses necessary to maintain these troops has been placed at US$1 million per day (*New York Times*, February 21, 1988). While popular analyses within Zimbabwe and Mozambique tend to confirm this figure, the government of Zimbabwe denies the expenditures are this high. The position of the Zimbabwean government may be a response to local resentment that much-needed dollars are being drained away to fight another's war.

12. President Banda of Malawi has had a long history of formal association with the Portuguese colonists in Mozambique and with the apartheid South African government; in fact, Malawi is the only country of the Southern States to have done so. Most think that Banda's support of Renamo stemmed from his desire to annex at least part of land-rich and sparsely settled northern Mozambique to overpopulated Malawi.

13. Finnegan (1992) provides one of the more detailed discussions of the many aspects of private militias and the impact they have had on the communities they guard.

14. Variously transcribed as *mujuba*, *majiba*, and *mujeeba* by Vines (1991).

15. In the literature on this movement, the term Naprama (or Naparama) is usually used. Naprama is a formal term that refers to the use of special medicinal plants to protect people in battle. I use the word Parama, however, as I lived in the center of the Parama stronghold and, in all my discussions on the subject, Parama soldiers and civilians alike used this term. Some authors transcribe it as Prama, but I found it was usually pronounced with a melodious inflection that lent three syllables and a rolled "r" to the name.

16. To the foreigner's eye, this protection was less than obvious. I remember the first time I arrived in a village recently freed from Renamo control by Parama. I was greeted by a group of village youths in tattered clothes. I asked if they were Parama. Yes, they said. I asked if they were armed. Yes, they confirmed. Where were the arms, I asked? Right here, they said as if it were obvious. Right where, I questioned? They pulled a man forward who had an old knife hung on a string slung around his shoulders. Here, they pronounced. I realized that each person had on some piece of red cloth, tied on an arm, wound around their head, sewn onto a piece of clothing: Parama's insignia.

17. See Nordstrom (1990; 1996) for a discussion of women's roles in war.

18. The *prazo* system took its definition from the Roman contractual agreement of emphyteusis, which granted a person a three-generation hold over the land, in this case passing through female lineage.

19. Vail and White sum up the situation with a quote from Villas-Boas Truão, Governor of Tete Province in 1806:

> While the slaves, male and female, work in the mines, the African traders pass through the bush, and the *colonos* cultivate the land. The *senhor*, lazy and inert, not needing to devote the least thought or combination of ideas to his affairs, passes his days sleeping or smoking or drinking tea, or at other times leaves his house when the sun is setting, offering the public the fatuous sight

of his stupid indolence and bogus grandeur, appearing lying in a *machila* and carried along by four miserable slaves. (1980:12)

There is another side to this picture. With their private armies, the *prazo* holders formed the bulk of the military weight in the area. Portugal was placed in a position of having to rely on the military strength of the very citizens against whom their decrees were often set. Needless to say, the decrees went largely unheeded. The strain placed on the entire *prazo* system by warfare and the wanton extraction of resources and people without regard to development caused the power of the *prazos* to crumble throughout the final half of the nineteenth century.

20. I have always found it interesting that the same verb in Portuguese is used for "to explore" and "to exploit."

21. Interview in April 1987 for the film *Mozambique: The Struggle for Survival.*

22. Habits of resistance, Isaacman continues, can be seen in the (1976) Tonga battle against the Muenemutapa forces.

Chapter 3
Ethnography of a Warzone

Dreaming bullets

    I grasp
    a humiliation
    and without leaving my homeland
    I emigrate to the north of Moçambique
    with the dream of bullets on my shoulders
             and there

I lunch on roots
I drink the rain water where the worms drink
I crawl
I crawl on my elbows
and knees

        Then
              Hidden in the middle of the bush
              The most red flowers blooming
              Of our beautiful freedom re-
              conquered with gunshots
                        —Susana

Renamo graffiti on walls of occupied town, Zambezia province, 1990. Photo by
Carolyn Nordstrom.

I present here an ethnography of a warzone—method, process, and theory—with the understanding that an ethnography of war is *not* the same as the ethnography of the effect of war on a particular locale.[1] When I first encountered lethal conflict, I discovered there was little in my anthropological repertoire that addressed immediate ethnographical and methodological necessities. I also discovered the discipline does not fully prepare us to make evaluations of the ethical considerations that surround studies of dangerous and often tragic circumstances. Thus in this book I stress ethnographic process as well as its theoretical implications in part so that others may not make some of the stupid and at times life-threatening mistakes I did for sheer lack of knowledge about the dynamics of violent conflict, and in part because the complexity of our contemporary world and the violence that marks it challenges anthropology to develop versatile and even unconventional research paradigms.

To capture war's complexities, I decided to shift my focus from relying on traditional ethnography rooted in a single locale to looking for an understanding of the arena of conflict itself. I grounded my ethnography in a topic and a process, not a place. War, then, serves as the "locating" topic of this study. It will be clear in the course of this chapter that what is one person's fact is another's fiction; what is one community's experience of war is different from that of a neighboring community. What constitutes violence, suffering, and survival is remarkably contested. In order to understand political violence it is important to follow its many manifestations unfolding across time, space, and culture.

The Art of Studying War: Five Stories of Listening

The Anthropology of Listening

Thousands of children have seen their parents die before their eyes, hundreds of children have been boiled in the presence of their parents. Heads of old people are used as stools by the bandits, unwilling farmers are nailed to trees. Every refugee, child or adult knows such a story. Seeing the war is to listen. (Dis 1991:44; translated from Dutch by A. Robben)

Antonius Robben, who sent me Adriaan van Dis's quote on Mozambique, struggled with the translation of "Seeing the war is to listen":

It is very difficult to translate the last sentence into English. In Dutch it sounds far more impressive. The author is saying that while one is listening to these stories one is actually seeing the war before one's eyes. There is a fusion of seeing and listening.

For people who have not conducted research in a violent context or among traumatized people, it may seem surprising that a researcher can elicit personal information of any kind. It is often assumed that war provokes xenophobia toward all outsiders, especially those neither intertwined within familial networks nor part of power regimes. It is further assumed that people will guard their silence because they are uncertain about how researchers will use the information they are collecting, and because they may fear reprisal. These assumptions are in many ways valid, but they are balanced by what Veena Das calls "the need to talk and talk" that characterizes victims of violence. Das's (1985, 1990) observations are based on her work on the severe rioting against the Sikhs sparked by the assassination of Indira Gandhi. "One man," writes Das (1985:5), "whose two sons had been killed, offered to raise fifty rupees later if we could have an account of their suffering published in a newspaper. We discovered thus that being subjected to brutal violence for two consecutive days had not been successful in stripping men of their cognitive needs, nor could it blunt their desperate need to have the truth recorded and communicated." Das then speculates that "they wanted their suffering to become known as if the reality of it could only be reclaimed after it had become part of a public discourse." A quote Das (1990) collected from a riot victim became the title of her work on this subject, "Our Work to Cry: Your Work to Listen."

Time and again my fieldwork confirmed Das's observations. Whether the violence extended across two days, as in Das's study, or two decades, as in the case of Mozambique, the need for communication and the complexity of what is communicated dovetails with violence. As both Das and Elaine Scarry (1985) note, it is essential for people to reconstruct their world after violence has deconstructed all they hold dear. Words serve to give voice to the unspeakable, and therefore render it at least somewhat more controllable. Words serve to mourn the dead and create meaning in a new and brittle world. Words serve to construct a tomorrow in the face of chaos. People also feel the need to convey their stories to challenge the "factx" of war spun by the politico-military institutions and by outsiders with vested interests—and thereby to break the "reality" these people have constructed upon the victims. In the words of several Mozambicans: "We are glad you finally came to ask us our story; up until now, everyone has come to tell us what our story is." When these stories involve life-and-death characterizations, the need to dispel what is perceived as dangerous myth with personal truth is a powerful incentive for many people.

Speaking these stories aloud carries another imperative. It validates the existence of those who have died, and those who survived to tell their tales:

The injunction to listen is the total interpellation of one subject by another: it places above everything else the quasi-physical contact of these subjects (by voice and ear): it creates transference: "*listen to me*" means *touch me, know that I exist.* (Barthes 1985:251; italics in original)

And it is in the act of listening that we can begin to understand the existence of those who speak. "Listening to the voice inaugurates the relation to the Other: the voice by which we recognize others (like writing on an envelope) indicates to us their way of being, their joy or their pain, their condition; it bears an image of their body and, beyond, a whole psychology" (Barthes 1985:255).

"Talking violence" will always have a dual nature: the need to talk will always be offset by a need for silence that preserves dignity and protects the survivors. Das writes about people who suffered two days of rioting. When days stretch into weeks and weeks into years—and violence and deprivation are compounded time and again by loss and tragedy— the need to talk and talk is tempered by a careful knowledge built experience by experience that both good and dangerous people exist, that every public conversation is political. Conversation demonstrates an agency that constantly juggles "Who wants to know what about whom and why?" Added to this is the fact that war experience is all too often grievous experience. Letting outsiders into a personal world of suffering, survival, courage, and confusion—sharing the tears of mourning, the angers of betrayal, and the fears of future atrocities—is not done freely. Yet, telling a history sometimes serves to commemorate the memory of the dead and missing and to reaffirm the traditions of the survivors the war has sought to destroy.

The Philosophy of Listening

Listening is not merely an auditory act. On the cultural level, it is not solely the process of interpretation. In a world that privileges the visual, the complexities of listening have been neglected. Collecting people's stories of hardship and tragedy is dependent on "listening well." But the value of listening extends beyond this. Roland Barthes and Brenda Ueland claim that listening is an act of creating.

Listening is a magnetic and strange thing, a creative force. . . . When we are listened to, it creates us, makes us unfold and expand. (Ueland 1992: 104)

When we listen to others, "we are constantly being recreated." As a creative force, listening goes far beyond the mere hearing of words, the simple decipherment of discursive meaning:

To listen is to adopt an attitude of decoding what is obscure, blurred, or mute, in order to make available to consciousness the "underside" of meaning. (Barthes 1985: 249)[2]

Just as the experience of terror, the pangs of grief, the painful yearning for worlds and homes irreparably lost to violence extends beyond the boundaries of words and text, so must the dynamic of hearing. For herein lie the clues to understanding the incommensurability of the mundane as it is infused with the incomprehensible and the unspeakable. In this sense, listening becomes an "art of the possible"—the possibility of subverting the transgressions of war, of surviving, of humanity, of tomorrow.

Listening to Silences

Sometimes it is as important to listen to what people do not say as to what is actually said. People "know" things on many different levels. Although people may be unwilling to express certain thoughts and feelings in particular contexts, sometimes they are truly unable to do so. People will let themselves know and feel things in certain situations that they will not let themselves know in others. People cannot be overwhelmed with grief for lost loved ones, fear impending attacks, or feel hopelessness in the face of starvation or anxiety over being able to protect their family twenty-four hours a day seven days a week. As Dostoevsky admitted, one cannot suffer all the time: one must also rest.

People's stories reflect the context in which they speak. The many quotes presented in this book are the product not simply of getting to affected areas and asking people for their responses, but of patient attention to creating a "space of listening" and respecting the many, and sometimes contradictory, responses.

Most people I encountered had formulated a variety of opinions and worldviews that were context-dependent, and these often demonstrated a wide, and contested, set of precepts. For civilians and combatants alike, there are many kinds of answers to a question: political (in the context of the government), political (in the context of tribal authority), military (in all its many contexts, FAM, Renamo, militia, the traditional army Parama, each of which demands different "answers"), community oriented, religious, familial, and personal. Survival depends on giving the right answers in the right contexts.

An example shows the importance of waiting to collect all, or at least a range of, responses any individual has to offer. William Finnegan (1992) says several times in his book on Mozambique that peasants often do not really understand that they belong to a creation called "Mozambique."

Isolation by rural distance, the war, illiteracy, and tribal alliances means that the idea of a "nation" is lost on many. He cites, for example, the fact that when he asked people who the president of Mozambique was, they could not say. I can understand how Finnegan came to this view, but, in my experience, villagers, no matter how rural and illiterate, *knew* what Mozambique was, who the president was, and what the harsh reality of the war was—but they might not say.

People have learned that, politically and militarily, knowledge is a dangerous thing. How did one come by such knowledge? Who was one fraternizing with to gain such knowledge? And worse, how are people using, or misusing, this knowledge? These questions can result in death. When I first asked people who did not know me what was going on in the war, who the president was, or just about any other question, I often got the reply, "I really do not know." As I sat and talked with people, shared food, explained my work and the people whose friendships I valued, made return trips, listened to their stories and shared my own, people's "answers" changed. They did know what Mozambique was, who represented the power brokers, the toll the war was exacting—and they had opinions about all of these. Gradually I came to understand their initial reticence. If people said they knew who the president of Mozambique was and this got back to Renamo, the latter might demand to know how they knew this: had they been associating with Frelimo, assisting Frelimo? Something as simple as this could threaten a person's life. Likewise, if a person spoke about Renamo troop movements, a topic people had to be familiar with if they were to stay out of harm's way, Frelimo troops might begin to question how they came to this information: were they collaborators? Again, a label that could result in death.

The examples of the importance of guarding information are extensive and subtle. For instance, I was always surprised that, when discussing the tragedies of the war, people talked about having or not having salt. It seemed a remarkably trivial deprivation when placed against the larger losses of family members and entire villages. During the course of my fieldwork, however, I discovered that "having salt" was associated with Frelimo, and "not having salt" was associated with Renamo occupation. People have been killed by Renamo for possessing salt—a "clear" sign that they had been "collaborating" with Frelimo, as far as Renamo was concerned.

The political and military contexts of guarding information are understandable. Equally important is the fact that within each community people had different loyalties and alliances. Chiefs and other tribal authorities demanded allegiances that people had to negotiate continuously. Chiefs often had very different political agendas from those of the Renamo soldiers or Frelimo administration, and sometimes they had different political agendas from those of the villagers themselves. These differences were often fraught with personal as well as political rivalries. Collaborators with the various military contingents existed in the civilian population and wreaked havoc with trust. Teachers and health care workers, for example, were targeted by Renamo, curandeiros by Frelimo. A mere statement of one's occupation to the wrong person could be dangerous, even lethal. Blackmarketeers and purveyors of other economic realities controlled access to necessities. Even finding food could be a politically loaded task. And this list covers only some of the differing loyalties and divisions that cross-cut communities with powerful repercussions. Speaking correctly, or not speaking at all, was important in each of these contexts—and each context required a different discourse or action. Set against this was the necessity of acquiring and sharing accurate information on troop deployment, economic networks, political realities, and community affiliations in order to withstand the onslaughts of violent and conflicting alliances and antagonisms. Knowledge was both dangerous and essential.

Listening to the Chameleon Text

In one of the locations I worked in Mozambique, I was repeatedly told the same story, albeit with a slight modification every time. The modification in each story turned out to be as important as its enduring quality. People would invariably preface the story with the phrase, "Carolyn, you are interested in things having to do with traditional medicine," and then proceeded to tell me about President Banda of Malawi. The speakers would say, with a significant look intended to convey the fact that I was to listen carefully because what they were about to say had a deeper import,

> You know—Banda is a powerful sorcerer [the word healer was not used] who can change his shape and fly instantaneously to wherever he wants in the world.

They would then go on to explain that he had recently visited a certain location in town (always the same location) and had materialized in a room and slept on the bed. He never went out of the room, people never saw him on the streets, but they knew he had been there because he always left something in the room. The only part of the story that ever changed was what he had left: one time it was his hat, the next his umbrella, the next his overcoat, and so on.

The story then proceeded with some observation such as:

You know, this sorcery, this changing to another shape and traveling instantaneously, well, you never have to worry about borders or visas do you? I mean, you can just come into a country and leave at will and no one is the wiser.

Or:

Now that hat that he left, why do you suppose he left that hat, what do you think it means for us that this sorcerer left his hat here among us?

Or:

You know, he left that umbrella, but why do you suppose he brought it—it isn't the rainy season now, hasn't rained for quite a while. You don't suppose that he bought one of our umbrellas here and took that back with him, even though ours are of an inferior quality and his was much finer?

And then the topic usually turned to the war, the problems, the tragedies, the deprivations, the troop movements and arms shipments, the blackmarketeers.

It was some time before I realized that people were not discussing traditional sorcery practices but the intricacies of the war process itself. Parable and metaphor were politically loaded dialogues. I do not think that anyone thought Banda himself actually came into the country to sleep in a certain bed in a certain locale. It was the network, the alliances, the transfers of arms, supplies, and people that was being talked about. I can only speculate as to what the hat, the umbrella, and the overcoat that Banda left signify in terms of actual support, supplies, and personnel.

The story took on more meaning in its context. President Banda incurred the disapproval of the Southern African Front Line States (Mozambique, Zimbabwe, Namibia, Tanzania, Zambia, etc.) for his alignment with apartheid South Africa. The disapproval turned to political outrage for many when evidence of his support for Renamo came to light. In addition to Banda's links with the South African government, many thought his support of Renamo stemmed from his desire to annex at least part of northern Mozambique to Malawi, a feat potentially possible through an association with the rebel forces in Mozambique. Because northern Mozambique shares a length of border with Malawi, soldiers and supplies have fluidly crossed the border: training camps for Renamo existed in Malawi, supplies passed through Malawi into Mozambique, and looted goods from Mozambique were carried to Malawi to

sell. While world opinion forced the Malawi government to disassoci-
ate itself from Renamo in the late 1980s, many people speculated that
covert supplies continued to move through these established networks
until the end of the war. In addition, the looted goods from Mozambique were attractive to Malawian traders. I remember one day when
I was flying with an emergency supply crew to western Zambezia. The
pilot flew over the Malawi border to show the dramatic change that was
immediately evident: the barren, brown, sparsely populated landscapes
and burned-out towns of Mozambique gave way to green fields and
teeming villages in Malawi. "Look," a Mozambican colleague pointed
out, "there are our tin roofs on their houses, our looted goods in their
shops . . . all bartered by Renamo and jackals."

The owner of the establishment that Banda periodically "visited" was
known to be sympathetic to Portuguese neocolonial aims. The owner's
son had in fact been indicted during the war by the Mozambican government as a Renamo agent. Long before his prison sentence was over,
his mother successfully got him out of the country. Interestingly, when
people spoke of this, they tended to use the same refrain: "He was just
spirited out of the country." They would then go on to speak of the
underground network by which questionable people and illicit goods
moved in and out of the country and around the provinces—a network
that was extensive, well-oiled (if one knew how to use it), and, however
nebulous it appeared to those outside it, efficient. So the owner's son
was spirited out of the country, presumably along the same lines that
Banda used to spirit things into the country.

Parable, myth, metaphor, and innuendo are the means by which
people, in Das's words, "talk and talk about violence," and protect their
safety and need for silence at the same time. Yet, as noted in Chapter 1,
these cannot be "read" as set "texts" of the war, intransmutable across
time and space. I encountered many instances when time-honored parables were invoked by a specific person, in a specific context, to refer
to specific circumstances. While the words were the same, the situation
being described, the warnings being dispersed, the comments on who
was trustworthy, dangerous, Janus-faced, and victimized were particular
to both the speaker's point of view and the community being discussed.
By "the telling," people listening knew exactly what specific information
was being conveyed, who were "the good guys" and who were "the bad."
In the next telling, the same story might implicate other people, other
problems, other solutions. Apart from the telling and the context, the
parable means little. It is, as people would say, "just a story we tell our
children before they go to bed."

These parables not only cross warzones, they cross peace accords as
well. During the height of the war, a friend told me a story as we were

in a health care clinic checking on some people. I did not have the time or paper to write it down. Later, as I began this chapter, I thought of her story but remembered only the main points. It had to do with an innocent man who was murdered and covered with a blanket to hide the body. As in many Mozambican tales, a bird sees the event and calls out the truth. The bird's calls are usually unheeded at first, and often the bird becomes a target of the person(s) trying to hide their nefarious acts. But at the end the truth prevails. The body is found, and the bird alerts the community to the killer(s) among them. As I looked around the clinic at the sick, wounded, and dying, I understood at the time who in the community was being implicated as dangerous and trustworthy in this "parable." So did the patients in the clinic. I could see them listening and nodding their heads in agreement as they looked at their own wounds and their wounded friends and family. It was a political story, a war story.

In 1996, while visiting this friend in Zambezia, I asked her if she remembered this story, for I wanted to write it down in its entirety. "Sure," she replied, "in fact my [ten-year-old] son is quite a storyteller, and he can give you a good rendition." The whole family gathered, and the son launched into the story. But this time the story was related several years after the peace accord had been signed. People had discovered that peace accords did not stop the profiteers from gaining at the expense of others in war-ravaged societies. Many in Mozambique in 1996 told me that their economic position was as precarious as it had been during the war. As the story emerged this time, three brothers were working on a plantation for minimal wages. They had only enough money to purchase one blanket. They sent one of the brothers to purchase the blanket they had all agreed on. The store owner was unscrupulous and sold the man the wrong blanket at a profit. When he returned home, his brothers were so angry they killed him. The bird in this case flies to tell the mother what has happened a son had been killed by his brothers, all because of an unscrupulous shopkeeper. Unscrupulous soldiers and political power brokers of the war years have in a small change of words become unscrupulous economic power brokers. The dangers of violence are as fundamental to peace time preoccupations as they had been during the war. Just as when I was in the clinic during the war years, I could look around postwar Mozambique and see the few who profited from the plight of the many yet again. Like the time in the clinic, I knew exactly who the story was talking about.

Seeing as Listening

I began the section on the Anthropology of Listening with the quote from Dis that reminds us that listening is seeing. The author, relying on verbal accounts, shows that by listening to the narratives of the victims of war, one "sees" the realities of the war unfold. I would like to stress as well the inverse: that seeing is listening. Social science has tended to rely strongly on the discursive. Language, it is commonly presumed, informs conception and grounds human endeavor (Saussure 1959). While most people recognize there are metanarratives and cultural texts, the idea remains that these are open to a textual reading and are ultimately discernible in discursive practices.

I first learned the limitations of this approach while witnessing violent mobs during riots. A tangible form of communication exists during rioting to convey where a mob begins and ends, who is a mob member and who is not, what the intents and actions of the mob are and will be, and what idea(l)s and emotions have fanned the mob into action. Yet this communication is nonverbal. While the information conveyed to me during rioting was as clear as information I gathered on more physical features—the number, gender, and dress of the mob members and the words they actually spoke—I could not explain the mechanisms by which nonverbal information was communicated. Other scholars on mob behaviors have noted a similar difficulty (Wright 1978; Berk 1972). Social and linguistic science have not yet fully developed tools by which we can understand and document communication that cannot be broken down into the logical tenets of verbal, discursive, and linguistically based information transferral. Compared to all the work produced within social science, research conducted in contexts of violence and social upheaval is relatively sparse, although it is here that the importance of nonverbal communication is most obvious.

Studying the war in Mozambique has underscored the value of these observations. As I brought out in Chapter 1, collecting the accounts of war experiences after the fact is a valuable part of ethnography, but narratives are not to be confused with the raw experience that provides the material of the narrative. Speaking about terror, grief, or the chaos of battle is not the same as being swept up in the initial immediacy of these realities. At the "ongoing present" in which these events unfold in actuality, little discursive interaction is taking place, though a great deal of communication occurs.

Social science needs to embrace the fact that grief and the experience of terror and chaos, as well as a host of other phenomena, are often "silent" at the moment of occurrence. Yet they speak volumes. As one sits at the site of a battle with a mother who has lost her child, one may find, as I did, that the mother says nothing, but conveys a tremendous amount of information about grief, suffering, and loss. Similarly, during the chaos of an attack, people may communicate little verbally about the terror they are experiencing or the means by which they will survive it, but I found I understood a great deal from the context in which people's interactions unfolded.

The importance of nondiscursive communication extends to day-to-day life in violent contexts. I found people negotiating survival on the frontlines by paying strict attention to the nondiscursive nuances of behavior and action of those around them in order to determine when danger was approaching, who was trustworthy, and how to respond. It was a skill people communicated to me, and that I began to adopt in my daily life, but that I am hard pressed to explain in either words or actions. As a final example, and one I will explore in depth in Chapter 4, people who have not done fieldwork in the context of socio-political violence may not understand the communicative (however nondiscursive) power the return of a torture victim or a kidnapped child has on the community the victim or child is taken from or returned to. The kidnapping or torture of even one person resonates through the entire community to shape viscerally the experience of many. Like a labored breath or a heartbeat, it is an inescapable truth, an undeniable presence. It is not "her" or "him"; it is "us." It is by such means that the insidiousness of a culture of terror and the optimism of a culture of resistance are inculcated, often at one and the same time, among a population at large.

It is in this sense of the profound depth of the meaning of fear and resistance in the daily act of living that I emphasize the fact that seeing is listening, a listening that goes beyond formal discursive analyses to the forms of communication that ground much of human experience. "Seeing comes before words" (Berger 1972:7). Listening, likewise, goes far beyond mere words. As Barthes (1985:252) reminds us, "listening speaks."

An Introduction to the Ethnography of War: Six War Stories

The ethnography of a theme, such as war, is a bit more difficult to introduce than an ethnography grounded in a specific locale. One cannot familiarize the readers with a layout of a place, the neighborhoods that comprise it, and the people who populate them. Instead, broad dynamics must be identified, complexities explored, contradictions brought to light, and shared experiences woven together across ethnic, linguistic, and experiential boundaries. Finnegan, who traveled widely in Mozambique, states, upon reaching a district in the Maputo Province, "Manhiça was typical of nothing in Mozambique" (1992:214). I have heard this said, and have said this myself, of many places I traveled to in Mozambique. And yet a shared culture of violence—and surviving violence—links most Mozambicans in a profound way. For anthropologist and local alike, the phenomena of (personal) experiences slowly coalesce into an understanding of the phenomenon of (shared) experience. Differences and similarities, contradictions and solutions are entangled in a *pas de deux* (or perhaps, more accurately, a dance of many) that comprises the core of experience. In exploring the vast complexity of the war that defined much of Mozambique for fifteen years, I will introduce six different war perspectives.

The Town of Ekani and Beyond

The town of Ekani[3] is one thread in a tapestry of war—unique, but meaningful in the larger pattern defining the country. The villagers' experiences are not the same as those in the neighboring village, the neighboring province, or the neighboring country. Yet themes of terror and hope—however different their manifestation from locale to locale—demonstrate similarities that allow understandings across time and space, village and culture. The victims of war have a greater understanding of this than do the perpetrators of war.

Ekani was one of my favorite places in Mozambique, and I made an effort to visit it as often as possible. It is not particularly beautiful, an expanse of rugged scrub savanna reaching across hot and dusty plains. It was difficult to reach, located in the interior of Zambezia, well over an hour's flight, or several days' walk, from any major town. It was far from secure during my field stays: it was located in a hotly contested region militarily, and had changed between Renamo and Frelimo control several times. The fighting was never far away, and the town was besieged as well by refugees and overtaxed resources. At the time of my first trip to the area, twenty-five people were dying *every day* of starvation, disease, and deprivation. Ekani was not luxurious: the town and all its buildings had been destroyed, and a sea of small mud and thatch huts sprang up in a circle around the destroyed town. No one lived in the ruins of the town, as they do in some other locations in Mozambique. Though I never asked why this was so, I suspect it is because the walls and rocks of all the ruined buildings are covered with charcoal drawings done by Renamo troops during their occupation—crude drawings of battle plans; assault guns; helicopters strafing villages; the odd animal long since killed off in the area by vicious troops and starving villagers; men with guns for penises; men with grotesquely enlarged penises raping women; salutary proclamations to Renamo and its leaders; and one curious picture of an old, stooped-over woman carrying a full-grown man on her back. A mausoleum of memories.

The first time I arrived in Ekani was in 1990, shortly after the town had been retaken from Renamo. But it was not Frelimo troops that achieved this. No one, including the Mozambican government and foreign observers, contests that it was Manuel Antonio and his traditional army Parama that retook Ekani from Renamo.[4]

Frelimo troops had not been able to rout Renamo during the years of control. Whether Frelimo tried very hard to regain Ekani, I do not know, but the area was a heavily contested military zone. Ekani is a strategic location: it has rich mines of precious metals and gems and its lands are fertile. The wealth of the deposits is attested to in the stories told to me by locals about the "white men" who came to oversee the mining and removal of precious materials during Renamo occupation—and who left all the mines and equipment smashed on their departure.

Parama defeated Renamo in Ekani in June 1990. Two months later the Frelimo troops arrived. It took the soldiers two more months to clear out the landmines from the area and reconstruct a dirt runway. As Renamo had fled only to the outskirts outside the Ekani area, overland travel in and out of Ekani was fraught with danger. When the runway opened in October, the first relief supplies arrived to a starving population, coinciding with the arrival of the first administrator, a handful of medical personnel and teachers, and an anthropologist.

The following account of what had befallen Ekani was narrated to me by an old man who had lived there all his life. We sat outside his little lean-to, smoking cigarettes—I brought some of the first to arrive in town for a considerable time—and he told me of the plight of the area and its people:

> When the Bandidos [Renamo] came in 1984 they held a reunion, they called all the people and talked to us. I went to those meetings. They told us they had come to liberate us, that we could live freely now, that everyone would have plenty and grow fat, and that Frelimo would never come again and cause trouble.
>
> Then they called a second meeting and we all had to attend. They said we had lots of things here, good things, chicken, corn, beans, and so on, and that we should give these things to them and keep the manioc for ourselves to eat. And we had to give.
>
> Then the Bandidos called a third meeting, and we all had to attend again, and this time, they told us we had to give them our women, and they took them off to their Base Camp to clean and to work and to provide sex and "other comforts."
>
> When Parama and then Frelimo came, we ran off to the bush to

escape the fighting. I had a nice big house here. When I returned, Parama had burned it, and a lot of other people's houses, to the ground. Now I have built this little stick lean-to here, I have nothing. Everything considered, my life was better when Renamo was here. I had a big house and all my family, and now I live like this with practically nothing. People tell me those of us who fled to the bush when the fighting started were thought by Parama and Frelimo to be with the Bandidos, and that's why they burned our houses; that those who remained did not suffer in this way. Maybe it's true, but still, there is no winning. If you try to protect yourself, you lose everything. If you stay, you may keep your possessions and lose your life. There is no sense to this war.

But no, I wouldn't consider returning to live with the Bandidos. Maybe I had my big house, but they began asking for this and that, then they began to take what they wanted, demanding this and that—using force whether they needed to or not. No, I would never want to go live with the Bandidos.

Not everyone's story was so considered. The following quote is my first notebook entry for Ekani: the words of a middle-aged woman who sat, amid a group of acquaintances, cooking a noonday meal.

We have suffered too much. For years now we lived under the Bandidos' control. Epah, our life was hard, it was awful. Parama—the traditional army—liberated us, they saved us.

Over there, you can see if you want, are the skulls that show what life was like under the bandits. You can walk along the paths and stumble over bones. They [Renamo] wanted something, they took it. They killed without reason. I saw this, we all saw this—more times than we care to remember. If I had on a cloth or a shirt they wanted, they would just pull it off of me. If they wanted sex, they just grabbed you and took it. If you said no, you would die. And if they liked a woman a lot, they just killed her husband and took her.

For nearly ten years now we have had no schools, no health clinics, no food, nothing. They gave us nothing, only took.

In June Parama arrived. They asked the village leader [non-Renamo] if they could come here and help us to fight the Bandidos and run them off, and they were given permission. They sent a chief and lots of locals joined up: boys and girls alike. It is not easy, there are rules Parama must follow in order for the medicine that protects them from bullets to work. A man can have only one woman, and a person cannot commit adultery. They must always act with restraint among themselves and the community. They must never get mad or provoke others; they must never use force or fight among themselves or the people they are defending. Men and women fight side by side. The women even advance first in the frontlines. They do not have to be scared—the bullets cannot touch them—they have been protected by the vaccination. You can shoot them and the bullets cannot enter the flesh, you can try and cut them and the machete will not penetrate the skin. Sometimes you see people, their shirts are full of holes where they have been shot, but they just brush the bullets off like flies.

When I first arrived in Ekani in October 1990, people sang the praises of Parama. Many felt Parama had freed them from slavery and oppression. Under Renamo, people's movements had been heavily controlled. Civilians were not able to travel freely, and on top of a heavy tax, they had to provide goods and services to the soldiers on demand. The wing of Renamo controlling Ekani was under the leadership of a commander well known for his brutality, so the penalties for violating Renamo regulations, and in fact the treatment of civilians in general, were severe.

But even from the beginning of Parama's "quasi-governance" there were indications that cycles of violence and control were not easily broken. Parama and FAM greeted the first relief planes and tried to sequester the emergency foodstuffs, tools and seeds, and other emergency supplies. This was patently evident when one arrived at the airstrip to be met by soldiers clad in cheerful pink, green, and yellow summer dresses. One of the first emergency shipments had included clothing: cotton frocks for women. The soldiers had quickly sequestered the supplies and, fearful they would be stolen if left unattended, they wore them on military maneuvers. Only the forceful personality of the administrator, who went to the runway and personally challenged the soldiers' rights to these supplies, kept the goods out of military (traditional and modern) hands, at least to some extent. Government supplies and pay to FAM were irregular, nonexistent in the case of Parama. Villagers were "asked" to provide food and other necessities to both sets of troops, and they complied. They had little choice.

When government administrators and emergency crews arrived in October, they assumed the massive starvation greeting them was a product of Renamo occupation. The barren fields lying unplanted must have been a result of the rebels' policies of control. But the story is more complex than that. People said that life was hard under Renamo, a time of deprivation and want, but not, for the most part, a time of starvation, but this was due more to the tariffs and taxes imposed by Renamo than to restrictions on planting and harvesting. Why then should twenty-five or more people be dying each day for months after the rebels were ousted from the area?

It appears that Parama, so antagonistic to Renamo and its practices, had, wittingly or otherwise, reproduced some of Renamo's abhorred tactics. With Renamo so close outside Ekani, people's movements were heavily controlled by Parama, and later by the FAM. As farmlands were often some distance from the village area, people were often restricted from traveling to them and possibly to Renamo territory. Planting season came and went, but the people did not. Moreover, people living in the lands surrounding Ekani were rounded up and brought to the town area, ostensibly to protect them from the rebels' wrath—but also to make sure no rebel support in the neighboring regions was forthcoming to threaten Parama/FAM security in Ekani. This essentially amounted to forced relocation. The population of the town grew to a size that could hardly be supported even if the surrounding fields had been producing normally. The civilians knew the folly of complaining about the situation to armed soldiers.

I do not know how strict Parama and FAM control was before the runway opened. At best, even recent histories can only be reconstructed from fragmentary and conflicting information. By the time I arrived, Parama had been controlling people's movements, but also providing one of the few secure means of travel. Once Ekani was freed from Renamo control, families sought to reunite, to return to their homes, to reestablish old friendships and rebuild family farm plots. Parama provided military escort protection for people returning to or coming from Ekani. As I tramped around the outlying areas of Ekani, I often encountered groups of people walking with their possessions on their heads, accompanied by a Parama soldier with a red scarf and a spear. I do not recall ever seeing FAM troops performing a similar function.

Parama managed to reproduce behaviors they disdained in Renamo in yet another way. On a return trip to Ekani several months later, I found some of the villagers had another set of complaints.

> Epah, some of these Parama are too much. We have to feed and support them. Oh, we always have, soldiers cannot be expected to farm, but now they are so demanding. They walk around like big men, strutting here, demanding this, taking that. They no longer listen to the cries of the people, sometimes they cause them. Sometimes they push people around, and sometimes they are violent with them. And what can we do? They hold the power, they are vaccinated to be stronger than a normal human. Who do they think they are? Renamo?

These villagers did in fact do something about their problems. Their difficulties with the Parama soldiers grew so severe that word was sent to Manuel Antonio that he had to come and do something to control the situation. At the time, Antonio was outside the provincial capital of Quelimane, several days' walk from the area in question. I was in Quelimane at the time, and, interestingly, Antonio took his problems to the government military. Concerned about his reputation, and possibly equally concerned about the fact that the government troops were being accused of the same excesses, often in conjunction with Parama, the military arranged to fly Antonio to the trouble spot. He arrived within a day, and conducted an all-night ceremony in which he removed the protective vaccines from these renegade Parama (and thus their status as Parama soldiers) and vaccinated a new set of troops. I arrived in Ekani the day after Manuel Antonio had performed the ceremony:

> Ah, Carolyn, the ceremony was magical. It continued all night. Manuel Antonio came and expressed his displeasure. Then drumming started and he went into a trance. We buried him deep in the ground, and he remained there for a long time.[5] When he finally emerged from the ground, he was filled with power. He took the power of the vaccinations from all the Parama here, he cast it out and left them ordinary men, and then he left them in our hands to deal with as ordinary men. He even stripped the powers from the Commander he left in charge here, the man that was supposed to be his trusted friend, but who tried to grab all the glory and power for himself. Well, he is no more. Then Manuel Antonio selected a new group of soldiers and vaccinated them in a big ceremony, telling them if they did not uphold their duty to him and to us, terrible things would happen to them. The vaccinations are magical: if you violate their power dire consequences will befall you.

Antonio left the ex-Parama in the hands of the wronged community after he had stripped them of their powers. When I arrived in Ekani shortly after the ceremony, a number of the ex-Parama were receiving a beating from the people they had so recently taken advantage of. Townspeople said they had changed from strutting strong-arms to meek and rather cowering repentants overnight. The message was clear: this is what happens when power is abused.

A number of people, both in Ekani and beyond, were convinced that Manuel Antonio and his Parama were not to blame for the transgressions that had occurred at Ekani. They placed the blame at the foot of the commander Antonio had left in charge. This commander, they explained, had wanted to form his own power bloc, and had convinced the local Parama troops to follow his wishes against those of Antonio. The deed was seen as particularly despicable because the commander had been a trusted friend and supposed ally of Antonio, and his power ploys were popularly viewed as a stab in the back of the supreme commander of Parama.

Whether this version of the Ekani commander's actions is true or not was impossible for me to discern. Need plays as strong a role as fact in the construction of explanation. People needed to believe in Parama. They represented a return to valued traditions and safety in the midst of oppression. They had, after all, liberated Ekani. Parama also provided a buffer against FAM excesses. As one FAM soldier himself told me:

> I think these Parama are a good thing—they are very important. You know, sometimes when there is only one force, they can do anything they please. There are problems with this, they can begin to throw around their power, make people do things they don't want to do, use violence against people to get what they want. When you have two forces, people now have an option. Each force has to be more responsible. People can say, "Hey you can't treat us this way, there are others to protect us." This puts a brake on unnecessary violence.[6]

Although the commander of the Parama forces in Ekani may have been attempting to carve out his own power bloc, Ekani was not the only place Parama abuses were noted. As with Renamo and the FAM troops, the actions of Parama soldiers varied from place to place and commander to commander. Parama were celebrated in some places, tolerated in others, and feared in yet others. But for many, they were all the people had to pin their hopes on. Thus the "facts" about the traitorous commander of Parama may have been more a reflection of people's need to believe that the transgressions were not a reproduction of the violence seen under Renamo and Frelimo, and before them the Portuguese during the war for independence, but rather the misdeeds of a greedy and misdirected few.

*   *   *

Ekani is a prime example of some of the profound settlement changes wrought by the war. Mozambique does not suffer from overpopulation. With only 16 million people living in a space nearly twice the size of California, there are no serious pressures for land. Mozambicans have traditionally preferred a dispersed settlement pattern, with clusters of houses spread across farm holdings. These generally skirt uncultivated bush, affording people access to wood, herbal medicines, wild game, and other resources. But after the start of the war thousands, even tens of thousands, were cramped together in a sea of small mud huts clinging precariously to some semblance of security based on closeness.

Tragically, that closeness was sometimes constructed through forced relocation or controlled refugee settlements. The wood and wild game were largely gone, and resources were few. Venturing out for medicinal plants, or to *machambas* to eke out some precious food, was fraught with danger: the war, from landmines to soldiers, waited at any bend in the road, over any hill.

The channels of authority in these circumstances become seriously entangled. Traditional chiefs, were overpowered by soldiers and undermined by the thugs and informers variously employed by troop leaders, yet they retained their rights to authority in the eyes of most civilians. Traditional healers were critical to the survival of the population and were a primary target of attack and control for both Renamo and Frelimo. Moreover, the simple act of trading could open one to accusations of being a spy. And the fact that people from widely divergent ethnic, language, and cultural groups were merged into one sprawling community of need constantly challenged whose authority, whose traditions should be given the greatest voice and respect, and whose should be rebelled against and subverted.

Entanglements of power, authority, and survival did not take place in isolated communities. Flows of *deslocados* (those dislocated from their homes), soldiers, and profiteers, to name but a few of the many who move about in warzones, linked Ekani with the needs and concerns of increasingly expanding sets of relationships that extended far beyond the borders of the town, even the province. A constant exchange of information, goods, problems, and solutions continually reshaped the social landscapes and cultural realities of people's lives.

I have related the story of Ekani to introduce the complexity of ways in which conflict, ever fluid, is simultaneously produced, endured, resisted, and reproduced, and how fine a line exists between oppression and liberation. But Ekani is not the story of Mozambique, nor are its citizens' experiences representative of all those suffering from the war in the country. It is but one note in the discordant chord of life in war.

The Three Wars of Gersony

Robert Gersony (1988), in his now classic study of Mozambican refugee conflict experiences, was one of the first people to look at the country-wide dynamics of the war and its impact on civilians. Interestingly, Gersony worked with the U. S. Department of State when he did this study—and at this time the Reagan administration was still aligned with Renamo on a Cold War playing field. Gersony's report played a significant role in undermining conservative western support for Renamo.

Based on refugee accounts, Gersony identifies three different types of Renamo-held areas: tax areas, control areas, and destruction areas.

Tax areas were generally found in rural locales with dispersed population and settlement patterns. Renamo troops moved freely throughout these areas. Renamo soldiers visited the farmers on a regular basis to demand "contributions" of food, clothes, women for sex, and adults to porter supplies. Although people were not permitted to flee the area, Gersony notes that instances of brutality, murder, and kidnapping were less frequent than in control and destruction areas.

In *control areas*, the population generally surrounded a Renamo base, and both the demands placed on the population and the measures for controlling and punishing them were more extensive and brutal than in tax areas. Gersony notes that around 20 percent of the people he talked with lived in Renamo control areas. These civilians formed two categories: indigenous local populations, and those who had been abducted from other areas and involuntarily marched to the control areas. The civilians were forced to devote six days of work a week to providing for Renamo, and were allowed only one day a week to produce all their own necessities, including crops, housing, and other essentials. Forced porterage was common, and unlike the case in the tax areas, the length, number, and arduousness of trips was greatly increased. As Gersony notes, the loads were heavy, the pace rapid, and food and water minimal. Food, military, and personal supplies were carried to bases and between bases, often transversing province lines. Equally common were the sexual demands placed on girls and women. They were, Gersony writes, "raped on a frequent, sustained basis" (1988:21). Failure to provide food and supplies, labor, or sex for Renamo resulted in severe penalties, such as beatings, mutilation, and death. Such retribution could extend to family members as well. Noncombatants received no remuneration from Renamo for their toils. "The only reciprocity the captives appear to receive or expect is the opportunity to remain alive" (28).

Even the opportunity to remain alive was denied those in Gersony's third category, *destruction areas.* These areas frequently had some form of Frelimo governmental representation or served as government-sponsored refugee locations. The governmental presence may have been limited to one or several administrative officials, possibly a government-sponsored health clinic or school, and in some instances a small contingent of Frelimo troops. When Renamo targeted such an area, it attacked civilians and officials alike, structure and infrastructure simultaneously.

Officials and their families were often publicly executed. Goods were looted, and people were kidnapped to porter them. In addition, a large number of civilians in these attacks and other contexts were reported to be victims of purposeful shooting deaths and executions, of axing, knifing, bayoneting, burning to death, forced drowning and asphyxiation, and other forms of murder where no meaningful resistance or defense is present. Eyewitness accounts indicate that when civilians are killed in these indiscriminate attacks, whether against defended or undefended villages, children, often together with mothers and elderly people, are also killed. (Gersony 1988:32)

Gersony concludes with the observation: "The relationship between Renamo and the population appears to revolve solely around the extraction of resources, strictly by force, without explanation, with no tolerance for refusal, and without reciprocation" (17).

Gersony's words are telling in themselves. But until I personally witnessed the ruins of some destruction areas, I could not envision the attention to destructive detail Renamo employed. In one instance I observed a village shortly after an attack, where every structure had been carefully burned to the ground. Acres upon acres of charred circles extended in all directions, the only testimonial to the fact that a village of houses and shops had recently stood on the site. In another area I visited, Renamo apparently did not have materials powerful enough to blow up buildings not made of flammable materials. The town was fairly large, and contained a school and a hospital as well as administrative buildings. Renamo's attention to destructive detail was dramatic: in each building all furniture, equipment, and materials that had not been looted were systematically smashed and destroyed, and troops had even taken the time to carefully break each pane of glass.

The Quiet War of Two Villages in the Northern Hinterlands

In continuing to explore the complexities of war, I turn to the northern province of Niassa, the most remote province in the country. I collected the data on the following two "quiet wars" when I was in the area in 1991. This sparsely populated province is as removed physically and bureaucratically from the governmental seat(s) of power as one can get in Mozambique. It has, however, a strong history of resistance, being an area that staunchly supported the Frelimo forces during the war for independence. Some people feel the government's interest has passed them by: few resources reach this province, though it has managed to remain fairly self-sustaining. The frustration with the lack of governmental support was fomented in the early years of Frelimo rule when "non-productive" people (the unemployed, thieves, prostitutes, street dwellers, and other "undesirables") were rounded up in the country's capital city and unceremoniously dumped in this province in an action called "Operation Production." Those who were not confined in "reeducation camps" were expected to develop farms and other productive businesses, but the failure to provide education, tools, and other necessities to urban dwellers unfamiliar with the demands of rural life meant that many were unable to adapt, and a number reportedly died.

Thus Niassa Province's strong historical sympathy for Frelimo has been tempered since independence by the perception that the government has "forgotten" the province into obscurity. In fact, a commonly heard phrase in the province is that "you know when someone has messed up really badly within the Frelimo system [all education, health care, and social services are government run], because they get posted to this province as punishment and left here forever." People think that incompetents and rejects are sent to administer to the province's needs.[7] Yet, even in this context, markedly varied responses to Renamo exist. The following two stories help illuminate this.

The first account concerned the northwestern part of the province, where certain areas had been under Renamo control for years. These areas are remote by Mozambican standards: few roads, trade networks, or governmental services have been developed. As far as I could tell, little FAM military interest extended to these regions. Renamo-held zones were essentially left to their own devices, and, from what I heard, most of the trade from these areas was conducted not with Mozambique, but with neighboring countries.

Both the story of this Renamo-held territory and the province's lack of infrastructure and resources became apparent to me in the small and cheerful riot that broke out in Lichinga, the provincial capital. The source of the good-humored upheaval was the first shipment of beer to reach the area in "a long time." The beer and I arrived in town at roughly the same time, though the beer had followed a more circuitous route from Zimbabwe overland through several areas of heavy fighting. Perched on rickety chairs with warm, flat beer in hand, people who hailed from the remote Renamo-held area explained to me about life in their homelands up north. Communication with the people under Renamo control was often indirect, sometimes transmitted through neighboring countries, but it was possible. And in these remote Renamo zones a stability appears to have been reached: life went on normally. Rudimentary forms of education, health care, and administrative infrastructure existed, and the relations between Renamo soldiers and the civilians were good. Horror stories of atrocities were minimal. I would assume this is due in large part to the remoteness of the area: Frelimo had never built strong inroads into the area, and its troops seldom, if ever, launched an offensive for control of the sites. The Renamo troops themselves were isolated from main contingents of Renamo and were largely unaffected by events taking place in other parts of the country. With external threats so low, the need for terror-warfare was greatly reduced. The picture painted during these conversations was not filled with the instances of unchecked brutality or repression one might expect from an area of virtual Renamo warlordry in a remote and uncontested area. Instead, these people discussed a productive community governed with concern for its well-being. The area was not rich, but the people were basically content. There was stability, sufficient food and resources, and relatively harmonious relations with Renamo control. Largely severed from the rest of the country and its devastating violence, people forged a viable sense of community.

This scenario is not restricted to isolated regions of this one province. Similar stories can be heard throughout Mozambique. In some cases expatriates (generally religious personnel from Europe) who chose to remain and work in locales overtaken by Renamo communicated analogous circumstances: equanimity had been achieved between Renamo and its subjects, however basic the lifestyle may have been in these areas (and data suggest it is generally fairly basic). They are usually isolated and removed from Frelimo spheres of influence. In these rural areas, life progresses much as it has for decades. These zones may not represent the norm, but these stories of cooperation between Renamo and noncombatants in uncontested areas are as real a part of the total war experience as are those of violence and hardship.

Not far from the Renamo-held areas in the northwest of Niassa province are areas that have staunchly attempted to maintain their independence from Renamo. The second account I will relate here has parallels throughout the country, and demonstrates the fundamental linkages politics, culture, and medicine have with the processes of war.

This second area was under the control of a famous and powerful *regulo* (chief), who was concerned with the well-being of the villages under his control and with keeping Renamo at bay. Far from the centers of Frelimo administration, the chief had worked hard to maintain a smoothly functioning and productive environment. He feared that Renamo incursions would disrupt the harmony of his protectorate. Chiefly power in Mozambique is strongly tied to the power of African medicine, which ensures the physical and mental health of Mozambicans as well as protecting the political and social health of the entire community. Military strength and the power to rule are reinforced through African medicine. In this case, the chief himself was skilled in certain medicinal traditions, and performed a set of rites common in contemporary Mozambique which protected the villages under his control from incursions by Renamo. All villagers within the protected area had to conform to a set of behavioral prescriptions and proscriptions to assure the continuing efficacy of the medicinal shield. The protective powers of the chief had functioned successfully for years, and his lands and subjects had prospered. Then, in the late 1980s, the chief took up with a younger woman without consulting his first wife. The first wife sat at home, as one Mozambican explained to me, "so very sad and lonely, thinking all day long 'why did he do this to me?'" Two days later Renamo over-ran the place. The Mozambicans with whom I spoke were convinced the chief's first wife was responsible for the military incursion. "There were so many proscriptions necessary to maintain the protection of the area—undoubtedly she violated one of these. Probably she ate something that was disallowed." Yet most of the people I discussed this with could not believe that she would knowingly break a proscription and welcome an attack by Renamo, no matter how upset she was. "Clearly," they explained, "she was so distraught she forgot all her duties, and in her sadness unknowingly ate something she should not have." (Part of the tragedy of this story is the tendency of all military cultures to blame women's actions for misfortune and defeat.) The story has a positive ending, however. The chief, recognizing the error of his ways and the impact of his actions on his first wife, quickly stopped his *brincadeiras* (games; playing around) and returned to apologize to his wife. Almost immediately, Renamo was routed from the area. A friend of mine from Lichinga traveled to his natal home, the chief's village, when he heard of the problems there. He arrived to find that the villages under the chief's control had suffered destruction from the Renamo attack—noncombat-ant casualties, burned houses, and looted buildings—but that they were quickly returning to normal life already free again of troops. Until I left Mozambique, the area never again suffered from Renamo attack, nor, to the best of my knowledge, did the chief further upset his first wife.

Geffray's War of Power and Politics

The existence of contiguous areas, one supporting Renamo and one supporting Frelimo, is not unusual in Mozambique. Christian Geffray is one of the first social scientists to conduct a study of the dynamics giving rise to such circumstances. With the support of the Frelimo government, Geffray did fieldwork in two zones in Nampula province in the north central region of the country: one which sided with Frelimo and the other with Renamo (Geffray and Pederson 1986; Geffray 1990).

Geffray[8] attributes much of village Mozambicans' disenchantment with Frelimo, and the early successes of Renamo, to Frelimo's practice of implementing socialist policies in the countryside. Problems revolved around two central tenets of Frelimo strategy: the production of communal villages and the proscription of traditional power structures and culture. The construction of communal villages was, according to Frelimo, intended to bring dispersed rural populations together into more productive units, so that farms, cooperatives, and trade networks would boost the economy. Quality of life would also increase, it was argued, as people had greater access to goods, communal labor, and the schools, medical clinics, and other services Frelimo would be able to provide to centralized locations. Geffray questions Frelimo's true goals and thinks the government was more interested in controlling the countryside.

Villagers were embittered by the villagization scheme. They were forced to leave their homelands and move to lands under the control of other chiefs, clans, and leaders. Infrastructure was not sufficient to meet the needs of the people, and hunger and deprivation, as well as the undermining of the integrity of entire clans, ensued. Communal villages were often nominal "villages" at best, and disruption of the countryside and home life was often severe.

Equally disastrous was Frelimo's policy toward the proscription of traditional power structures. Bloodline chiefs and African healers—mainstays of African life—were marginalized from power and, at times, actively persecuted. Geffray gives the example of elections held for local assembly in 1977, which he sees as a battle between the old power and the new. Local chiefs won a decisive victory, and the district administrator (a Frelimo representative) immediately annulled the election results, called new elections, and prohibited the chiefs from running again. The villagers elected the village idiots in the second election.

Renamo seized on this opportunity to further its cause. Its representatives spoke of their support of traditional chiefs and culture, and attacked the communal village scheme, telling villagers to return to their homelands. Renamo then used the chiefs as their liaison with the villagers under their control. Geffray notes that the initial flood of people leaving the communal villages was surprisingly large, attesting to the animosity Mozambicans had toward these enforced settlements.

However, differences did emerge in villagers' attitudes. Geffray identifies three groups who were most receptive to the rebels' claims: marginalized local authorities, the poor and the disenfranchised in the communal villages, and youths who felt they had no future. Marginalization was in part a function of clan identity. In the province of Nampula, the Macuane were known as warriors, and they were basically a scattered and rebellious population. The Erati, on the other hand, demonstrated a more centralized and organized clan structure and system of rule. The latter were more likely to have been closely linked with Portuguese colonial rule, and in fact profited in many ways under colonialism. When Frelimo came to power, the Erati simply shifted their loyalties and remained in positions of leadership, while the Macuane found themselves at the bottom of the hierarchy. Renamo provided the Macuane with an outlet for their grievances, while the Erati continued to maintain a loyalty toward Frelimo. The Frelimo army did not always help engender loyalties. Troops murdered chiefs suspected of supporting Renamo and burned villages thought to be colluding with the rebels. Like their Renamo counterparts, they were known to use terror tactics to intimidate and control the population.

In an interesting aside, Geffray notes that in the area he studied he found an oasis from war similar to the one I described above in Niassa province. In Nampula province, Geffray writes, a great Erati chief was respected for both his ruling and his magical powers. His village suffered no Renamo attacks, and people ate and slept without worry. In contrast, just seven kilometers from this chief's protectorate, the area lay in total ruins from military attacks.

Geffray underscores what has been observed by many others: during the war Renamo had little political identity. He stresses that Renamo's primary goal was to sustain itself. It had little interest in the domestic life and disputes of the people under its control, and relied on chiefs to manage these local issues. Chiefs were largely responsible for providing for Renamo's needs: food, goods, and taxes were collected from villagers and delivered to Renamo bases. *Capiceiros* (local "police" recruited by Renamo) and *majubas* (local Renamo collaborators) assisted in the collection of goods and the control (sometimes extortionary and brutal) of the population. They generally worked through the chief, and thus had a guise of authority that spanned military and traditional power bases. While some chiefs disagreed with the policies and practices of Renamo and their collaborators, they had few avenues for disagreement without endangering themselves. Geffray estimates that 300 soldiers eating 300 grams of manioc flour (a staple in the area) twice a day consume 66 tons of flour a year. This produced a severe drain on the resources of the villages Renamo controlled, and villagers often suffered serious privation due to these demands.

The demands for food were not the only strain Renamo placed on the populations it controlled. Demands for women and porters, harsh penalties, and a lack of political agenda undermined the support Mozambicans once had for Renamo. As abuses mounted, people became more and more disillusioned with the rebel group. In many areas, Renamo disallowed people from leaving Renamo-held lands, and punishment for infractions was severe. Captives were often subjected to, and forced to witness, brutalities and murders—actions intended to break people's associations with their former lives. People were also reluctant to leave Renamo lands, as Frelimo soldiers had been known to kill and mutilate people returning from Renamo areas as a warning to others. When

Frelimo, recognizing the error of these ways, instituted a policy of amnesty for all civilians and soldiers abandoning the rebel cause, Renamo banned all news of the amnesty program, and, when news of the program filtered in, worked hard to convince villagers it was a fictitious and lethal ploy.

Geffray stresses that the chiefs did not rebel against the state because it was a state per se, but because they had been marginalized from power and dignity. They thought Renamo offered them a means toward an independent existence where they could maintain a valued lifestyle. But chiefs, too, became pawns in a larger military contest, and people, freed from the communal villages, found they were yet again displaced to Renamo control areas for security reasons. Little if any improvement was gained under Renamo, and the enthusiasm for Renamo promises waned. At the same time, Frelimo corrected some of its earlier policies. The villagization schemes were virtually abandoned toward the end of the war, and the party increasingly recognized local village chiefs in the power structure. Because many Mozambicans felt the conflict in Nampula was a direct result of the marginalization of traditional chiefs, such recognition of political authority helped dispel some of the deep-seated resentments the populace had against Frelimo. Of course, Frelimo military excesses and enforced strategic villages in battlezones perpetuated lingering distrust.

In essence, what the villagers encountered was a continuing cycle of violence. The final picture Geffray paints was one of contending armies fighting over unarmed civilians. Frelimo forced people into communal villages and burned their family homes. Renamo arrived and burned the communal villages. When people returned to their homelands and rebuilt their old homes, Frelimo arrived to burn these down once again. Both sides captured people and forced them to march to new locations: Renamo relocated people to control areas around their bases, and Frelimo moved people to government-sponsored relocation camps. People faced a harsh life in both locations. The only difference Geffray notes was that the Frelimo army, unlike Renamo, is subordinate to a civilian authority.

Roesch's Rejoinder to Geffray: Questions of Differences and Similarities

The anthropologist Otto Roesch (1990) has challenged the applicability of Geffray's analysis to the whole of Mozambique. Roesch's work in the southern province of Gaza demonstrates the difference time, place, research style, and ideological orientation make to scholarly analyses, as well as supporting the contention that conflict is expressed very differently in various parts of a country at war. Roesch is certainly right in his contention that the war experience is different in the various provinces of Mozambique. I, too, traveled to Gaza and found circumstances there different from the other locations I had worked, though I found certain generalized tendencies that appeared to apply to the country as a whole. Roesch concludes from his observations that, "In contrast to the situation described by Geffray in Nampula, Renamo enjoys very little popular support in Gaza, or the rest of southern Mozambique, where it essentially operates as a predatory band, terrorizing and despoiling the rural population" (1990:25). He goes on to say that

At the same time, Renamo must be recognized as having taken on a local grass-roots dynamic of its own that is rooted in traditional ideological discourses, a narrow Ndau [the tribal group from the central provinces of Mozambique, generally credited with forming the bulk of elite Renamo] ethnic base, and the conditions of economic crisis and social breakdown which Renamo's own actions have played a major role in fostering. Though Renamo's traditionalist ideological discourse gives it a certain potential for mobilization in the rural areas, its ability to garner support would appear to be limited only to areas where local traditional leaders with popular followings are willing to make alliances with it. (1990:25)

The curious thing is that Roesch's observations match Geffray's in most instances. Three factors may help explain Roesch's conclusions. First, there are areas under Renamo control in the outlands of Gaza that were not accessible to outsiders (including Frelimo affiliates), and no one has a clear idea of the circumstances characterizing people's lives there. In contrast, Geffray conducted fieldwork in an area that supported Renamo with the assistance of the Frelimo government, which was concerned to discover why certain segments of the population supported Renamo. Second, in several areas that are accessible in Gaza, the villagization schemes put into motion by the Frelimo government were not met with the same hostility as they were in Nampula. In some instances, people received much better land and did not suffer from being subjected to living in regions traditionally controlled by other clans and traditional chiefs. Because of this, their loyalty to Frelimo was greater. Also, many Frelimo leaders are from ethnic groups represented in Gaza, and the linkages between the party and the people from Gaza have traditionally been strong. Moreover, traditional antagonisms between Gazians and Ndau (whom Roesch argue form the controlling faction of Renamo) have made Renamo incursions into Gaza particularly brutal. Finally, Roesch presents his findings based on research done in 1990. Geffray conducted his fieldwork from the mid-1980s on. Geffray himself states that, by the late 1980s, many in Nampula were disillusioned with Renamo and failed to maintain the support that they had initially shown. Had Roesch been in Gaza during the 1980s, he might have noted more complex and changing loyalties.

Tragically, Otto Roesch died in Mozambique. One of a handful of anthropologists who traveled in country during the war, he was killed in an automobile accident after the Peace Accord was signed.

The Living and the Forgotten to Death

These various accounts of the war in Mozambique are not intended to convey a string of circumstances connected only by location in a country at war. They are introduced here to demonstrate the depth of complexities that characterized the conflict experience in Mozambique. Yet the discussion does not do justice to the true diversity of experiences typifying a country at war. Against the tragic flux that is Ekani, the destructive capacity of Renamo portrayed by Gersony, and the logic of power and marginalization that Geffray illustrates are a host of people who suffer the weight of a war that is neither horrific nor calm, neither logical nor incomprehensible — a war that wears them down by its endless demands on dignity. Everywhere I traveled in Mozambique I heard stories similar to the one a friend relayed upon returning from a visit to her homeland in the interior of Zambezia province.

> I walked nearly a week to get to my homeland, the place of my birth, after taking the convoy as far as I could. I went because I had heard my mother was ill, and I was afraid she might die. I knew it was time to go to perform the ancestral ceremonies I had been forced to neglect for so long, and to reacquaint my parents and relatives with my own children and family. My mother was sick, but it was the war she was sick of. Ahye, I remember my home as it was when I was young. This memory calls to me daily, making me want to return to life as it was there and then, to let my children know what our life is really all about. The lands were beautiful then, green and full of crops. We grew everything we needed, we had manioc, we had vegetables, our trees were full of tasty things to eat. You would look out from the house and there would be chickens, and goats. And you should have seen the cows, they were beautiful. I loved our house — it was full of laughter, and it had plenty of room for us children.
>
> But you should see it now. Years of the Bandidos coming through have reduced it to a sad and barren place. The cows and goats and chickens went first, robbed and slaughtered by passing soldiers. One of the times, they burnt and destroyed the house, but not before they looted it. All our possessions are gone. Even the trees and the crops were destroyed that time. After they killed my brother, my parents

were never quite the same. They did not have the heart, or the manpower, to keep the machamba producing like it used to. I think they lost the will to work—the bandits might come and destroy it all again. They built another little house, but it seems so empty and lifeless. The whole area seems empty and lifeless: so many people have fled to other safer places, or have died. But my parents will not leave. They are old, and it is their home. The Bandidos may take all their goods, but they cannot force them to give up their ancestral lands.

When I took my youngest son to visit this time, my parents were so happy to see us, it brought some happiness and hope back into the house. But hope is so hard. I dream of returning to my birthplace to live, but I cannot stand the thought of living there like it is now, so desolate and full of fear. I pray for a future that can be like the past, with the fields green and full of good crops, and chickens and cows outside the door. But even if the war ends, what do we have left to build with?

All these war portrayals deal with what is known, or knowable. They come to define the war experience. A great deal of the war experience takes place away from the eyes and the pens of those recording conflict processes. In my field journals, I often label these places "forgotten to death."

Consider the place I call in my notes "north of A." I call it this because no one is quite sure precisely what area "north of A" covers, only that it exists. It is an area that is remote in terms of communication and roadway linkages. It has no runway, nor did it have any developed linkages with Frelimo administrative structure during the war. It did not escape the war, however. I had been interested in the stories filtering out from the area, because it showed the way in which conflict dynamics, and Renamo tactics in particular, changed with the introduction of FAM troops. While no Mozambican traders, administrative representatives, or foreigners traveled to the area, I made an effort to talk with people who had relatives and friends in the area and tried to remain in contact with them.

The people in this area of north central Mozambique lived in relative peace for many years. Renamo passed through on occasion and demanded goods, which the villagers gave them to avoid violent reprisals. Because there was little in the way of Frelimo representation there, Renamo did not feel the need to set up control areas, nor were there (potential) Frelimo supporters Renamo felt they had to make examples of by murdering. Essentially the population was left unharmed, if periodically depleted of resources.

FAM then "took" the area. They established a base on top of a hill commanding the area and forced the population to relocate around the base of the hill.[9] Around the civilians was a circle of Renamo troops. The civilians served as a buffer between the FAM troops and Renamo. The FAM troops controlled the movements of the villagers completely. During the day people were not allowed to move freely or to go out to their *machambas* to work their crops. At night, people were expected to maintain their presence in the locations set up at the base of the hill by the FAM troops. Furthermore, the troops were short on food themselves, and demanded food from the villagers. Marasmic kwashiorkor (a syndrome resulting from severe protein and calorie deficiency, with symptoms including retarded growth, changes in skin and hair pigmentation, edema, severe tissue wasting, and liver pathology) soon came to be known as "the disease of north of A." The few details about the area available to outsiders spoke of an entire population of children that suffered severe marasmic kwashiorkor.

Frelimo stated at this time that the area was under its control, and, apparently, by day it was. But at night Renamo made raids into the civilian area, looted goods and food, and mined all entrances and exits into the area. No one could get in or out. With Renamo's raids on food sources, Frelimo's sequestering of goods escalated. The population rapidly descended into abject poverty and starvation. In response, Renamo raids became more brutal. Now that people were "affiliated" with Frelimo, even if under conditions of forced relocation, Renamo's earlier policy of leniency was shelved for a harsher and more combative approach. Yet, as is so often the case, soldiers did not engage with soldiers but with unarmed villagers.

For a while, people outside the area heard of the situation mainly by communiqués passed through friends and relatives and by the few villagers who escaped. Mozambican relief agencies tried to get emergency supplies into the area, but all entrances were mined. Suddenly, no word was available about conditions in this zone. News simply dried up completely. No one could figure out what was taking place, but speculations were rampant. Did Frelimo retreat from lack of food and reinforcements, leaving the population to fend for themselves? Did the population finally die off from starvation? Did Renamo win any kind of victory in the area? Regardless of which scenario prevailed, those who remained alive, if any, were consigned to difficult times.

Within a month of the time the news from this area had dried up, people no longer talked about "north of A." It was, literally, "forgotten to death." For the remainder of my stay in the country, I heard nothing further about the area. I do not know whether people turned from the possible horror of a population that may have died out en masse, or whether they turned their attention to new areas undergoing similar fates where they felt they could lend assistance.

*   *   *

If it appears that this section portrays fragments of war contes—variously related and disjointed, incomplete, fluid and contradictory—then I have succeeded in accurately conveying the ground experience of war. People's lives are lived amid bits and pieces of information and misinformation, and their survival depends on trying to gather these into some pattern of meaning. People "know" their experiences, but these are not sufficient to predict future behaviors: a new commander, a rogue soldier, a change in the prevailing political winds, a revision of policy, a vengeful neighbor, a mercenary far from home, may come down the road exacting new tolls on life—unforeseen and potentially lethal. Surviving war entails the fundamental irony of simultaneously creating meaning and embracing (the reality) of chaos—a demand on cognitive process that confounds even the best philosophers.

Notes

1. I do not mean to imply that single-locale ethnographies on war are invalid. Hopefully in-depth studies of various communities' responses to war will provide a framework for a more sophisticated understanding of socio-political violence. Even producing such studies is fraught with dificulties. Few researchers are willing to risk living in a town under direct siege. In the case of covert warfare, few would be able to penetrate the political secrets and military institutions through which terror, torture, and murder are carried out. And if they elect to collect data in the capital cities and urban centers largely free of direct aggressions, they are no longer conducting an ethnography of war proper, but reconstructing the reconstructions of war available to them. All these forms of research are both cogent and necessary, but they should not, in themselves, be taken as definitive statements "on war."

2. Barthes (1985:258) further explains: "First of all, whereas for centuries listening could be defined as an intentional act of audition (to listen is to *want* to hear, in all conscience), today it is granted the power (and virtually the function) of playing over unknown spaces: listening includes in its field not only the unconscious in the topical sense of the term, but also, so to speak, in its lay forms: the implicit, the indirect, the supplementary, the delayed: listening grants access to all forms of polysemy, of overdetermination, of super-imposition."

3. Ekani is not the real name of the town, but a Chuabo word meaning war.

4. Parama was introduced in Chapter Two. To reiterate, Parama was a spontaneous, grassroots traditional peasant army that was protected against harm by vaccinations of traditional medicine, and fought only with *armas brancas*, the white weapons of traditional spears and knives. Their sole purpose was to rid

their lands of Renamo troops, and they operated mainly in two of the north central provinces of Mozambique.

5. Manuel Antonio here is enacting his own resurrection from burial, and, by implication, his links to Christ. As I wrote in Chapter Two explaining Manuel Antonio's history, the themes of burial and rebirth are common in Mozambican medicine and power.

6. A colleague, Tamara Jane, read this manuscript before publication and wrote in the margin: "This is amazing in terms of how *mass* daily compliance is essential to legitimize power—unless the power is used to control people solely through terror—and how both of these constantly interact. I resist mentioning Foucault . . ."

7. Whether this is true I cannot say, but I found a dedicated group of people working within the province doing as best they could with very limited resources. The twenty minutes of water and several hours of electricity a day serving the provincial capital (and this during "good" conditions) convinced me that at least some apathy on the part of Frelimo existed toward this area.

8. I am indebted to Karl Maier for aiding me in understanding Geffray's book *La cause des armes*, which is written in French.

9. Reminiscent of Foucault's panoptican.

Chapter 4
Living on the Frontlines

Departure

Anger is creaking and
authoritarian forces vibrate
strange things are advancing without scruples
in a bewildered way and
a hoarse voice
cries out without hope or fear
resounding in his heart
pain and grief.
Pools of blood and evil
emerge criminally in the land and
escaped souls
drown life without distinction!
How it hurts to evoke a destiny!
Splendid sunbeams
tearing the yellow belly of the dawn
will shine through
eyes rebelling against death and sleep
in one beautiful morning of departure.

—Bernardo

Displaced people, Moatize, Tete province, 1987. Photo by Anders Nilsson.

Violence

> They have not just killed my family and taken my home, they have killed my soul. They have spit on it and killed it. (Mozambican woman, at the height of the war)

It may at first seem curious that in a book entitled "a different kind of war story" this chapter is devoted to issues of violence and its resolution, not "war." There are several reasons for this.

The most important involves the pursuit of the definition of war. Not war in the abstract, as in a Clausowitzian treaty, but as enacted by real people in real places. If I am to conduct an ethnography of a warzone, what exactly is this war I plan to study, where do I go to find it, what does it look like? Traditional political science would have it that going to the offices and institutions of (elite) political and military actors constitutes a reasonable place to study (the phenomenon of) war. But both the people who populate the institutions and the structures and ideologies that shape their expression exist across war and peace. How, then, can they be said to be indicative of war if they exist and operate equally in peace? Political alliances and antipathies, clashes of ideologies, the intoxication of power, and the activities of militaries define the very institutions and actions of militaries and political power brokers, in war and out. The institutions that are defined as carrying out the enterprise of war—political and military—are fundamentally concerned with controlling the definitions of what war is, not with making the definitions responsible to the realities of war. In fact, one can argue, these institutions have a vested interest in defining war in precisely nonrealistic terms. If any warmaking institution in the world were formally to publish strategic texts or policy statements that included, for example, the 1996 United Nations statistics that more children are killed in war than soldiers or data on the extensive international profits that accrue to war, public support for war could evaporate rapidly. Therefore studying the nature and culture of war from a purely institutional vantage is less about the actuality of war than about the politics of power.

If the staging ground of war is not to be found in institutions and their ideologies, where, then, is it? Logic supplies a single answer: war comes into existence when violence is employed. Political aggressions may become flamed, threats may be flung back and forth, military exercises may take place, but it is only when bullets are fired and people are maimed and killed, when bombs destroy strategic targets, that war is said to exist. It is in the act of violence, then, that the definition of war is found. Militaries operate on one single truth: the strategic employment of violence. Politics is rooted in one paramount definition of security: military might that is ultimately predicated on the ability to employ (and deploy) violence effectively.

To understand war is to understand not only the places where it is formulated and directed, but the places where violence is enacted in the name of war. It is perhaps a profound irony that the political and military institutions themselves are precisely where war does *not* take place. Politicians may launch war, but they are seldom out on the frontlines facing and inflicting violence. Military command centers may direct battles, but the ground soldier advancing weapon in hand, the bomber flying toward a target, and the ICBM launchpad constitute a reality far removed from these command centers and their personnel.

Yet it is notoriously difficult to study the actual sites of violence. In fact, it is as hard to study the actuality of war as it is easy to study its institutions. This fact, perhaps more than any other, explains why so many studies of war have focused on political and military leaders and their institutional bases—as unrepresentative of actual war as this may be— rather than following the actual deployment of violence in situ. How many researchers collect data and hone their theoretical acumen in the midst of firefights, are witness to massacres, are allowed to observe and take notes during torture sessions in military prisons?

Locating war in the strategic use of violence does not provide easy answers to studying either war or violence. The question then becomes: what is nonviolence, and how do we study it? Answers are far more difficult to obtain than either popular or scholarly theory would suggest.

A major conundrum in the study of violence is the definition of violence. To sum up the dilemma: violence is not defined. This statement at first appears patently incorrect or frivolous, but it is not. It is a serious statement about the politics of power and about the way war is, and can be, conducted. Let me begin with a simple observation. In the decade and a half I have been teaching and researching issues of violence and its resolution, I do not recollect ever hearing anyone ask for a definition of violence. Because, quite simply, speaking at the level of cultural epistemology, people simply *know* what violence is. This knowledge of violence brooks no question into the accuracy of these definitions. It is what I call an "essentially defined concept." The knowledge people hold about violence they take, quite literally, to be true. It is accepted as a given, so much so that its givenness is not questioned. It is knowledge that is "always already" in social epistemology—the foundation from which all questions derive, but which is itself not questioned.

Nor, observation would indicate, can it be questioned. At a certain point, again speaking at the level of cultural epistemology, the basic assumptions "defining violence" become incontestable. A second observation joins the first: in my experience people are as loathe to accept definitions of violence as they are to ask for them.

There is what may be termed "definition by a strategic lack of definition." For ultimately the key to controlling a phenomenon or event is defining it. If these definitions are essentially underdefined, the harsh realities of violence on the frontlines remain obscured from formal discourse and censure. If the lack of definition surrounding violence is not apparent, think of all the presentations available on violence and ask exactly what is violence?

- an act, a drive, an emotion, a sensation, a relationship, an intent to harm?
- a thing, an event, a concept, a process, an interaction?
- an intangible threat, a tangible force?
- something physically felt, something emotionally registered, something conceptually recognized?
- something that is over with the end of the act, or something that reconfigures reality in its very occurrence, making the concept of "over" meaningless?

Can the ontics of violence (the lived experience of violence) and the epistemology of violence (the ways of knowing and reflecting about violence) ever be realistically separated? Should an attempt even be made to situate violence in any of these domains? While recognizing that violence may be expressed as actions, emotions, responses, drives, or states of being, is it not dangerous to essentialize the definition of violence? To do so stereotypes core dimensions of human existence and leads to a tendency to fix violence as a "natural" category with "universal" expressions. To essentialize violence theoretically is to reify it, and to do so from the idiosyncratic cultural heritage of the theoretician is to lose not only the experiential force of violence lived but to endanger an adequate understanding of complex dynamics that define this phenomenon in thought and action.[1]

If reality is indeed culturally constructed, then fixing definitions is at once both political and impossible. In fact, I will suggest, the widespread Mozambican redefining of violence constituted one of the most profound acts of resistance to war's oppression I have ever encountered. It was the very flexibility of definition, hidden behind the hegemonic presentation of "what war is" so common in formal and popular thought, that noncombatant Mozambicans used to their advantage.

Regardless how we answer these questions, there is a truth of violence that cannot be ignored. Simply put: every military, every police repression, and every war or battle of the modern era has one and only one thing in common: reliance on the use of violent force to accomplish political goals, to vanquish enemies, and to enforce power over others. In this sense, violence is deconstituting and profoundly enmeshed in the politics of unequal power hierarchies. The millions of victims of political violence emerging each year share a significant experience of power politics in its most ontological dimension. What exactly is this ontological experience of violence that makes it the handmaiden of politics?

This book has continually demonstrated the difficulty of studying violence rather than a second-hand account of violence-passed. Even investigations into violence first-hand are fraught with possibly unanswerable questions. The foremost of these questions, and one that undermines the definitions of violence discussed above, is the issue of where we *situate* violence.

To study violence, even to talk about it, is to make a determination as to what constitutes violence where and among whom. Before we can study it, before we can even ask about it, we must situate what we deem to be violence. In the most basic terms, to what person or text in what location do we as researchers go in conducting a study of war and violence? The decision, from military commander to maimed civilian, situates our definition of violence and thus determines our definition and approach to violence. Do we situate it:

- in the leaders who define and command, the soldiers who enact, or the civilian population who constitute 90 percent of all war casualties in the world today?
- in actual troop actions in war and peace, only in troop engagements engaged in violence, or in the whole of the politico-military enterprise?
- in the perpetration of violence, or in victims and target populations?
- as outside everyday society, or as within it?
- in war, or in the mere possibility (threat) of war?
- in (violent) actions, or in narratives of violence?
- at the nexus where violence meets resistance and conflict resolution?

Do we locate violence in action, culture, society, physical realities, conceptual ideologies, biology, ontology? Does a child's song about an encounter with violence carry the same analytical weight as troop deployments and adults' resistance movements?

Where do we locate viable discussions of violence? In military texts, military accounts, political policies, academic treatises, with the victims, the onlookers, in the stories true and false that circulate in and throughout everyday society and life?

If the answer is all of these and more (which I would strongly agree with), the next question of course is, how many researchers require how many years to make even a dent in collecting representative information? Given this restraint, how do we make the study of violence responsible? Where does one person turn her or his focus to collect information on violence?

The Question of Violence and Anna's Story

So, what is violence? I hold with philosophers like Nietzsche who say that all too often theory is a mirror held up to reflect one's own presumptions and worldview, not one positioned to reflect the world outside. Or, as Bacon—ironically, one of the forebears of scientific realism—observes:

> The human understanding is no dry light, but receives an infusion from the will and affections; whence proceed sciences which may be called "sciences as one would." For what a man had rather were true he more readily believes. (1960:52)

This is nowhere more evident than in considerations of violence, a topic so politically loaded and emotionally charged that opinions often speak more to how people want to see the world than how it really is. Violence is a cultural construct, as are the theories intended to explain it. Each is embedded in a spiral of personal, social, and cultural histories and experiences that color one's orientation toward the topic, researcher and informant alike.

Violence fits well with Bacon's list:

> There is no soundness in our notions, whether logical or physical. Substance, Quality, Action, Passion, Essence itself, are not sound notions; much less are Heavy, Light, Dense, Rare, Moist, Dry, Generation, Corruption, Attraction, Repulsion, Element, Matter, Form, and the like; but all are fantastical and ill defined. (1960:42)

The *notion* of violence is an abstracted category, by definition an order of reality altogether different from that of the experience of violence. As a "notion" it is removed from "actuality" as we live it. Moreover, notions are conceived, politicized, even poeticized in ways experiences never are. Many of the definitions of violence I held to be "true" before I began to study it were dispelled as I listened to the hundreds of stories of people living on the frontlines of conflict. I realized that many of the assumptions we take to be valid are more a part of our cultural heritage than a product of scholarly endeavor. To illustrate the complex nature of violence and the questions that accrue to it, consider the story of Anna, whom I met in 1991.

Anna lived on the outskirts of one of the larger towns in Zambezia. She had arrived a year or two before—a refugee from the war in her own village. She had fled an attack, and before fleeing she had seen one of her sons, and a number of her friends, brutally murdered. When she ran, she took her youngest child with her, but lost track of her husband and the rest of her family, who had scattered to avoid the violence. As she paused to look back at the village where she had grown up, she saw flames consume her home, the market where she bought her goods, and the houses of her friends where she went to talk and share chores.

As she tried to reach safety, she was captured by a group of Renamo soldiers. She was raped and beaten, and forced to carry the loot of her own village for seemingly endless days through the bush, heading toward, she guessed, the Renamo base camp. Other people from her village that were kidnapped during the attack shared her plight. One older man could not keep up. He had a cough and the loads were too heavy for him. He was beaten and left to die. She hoped he somehow had made it to safety.

One night when the soldiers seemed to relax their guard, lulled into complacence by the vastness of the bush and the distance from any village or Frelimo base, she and her child slipped off quietly into the night and ran, hungry and full of fear, until dawn. She walked, her child in her arms, for days, living on what little she could scavenge from the land, until they came to a town. There she was told she should try to make it to a larger town several days' walk away—the town where she now lived—for there she would find refugee assistance. Along the way she met several others in her predicament, and they made their way to the new destination.

There was a refugee center, but it was like nothing she had ever seen before. There was food, but not much; there were houses, but they were small huts all crammed one on top of the other, stretching as far as the eye could see. Not long after she arrived, she and her child moved in with a man she had met. He was all right, but he beat her when he became angry or frustrated, which was often. But she told herself it was better than being alone and on her own.

Food was more than a daily preoccupation, one she, like all of the deslocados, worried about hourly. The food made available through the center was not enough. By the time the distributors had their cut and the blackmarketeers had siphoned off what they could to sell, there was little left for the many who were hungry. The village leaders and the military, if present, often took the lion's share of what was left. People were encouraged to make and farm their own machambas, but that was fraught with danger. The townspeople were embittered with the arrival of so many deslocados competing for resources, and fights over rights to farmland often became bloody. The townspeople usually won—they had rights to land that spanned generations and bureaucracies, and they had the force of family and friends to back them up. That meant the recent arrivals like Anna had to go far into the bush, often several hours' walk, to plant a machamba. Traveling so far on one's own left a person vulnerable to attack from soldiers in the bush. For those who had already escaped from Renamo attack or capture once, this was an unbearable possibility. However, so was starvation. The dilemma became whether to risk kidnapping or death at the hands of Renamo while traveling to and from one's machamba, or to procure food in the camp or in town either legally, which was sometimes impossible, or illegally, risking imprisonment. In addition, even if one could procure land to farm, a newcomer had no ancestral rights to it. Ancestral rights were significant because of the traditions that linked lineage and ancestral rights to specific land(s). One's ancestors came to live in the land, ensuring the right of their descendants to live and work the land, and ensuring fecundity. Living on someone else's land meant that deslocados either lived without the protection of their ancestors or, if they chose to perform ceremonies to bring the protective spirits of their ancestors with them, lived on land under the rule of someone else's ancestral lineage. Many people told stories of becoming sick because their ancestors fought with the ancestors who had historical rights to the land, the former hating to succumb to the domination of the latter.

Amid all this, Anna was profoundly troubled by the fact that she had not been able to do a proper burial and ceremony for her son who had been killed in the attack on her village. She worried about what would happen to his spirit, and what that meant for both him and her family. She was never able to express the grief she felt.

Anna was hungry, her child was hungry, and she had nothing; all her possessions had been lost when she fled her village. Many people were in her position: refugees who had lost everything and fled here for safety. Embittered, angry, exposed to too much violence, and unable to work or farm, the more aggressive and desperate turned to thievery and violence to put food on the table. This was especially true in the town areas, where even walking in certain places or at certain times was unsafe. You never knew when someone might catch up with you walking at night and take your last piece of clothing, the few coins you had, or the bit of food you had been able to coax from the ground or another person. As Anna spoke a different dialect from that spoken in the area she now resided in, she feared this might leave her even more vulnerable to the unscrupulous.

The thing that kept Anna going was dreaming of returning to her home village, of finding her husband and the rest of her family, of rebuilding her house and replanting her machamba. But she was pregnant again, and what would her family say to that? In all likelihood, the pregnancy had resulted from the rape she suffered at the hands, so to speak, of Renamo. She had heard women gossiping about other women who returned home with one more child than they had left with, only to be cast out by their husbands.

I met many Annas in Mozambique, and I tell her story here to explore the question of what violence is. The question is complex, and the layers of violence to which people are subjected are stacked one on another in an experiential whole that can be understood only by investigating all the strata. Military assault is the most compelling font of violence, but from where Anna stands, violence extends out from her world in many directions. The layers of violence in her daily world are manifold and indivisibly intertwined:

- There is the violence that extends into her home. Probably most immediate to her is her child's hunger, a product of a world of inequalities whereby some can feed their children and some cannot. Yet it goes deeper than this: her child's normal destiny has been taken from him. Her son does not play lightheartedly with the other children of his birth village, grow strong on the stories and the food of his extended family, delight to the tales told by his grandparents. He does not learn the landscapes, the animals and the plants of his village, but the harshness of a town of strangers and how to listen for the attack of soldiers or thugs. There is the violence done to her murdered son, and to her in watching him killed—an unresolved pain for Anna because she has never been able properly to express her grief, conduct the ceremonies necessary to ensure his place among the dead, and to mourn him and his spirit in a healthy way. Then there is the violence of her home life: her partner who beats her and has little respect for her traditions and values.
- There is the violence unleashed on the community: of people competing, at times viciously, for insufficient food and goods; of crime and feeling continually unsafe.
- There is the violence of being a *deslocado*, a person of a different language group, of being an outsider. This is an everyday fact of life that ultimately impinges on her very identity: to be dis*placed* is to be uprooted from that which grounds notions of self and self-worth, suddenly to confront a world lacking in signifiers that give meaning and sense to being-in-the-world.
- Then there is the violence of her memories. As she describes it, each thought of her family, of not knowing if they are dead or alive, is

like a knife wound. Her yearning for her once-happy home life is, she says, like a crippling pain. Her nightmares of her village burning make her physically sick.

• And then there is the physical violence of the war itself, both that done to Anna and all those like her, and that which they were forced to witness. It is a violence, Mozambicans tell me, that goes far beyond the physical bloodshed to injure family stability, community sustainability, and cultural viability. The continuity of the historical present is obliterated, respected traditions are dismantled, values rendered moot. Psychological peace and emotional security are bygone memories. Tomorrow, once taken for granted, now becomes a tenuous proposition.

Multiply Anna's story not by the thousands but by the hundreds of thousands, even the millions, and a picture of what the war in Mozambique was like for the citizens begins to emerge. Widely accepted figures demonstrate that fully one-half of the population, more than eight million people, were directly affected by the war.

Nuancing Our Understanding of Violence

What does this say about Mozambique? In terms of sheer overt violence how do we compare the experiences of the people who are mutilated in individual acts of terror; the villages that are totally destroyed; the communities that bribe paramilitary soldiers not to harm them; the districts on the margins of the fighting that have never seen actual warfare but slowly starve because of ruined infrastructure; the children kidnapped and forcibly trained to become soldiers; the refugees who continually flee war and never see it but lose family members to it; the traditional healers who treat the devastating wounds of war but are then placed at the center of fighting as targets and booty for both armies alike; the people who make fortunes selling information and acquiring loot; the war orphans who have seen their parents killed; and, finally, the experiences of the soldiers and political leaders themselves? How do we successfully juxtapose the violences Anna has endured to those of the woman who told me:

> I love this country and I hate it. It is my country, its blood flows in my veins. No one who has not lived like this can understand. The war has gotten into us all, it lives in us, affecting our every move and thought. If I walk outside, I wonder if today is the day I will die. If my brother is late coming to visit me, I wonder if he has been kidnapped or killed, and the terror lives in me. I have not heard from my mother—she lives in an uncertain area behind Renamo control—and I live daily

not knowing if she is dead or alive, whether her spirits are calling for
me to do a proper ceremony for her, or if her body is calling for food
and family. You do not have to see the war to live the war, and the war
lives in all of us.

Each story, each experience, is as personal as its narrator; but all,
taken together, begin to make up the cultures of violence and survival
that shape the lives of Mozambicans. And this culture of violence is in-
serted into the daily life-worlds of people on myriad levels, from the
actual to the symbolic, from parable to representation, from personal
interaction to dream. It is less about actual institutions of violence than
about the reality of violence as an inescapable fact of life. It is the
knowledge systems made necessary by war and threat; it is the site of
resistance. This culture of violence is not activated only during or near
actual encounters with physical violence; it does not disappear when the
physicality of violence ceases. Violence becomes a cultural fact, a per-
sistent enduring dynamic. This cultural force of violence maintains the
reality of violence beyond its mere physical expression.

Because violence was so widespread in Mozambique, stories about violence—stories of suffering, of compassion, of survival—circulated constantly in everyday conversation. These discussions were a survival skill
intended to take care of the victims of violence and to warn others how
to avoid victimization if at all possible. But to accomplish this, an accurate understanding of how violence is experienced was crucial, and thus
many discussions revolved around the many "casualties" of violence, the
many ways it could harm. This knowledge was essential to understanding how the harm could be ameliorated.

Readers may have noticed that the songs, the stories, and the quotes
so far presented in this book do not often deal solely, or even mainly,
with actual physical acts of violence, but rather with a type of violence
that is much deeper and enduring. This perspective stands in contrast
to the more official accounts of violence in global culture. In journalistic
reports, official statements, academic publications, and popular movies
physical acts of brutality are the main focus, and stories of gruesome
mutilations, rapes, and murders abound. The stories that most violate
notions of human decency tend to be the most circulated. Yet when I
listened to average Mozambican civilians discuss the war, these barba-
rous accounts, while present, were not the focal point. The destruction
of home and humanity, of hope and future, of valued traditions and the
integrity of the community resonated throughout these conversations.

To illustrate these nuanced perspectives of violence, I start with a
classic example of violence, and move on to examples of some of the
more common themes surrounding the experience of violence Mozam-

bicans frequently discussed. Lina Magaia's well-known book on the war in Mozambique, *Dumba Nengue—Run for Your Life: Peasant Tales of Tragedy*, contains what many consider classic accounts of violence, no matter what culture or position one holds. Magaia's book is a compendium of accounts of military (Renamo) attacks against noncombatants, each a story she collected in the course of her work with the Ministry of Agriculture. Magaia is careful to point out that these stories are not the worst or most uncommon, but just the opposite, the most commonly heard war stories of the most average of civilians. Her book opens with the following account.

Classical Example of Violence

It happened at night, as it always does. Like owls or hyenas, the bandits swooped down on a village in the area of Taninga. They stole, kidnapped and then forced their victims to carry their food, radios, batteries, the sweat of their labor in the fields or in the mines of Jo'burg where many of those possessions had come from.

Among the kidnapped were pregnant women and little children. Among the little ones was a small girl of nearly eight. . . . And the hours went by and dawn broke and finally there was a halt. They put down their loads and the bandits selected who could return home and who had to carry on. Of those who had to keep going, many were boys between twelve and fifteen. Their fate was the school of murder—they would be turned into armed bandits after training and a poisoning of their conscience. Others were girls between ten and fourteen, who would become women after being raped by the bandits. Others were women who were being stolen from their husbands and children.

To demonstrate the fate of the girls to those who were going back, the bandit chief of the group picked out one, the small girl who was less than eight. In front of everyone, he tried to rape her. The child's vagina was small and he could not penetrate. On a whim, he took a whetted pocketknife and opened her with a violent stroke. He took her in blood. The child died. (Magaia 1988:19–20)

Nuancing the Classical

Such stories as this have come to be associated with the very nature of violence. They have come to define it. But violence is not so easily rendered. While Magaia lived with the truth of this violence in her everyday life, readers outside Mozambique do not have this same depth of knowledge. If we take this description alone, as journalist reports and anthropological vignettes are wont to do, what do we learn about the ontological dynamics of violence? How did the act described above reconfigure the definitions of self, the lives, and the daily realities of the people present? What does it convey about the nature of grief and fear? How did this act of violence insinuate itself into the society and culture of those who witnessed it or heard of it? How did it reconfigure cultural truths? What is it that is so powerful about this kind of violence that it is found in virtually every war taking place in the contemporary world? If war is about hegemony and control, and violence is fundamental to the carrying out of war, what is the relationship between violence and the abuse of power and control?

We also need to ask: would we as readily see violence in the plight of the mother whose son works in an area behind Renamo lines, who has no way of knowing if he is kidnapped or safe, dead or alive? Would we label as violent the situation of the child who may never have seen bloodshed, but listens, in both fascination and fear, to the stories told around the cooking fires at night of the treachery and terror the war has brought to the child's land? And whose definitions of violence do we take to be most true?

> The war brings many types of violence, and some we can deal with better than others. The physical mutilation and massacres are horrible. . . . There is no excuse for this, no easy solution to the suffering it causes. The foreigners, the government representatives, and the journalists all talk of this as if it were the only kind of violence there is—when you see the blood run. But this may not be the worst form of violence. We have seen people hurt and killed in our lifetime. We know there are dangerous people in the world. We have seen people mutilated from war and accidents. We know there are sorcerers in our midst who wish us harm. Our traditions teach us how to deal with these difficult aspects of life. This war has elevated death and mutilation to a terrible level, worse than anyone should have to live through, it is true, but these things we have seen before. But you want to know what I think is the worst thing about this war, the worst violence I suffer? It is sleeping in the bush at night. The Bandidos come at night and attack while we are sleeping, so we all sneak into our villages, our homes, during the day to do our work and tend our crops, and then sneak back into the bush at night to sleep hidden by isolation in some distant location covered only by the sky at night. Animals live in the bush, not humans. Forcing us to sleep out with the animals makes us no better than them—these Bandidos, they take away our humanity, our dignity, they make us like animals. My marriage bed is the center of all the things I hold dear. It is the center of my family, my home, my link with the ancestors and the future. This war, these soldiers, have broken my marriage bed, and with that they try to break my spirit, break what makes me who I am. This is the worst violence you can subject someone to.

Violence reverberates across personal and social landscapes in ways that move beyond the sheer physicality of the act of harm. Adding to

Magaia's stories, consider the following perspectives on violence I found common in Mozambique.

Grief as a Weapon

One day, during a visit to a town that had recently shifted control from Renamo to Frelimo, several Mozambicans and I walked past a hut where a man's body was being carried out. We had been talking about the fact that more than a score of people were dying each day in the town, and the many ways war kills. One of my compatriots turned to me and said:

> His child died some days ago, and now the war has taken him too in its own awful way. You see it all the time, a young child will die, and in a few weeks the parent will be dead. He had to watch his child waste and die in his house before his eyes, unable to do anything, unable to get medicines or food or help because the war has made all this impossible. And he sits and thinks all during this time, "I am the father, I am supposed to take care of my family, to protect and nourish it; and yet here I sit watching my child die and I can do nothing." And then when the child dies, he just locks himself in his house and his grief, and he doesn't come out—and pretty soon we must perform another funeral.

Attack Against Hope and Normalcy

This is a particularly insidious form of violence. One day, I was speaking to a child of five or six years of age who had walked hundreds of kilometers with his family after his own village had been attacked and burned. He had the countenance of an adult and the weakened body of a child half his age, and he spoke with the detached seriousness of an old man about the violence he had witnessed. At one point I asked him about a wound on his leg, the type of injury children are prone to get. My question was intended only as a demonstration of concern—the wound was not serious. I was quite shaken with his response, a pronouncement delivered with the utmost seriousness:

> The wound? I will die of it. We walked here many days, and we had nothing while we walked. I watched my brother die during that time. We had to leave our home because the Bandidos attacked it, and I saw them kill my father. Now we are here and I watch my mother dying slowly, because we have nothing. I will die too.

Tactical Use of Contradictions

Consider the all-too-common scenario related by Mozambicans who have been attacked by Renamo. When the soldiers came, as they often did at night, they sometimes broke into a home and raped the wife in full view of her husband and children. In fact, they often commanded the husband to remain and watch, or be killed. Sometimes family members were forced to hold the wife down during the assault. Both soldiers and victims know all too well that this is a broad-spectrum form of violence intended to undermine personal integrity and family relations in their most profound sense. Trust, normalcy, power, and control over one's life are all attacked. It is a spectacle of violence. The injustice is made worse by the actions of some of the FAM troops. I have been told by a number of FAM soldiers that if they hear of such a rape, they immediately assume the husband must be a Renamo collaborator—for how else could he sit and watch such a scene? So the violence is carried one step further, compounded layer upon layer. If the husband is incarcerated or killed by Frelimo troops because they assume he is a Renamo supporter, his wife and children suffer yet another assault in a spiral of violence—the survival of their family.

Thwarting Solutions

When chaos comes to define a person's life-world, Mozambicans seek to remedy the situation by returning order and meaning to the world through ceremonies. A constant refrain I heard among people was that, precisely because of the war, they could not perform the ceremonies they needed to. Ceremonies were usually performed at night, and the noise would alert soldiers in the area, potentially eliciting reprisals or attacks. For many Mozambicans, one of the greatest violences they were forced to endure was that they could not perform these ceremonies in order to begin healing the violence in their lives.

Emotional and Existential Violence

These rank equally with, and in many cases outrank, physical violence. The following is an excerpt of a conversation I had with a man in the interior of Zambezia the day after he arrived in town after having escaped from the Renamo band that held him. He was middle aged, his speech was halting, and his affect undermined. He was both a strong and a broken man. The first attribute had allowed him to escape; the second was a product of what he had to escape from. Speaking to him was like conversing with someone who is simultaneously present and looking off into the far distance.

> We were under Renamo control for several years. They came and took everything, including us. We were forced to move around a lot, carrying heavy loads for Renamo here, being pushed there for no apparent reason. People died, people were killed, people were hurt, assaulted, beaten—there was no medicine, no doctors, no food to help them. My family is gone, all of them. Only I am here. But the violence and the killing is not necessarily the worst of it. Worst of all is the endless hunger, the forced marches, the homelessness—day in and day out a meager and hurting existence that seems to stretch on forever.

Ongoing Violences

But what the above quote does not capture is the fact that the man's suffering is not over. An acquaintance had taken me to see the man, who was staying on the outskirts of town in a bombed-out and deserted quarter that had seen the ravages of the war come and go. Someone was sent to find him, and we spoke to him outside, on the border of a field lying fallow. At the time, I thought it unusual: Mozambican etiquette normally involves making one's introductions, and then sitting and talking inside, on a verandah, or on a patch of ground under a tree or in a clearing. In this case, no introductions were made, and we stood, isolated from paths where others might appear unannounced or rooms where others might overhear. In the harsh sun and on a flat plain, we could see anyone coming from a distance.

Only slowly did I realize that the man's ordeals continued. I remembered a phrase I had heard repeated frequently, both by civilians and soldiers: that one was never sure about these people who had been with Renamo for such a long time, kidnapped or not—for the violence and the way of life, maybe even the ideology, under Renamo might become absorbed, become a habit, become reproduced. Soldiers and civilians grappled with this dilemma in different ways. The soldiers said they investigated the person to try to determine if he or she might become a Renamo collaborator. If the evidence was strong, the person might be shot or taken to prison. Sometimes this was done even if no apparent proof of collaboration existed, or if there was evidence the kidnap victim had been forced to participate in raids. The soldiers explained these were not necessarily punitive actions. They justified their deeds by arguing that most kidnap victims escape far from their homeland, and without money or family connections they have little means of returning to safety. Should such a person fall back into the hands of Renamo, he or she will certainly be killed, the soldiers say. So for their own protection, they may be incarcerated. For others' protection they may be killed. Personally, I did not find the soldier's actions to be so reasoned. I encountered a number of towns where FAM troops had arrived and shot Curandeiros, village leaders, traders, and people suspected of being collaborators on the flimsiest of reasons. *Deslocados* were often suspect merely because they were "dislocated," and even for the most innocent victims of war the fact remained that soldiers and officials kept a close eye on *deslocados*.

Civilians have a different means of dealing with the recently escaped, means generally far more grounded in creative resolutions than in violence. Fluent in the realities of life under war, they recognize that the violence to which people have been subjected can remain with them, capable of erupting at a later date, and that this violence can ruin normal sensibilities. The solution, however, is to recommend African medical therapy from a curandeiro or curandeira who specializes in war trauma. Such a professional is adept at recognizing the psychological and emotional as well as physical wounds of war, at treating them, and at helping the patient begin to reintegrate into a normal community life.

But the end point was that everyone was concerned with those who have suffered under Renamo, and were watching them carefully. Because the man I spoke with had just arrived, and had not been interrogated by the troops, embraced by the community, or treated by local methods, his position was volatile. And because he had not undergone these rites of passage, he had not learned how to respond appropriately. As is often the case with people in this condition, they are extremely honest about their ordeal, almost carelessly so—they have not yet learned to "edit" their conversations to fit social and political requirements. It seems clear that my acquaintance felt for the man and was concerned with his protection, but also thought it important that his story be known, and for that reason he took me to see him. So we stood at the edge of a field in an isolated area talking and watching for anyone to approach. I have often wondered if that man finally made it to the safety of his home village, if he languishes in prison, or if he is dead. I never heard of him again.

Destruction of the Future

One day I was speaking with a man in the clinic who had just had his testicles cut off by a contingent of Renamo soldiers he had the bad luck of running into. Although bandaged and clearly in pain, his concern was not with the overt violence to which he had been subjected, or with the wound itself, but with what this wound meant to his future.

I have two wives. What will they say to me when I return home? I am
not like I was before, now I can give them nothing. How will they
want to stay with a man who has no sex?

Is the cutting off of the man's testicles the violence? Is it the cutting off
of his identity as a man and a husband? Is it the cutting off of his lineage,
of the children he will now never father? Or is it something more profound and enduring? The Mozambican scholar Sergio Viera once said
to me that the aim of the war was to create a *nonsociety*, and that is why
tactics like castration are employed. The spectacle of violence cannot be
detached from its experience, its aftermath, its enduring reality. Dirty-
war specialists know the actions of today define the truths of tomorrow.

One of the most insidious and powerful targets of violence is the very
sense of future that gives definition and direction to people's lives. In an
uncertain present, a future is impossible to determine. But to be human
is to have a future, and this lack of future, people said, can fuel further
violences:

> People do what they do, the atrocities and responses, because they do
> not see a future. They have no sense of themselves in the future. Thus
> a man who kills doesn't think of the repercussions of his act—that the
> spirits of those he has killed will return to harm him, that the society
> he has violated will hold him responsible.

The assault against a viable future carries a great weight in everyday
life. When a friend who lived in a different province asked me to stay a
while longer during a visit, I told her I had to go, but that I would return. She responded:

> Don't talk to me of the future, don't talk to me of coming back. Maybe
> I'll be dead, killed by the soldiers, maybe I'll have had to flee and
> no one, even me, will know where I am, maybe they'll blow up this
> damn town with everything and everyone in it and then what will you
> have to come back to? No, don't talk to me of tomorrow—stay here
> for we may only have today.

The reverberating effects of violence projected onto uncertain futures
is nowhere more evident than with people like Anna, whose story
opened this chapter. Her chronicles of violence, from watching her village burned and her son killed to the indignities of life as a *deslocado*, will
not be over with the end of the war. In discussing Anna and the people
like her that have come to populate the desperation of the Mozambi-

can landscape, Joaguim Segurada, a Portuguese anthropologist working with Action Aid in Mozambique said to me:

> So what happens when these women go back to their homelands? Still they are missing their husbands, their families. Who will want them? Maybe they return to find their lands missing—that they have lost the rights to them when they lost their husband, or maybe some avaricious person or enterprise has taken their land over, and the women have no means, no strength to fight this. But worse than that, they will have lost "normalcy": the context of their family and home can never be the same again—it has been irreparably destroyed. Healthy culture, as they knew it, is gone. How are they to live and thrive, to find new husbands, to find land to work, to build a home where they can raise their children well, to reestablish family ties with a family that has been shattered? Unfortunately, isolation is their plight now, and it will be their ongoing plight in the future; and for Africans, isolation is an impossibility.

I had just heard a woman's account of her experiences that gave tragic illumination to Segurada's words and am reminded with this story that it is not just this woman's, this family's, future that is a casualty of war. This is a stark example of the conditions necessary to reproduce violence across generations if left unsolved.

> I was kidnapped by the Bandidos Armados several years ago when they attacked our village, and forced to march back to their base camp. Life was awful: we had only the clothes on our backs, a fist in our face, heavy loads on our heads to carry, nothing in our bellies, and a soldier with his penis out coming at us every time we turned around. I was "given" to many men, and in the way of nature, shortly became pregnant and gave birth at the Renamo camp. It seemed like I was gone forever, for a lifetime. Sometimes I could not believe I was still alive. Times were always hard for us at the camp, but it became hard for the Bandidos as well. Food became scarce, and there were some attacks a distance away which forced some of the soldiers to leave and lend help in other places. With the confusion, some of us saw the chance to make our getaway, and slipped off one night into the bush. All those long days walking back to my village, all I could think about was how happy I was to be returning to my home, my husband and family, my machamba, my parents, and the land of my ancestors. Little did I know another war was about to begin. When I arrived home, my husband had taken up with another woman. I was disappointed but

not surprised, I had been gone away a long time. I still expected to live with him [her society is polygamous], but he could not stand the fact that I had a child by another man, even though it had been conceived in rape. He hit the child and called it filth, and threw me and the child out. My parents were still alive, and I moved back with them. But my father felt much as my husband had. He would hit my child and call him Renamo dirt, and tell me I was dirt to have produced him. He would constantly say, "You should take this filth back out to the bush and leave it there along with the rest of the Renamo garbage." No other man will consider me now. I see no future for me. I live with my parents now, but they are growing old and will die someday, and then I have no idea what will happen to me. I cry, and my child cries. But it is worse for him. He is treated like dirt, and he is starting to act like it: he is angry and aggressive, withdrawn and difficult. He does not play and grow and learn normally like the other boys. What will he grow up to be? This war has killed so much, and it is killing generations to come.

Resistance

In the safety of refugee camps people laughed at how a single Renamo soldier or auxiliary, often without a gun, had managed to demand goods and even rape women without the villagers being able to resist. To emphasize this point people told me about a woman in northern Tete who was suddenly overcome by the situation, and axed the Renamo soldier to death herself rather than see her home and family destroyed. People spoke in awe of the woman who had broken the Renamo-spell. (Wilson 1992:537).

Phantoms; and Bento's Story

One day, during a discussion of the war, a man said to me:

Do you know why, when you meet a phantom on the path at night, you run back the way you came, and never look behind the phantom? Because if you pass him and turn around to look back, you will see there is nothing there. This war, it is a lot like that phantom.

Phantoms and the phantasmagorical are part and parcel of African life. Time-honored traditions enunciate the dangers phantoms bring, the emotions and fears they elicit, the correct behaviors one is to engage in when meeting a phantom, and the curative interventions one must seek if damage has been done. The war has expanded on all of that.

Renamo usually come at night, and follows footpaths across fields and into villages. If people must travel home at night or go out to relieve themselves after dark, they risk walking the same paths as those who may be coming to do them harm. It is not unusual for a small contingent of Renamo to stand outside a village hidden from sight, capture an unwitting walker, and try to force information from her or him as to the layout of the village; the names and locations of administrators, teachers, health care personnel, and stores of supplies; the existence of any Frelimo collaborators in the village; and any information the person may have on Frelimo troop movements. Then, at their leisure, they can come back to attack the village. Anyone walking at night may be suspect: the point is not to brave a potentially dangerous encounter and risk violence, kidnapping, and even death.

Do not pass a phantom,

for to do so means the phantom is aware of you and can then interact with you. But the next line is even more powerful.

Do not look behind the phantom, for you will see there is nothing there.

This is perhaps one of the most profound statements on the war. The phantom like all dangers, conveys a terror that is truly multivocal. Its face is well defined and recognizable, and its countenance, along with its great size, can threaten the average civilian without effort. It speaks, it is full of stories and threats. Its footfalls are silent and its path unerring. And it is, if not invincible, at least perpetual. There are always phantoms. But behind all the many layers of violence and bravado, actions and words, there is . . . nothing. There is, ultimately, no substance, no sense. To die at the hands of violent meaninglessness is the paramount paradox, the source of terror, and the existential absurdity Mozambicans recognize.

Existential absurdity highlighted in the lethal force of war is a theme common to many narratives throughout Mozambique. Folktales, whether produced and reproduced around village cooking fires or by the literary elite of Maputo, capture this powerful dialectic intruding on people's lives in war. One of my favorites is "The Whales of Quissico" by the Mozambican poet Mia Couto (1986:55–62).

The story opens with Bento João Mussavele sitting, just sitting. One has the impression he has been sitting a long time, for although people pass by and talk to him, they do not worry about him. That is how he is. But one day he decided to get up, and his friends began to worry, assuming he was going back to his home and *machamba*:

But where are you going? Where you come from is full of bandits, man.

But Bento had a plan, and he disclosed it to his uncle:

You know, uncle, there's such hunger back there in Inhambane. People are dying every day.

And he went on to explain that these people had told him that a whale comes up to land on the beach there.

It comes from the direction of the night.

As it lands, it opens its mouth and it is full of things, just like a store.

Like a store from the old days.

All anyone needs to do is fill up a van and take it back into the city.

His uncle laughs, explaining that there is no whale, that it is a product of the imaginations of hungry people. But Bento refuses to be swayed so easily from his belief and his goal, and resolves to talk to two local wise men. The first, the schoolmaster, told him that

whales are prone to deceive,

adding quickly that this was because they looked like fish, but were in reality mammals. The second, the local white man, replied only that:

The world was going crazy, that the earth's axis was more and more inclined and that the poles were becoming flatter, or flatulent, he didn't quite understand.

So Bento sets out to find the whale, and finally arrives at the beach, lined by abandoned beach houses.

Now, all was deserted and only he, Bento Mussavele, ruled over the unreal landscape. He settled in an old house, installing himself among the remains of furniture and the ghosts of a recent age. There he remained without being aware of the comings and goings of life.

Several weeks later, he was visited by some of his friends who had risked the journey over war-ravaged roads where each bend in the road was a fright to ambush the heart.

Finally one sympathetically explains to Bento:

> You know, Bento, back in Maputo it's being rumored you're a reaction-
> ary. You're here like this because of this business of arms, or whatever
> they're called.

And he goes on to explain that South Africa is supplying arms to Renamo, which come via the sea. Bento, agitated and confused, reiterates
he is only waiting for the whale. One friend, who is a cadre member,
replies;

> The whale is an invention of the imperialists to stultify the people and
> make them always wait for food to arrive from abroad.

His friends left and the days went by. One night Bento awoke fevered,
sure that the sea was calling him. Giddily he walked naked to the water,
convinced the dark patch out to sea was the whale. As he waded out
into the sea, a voice of reason cut into his senses, telling him there was
no whale, and that the water was going to be his tomb.

> But to die just like that for nothing?

And he continued out, wading into his dream.

The story ends with the ruminations of those who, finding Bento's
clothes and satchel in the abandoned house, claimed they were proof
the enemy who had been responsible for receiving arms had been there.

In the story of mad Bento, who is ultimately condemned as an enemy
arms envoy, Couto has captured much of the absurdity and pathos that
defines the war. And he has brought home the way the war has in-
sinuated itself into every aspect of people's lives—into their hopes and
fears, their friendships and politics, their madness and sanity. Each set-
off phrase in the rendering of the story above is a theme that comments on the realities and tragedies of the war, themes that are heard
in story after story, told in province after province. Each contains a
message, an existential comment on the war—existential in the sense
of both a philosophical rumination and existence as survival. Following
the quotes through their sequence in the story, an example of themes
invoked include:

But where are you going? Where you come from is full of bandits, man.

There is no going home. A concept of home is itself a madness in the midst of war. But if there is movement, people assume it is toward finding "home."

You know, uncle, there's such hunger back there in Inhambane.

To be full of war is to be full of hunger. But hunger is a complex phenomenon, including, in addition to physical hunger, a hunger for reason, hope, cultural coherence, and equality—at least enough equality to get a piece of the very large pie that is feeding some while starving others.

It comes from the direction of the night.

Renamo, atrocities, and chaos come with darkness. Attacks come at night, and the arms that make the attacks possible come from the direction of night—the West.

like a store from the old days.

Millenarianism reconstructs the chaotic present by projecting a (safe) history, a respected traditional culture, onto an unknown future. But as well, the "stores" of the past were owned and run by colonists, like the war is today.

Whales are prone to deceive . . . the world was going crazy.

The information you ask for is not the information you get. The African schoolteacher warns of the threat of treachery and deception, while the white man is paralyzed by incomprehensible chaos, unable to distinguish flat from flatulence.

Now, all was deserted.

The war is a scene of intellectual, emotional, personal, and sociocultural desertification. It empties people not only of life and living but also of reason and reality. As one travels in Mozambique, one sees these deserted communities, goods left intact under layers of dust in a silent testimonial that dreams of coming home exist simultaneously with the recognition that one can never go home. These eerie borderlands run parallel to the margins of animated communities and through the center of the thing called war.

Each bend in the road was a fright to ambush the heart.

Even the mundane, especially the mundane—a bus ride—is fraught with unreal terror elevated to heart-stopping reality. Death is a very real possibility at each bend in the road, and the threat is of death to more than the corporeal body, it is a threat of death to the spirit and the soul.

You know, Bento, back in Maputo it's being rumored you're a reactionary.

Even the mad and the innocent are defined in terms of the polemics of war. And in the capital city, the center of war endeavor and analysis, people do not know the difference between the mad, the innocent, and the political.

The whale is an invention of the imperialists.

The mundane and the mad, dreams and hopes, become parables of power. For the uncle the whale is an invention born of hunger and desperation; for the cadre member it becomes a statement about imperialism and neocolonialism.

But to die just like that for nothing?

Like the phantom one must not look behind, the reality of death at the hands of meaninglessness is insufferable. Dreams, even dreamed in madness, are better than embracing the emptiness of an unintelligible war.

Finally, the interpretations of a poor mad man's fever-ridden death in terms of enemy networks of arms transfers brings the ironic, and the violence it speaks to, into the center of lived experience. The war has permeated every aspect of society, and is capable of turning innocence into complicity, fever into treachery, and dreams into strategy.

Lest we become complacent about the term "folktales"—seeing them as civilian parables attempting to make and convey some sense of the war, however filled with metaphor and fantasy they may be—I will set down a dialogue a colleague of mine had. This person had gone to speak with the head of security of a large international corporation with extensive holdings in Mozambique. My colleague was considering traveling to an area where the security might be dicey, and he thought that, as the corporation had representatives in the area, its personnel would have a good idea of the current security situation. The head of security told him that travel was possible, but that he should be careful, especially around the first of the month, for:

> That is when the submarine carrying supplies and weapons for Renamo arrives at the beach, and, for days before that, all the Renamo troops in the area are coming down from the hills and out of the bush to rendezvous with the submarine. Then, after the submarine leaves, the troops, brimming with supplies and weapons, make their way back to their camps. Anyone traveling at that time not only has a greater chance of running into Renamo, but of running into a Renamo war-giddy and heavily armed.

I do not intend to cast aspersions on the head of security of this large corporation, but I knew the area he was referring to fairly well and had never seen "hordes of Renamo coming down from the hills on the first of every month." Nor was there any indication, in local gossip or action, that a submarine came to the area with any regularity. Submarines may come and go, they may populate the landscapes of parables and folktales, but the average Mozambican knows that, regardless of the potential technology and weaponry available to Renamo through outside contacts, in fact the war is predominately a ground one. The reason Renamo not only attacks but loots villages and towns is that they are carrying, often by foot, their plundered goods to Malawi and other international destinations to pay for their war effort. For the Mozambicans, whether the submarine actually exists or not is unimportant, for it stands as a symbol of the intricacies of power and the international networks of military exchange that fuel the war they suffer. But for the international company, the submarine had become a reality.

Children's Stories

Child

To talk about a child
is to talk about the causes
of so many wars
is to remember the reasons
why parents are lost.

To talk about a child
is to talk of millions

of ragged faces
innocent victims
of excessive ambitions,
is to talk of hunger
of illness
and of starvation,
is to talk about nakedness
of misery
and of cries muffled
by human wickedness.

To talk about a child
is to talk of the future
of a people
is to talk about the construction
of a nation.

To talk about a child
is to shout loudly
DOWN WITH CORRUPTION
DOWN WITH WAR
LONG LIVE PEACE.

—Vitalina
(written by a secondary school student in Zambezia province
when I asked what her experience of war and peace was.
This was written in 1991 at the height of the war.)

I have focused primarily on adults as storytellers. Children tell their
own tales. One day I was near a coastal village on the beach of Zambezia province. A group of children were singing, clapping, and dancing
together. I wandered over to them, and asked if they would teach me
their song and dance. While I could master the dance with some ease,
having been a dancer in my earlier years, the song was in Chuabo, the
local dialect, and I stumbled over the words to the unmitigated delight
of the children. After some time, the mother of one of the children came
over to join us, and I asked her to translate into Portuguese the words
I did not understand. She and the children sat conversing, working out
the translation for me. Expecting some ditty children often compose in
play, I was surprised to hear:

Papa Chissano [the president of Mozambique],
Papa Chissano,
come and see,
come and see,

the Bandidos Armados are here,
they have taken my shirt,
and my crops don't grow.

I asked the mother if, the next time I was in the area, I could come to visit her at her house and collect some more of the children's songs. She agreed, and some days later I went to call on her at her home. When I arrived, we chatted a bit, and then I asked her about the songs. At that time, all the children except the youngest were outside playing, and she went to call them in. As she went, she said what stands to me as one of the saddest commentaries on the war:

We adults, we don't know these songs. It is the children who know. It is the children who make these songs up and sing them.

I was reminded of Veena Das's (1990) work with children who were exposed to the rioting in the Punjab. She points out that all too often adults treat children as if they have no philosophies, no feelings on war themselves. Yet they have developed remarkable social commentaries, if we only remember to ask.

The children sang a number of songs for me that day, some chronicles of their lives, some chronicles of bravado from those most vulnerable to the war:

On Friday when I was sleeping
I heard the gunshots of the Bandidos Armados
Then we ran away, we climbed, to Micaune
to the islands of Idugo.
We will return to Pebane
Oh Pebane,
Oh Pebane,
I dream of Pebane.

These children had fled Pebane after it was attacked and were now living as *deslocados* several days' hard walk from there. "All we dream of," they told me, "is going home."

The Bandidos Armados sabotaged our District,
called Pebane.
In Zambezia, no one plays [threatens] with us
we have cannons,
we have bazookas,

pistols at our side,
for the enemy.

The pathos of this song lies in the fact that children of five and six
have made it up and sing it as they play—children who are refugees,
who have been left with little, and who certainly have no means to protect themselves. Nor do their parents, who had no weapons, no means
to stave off the attack on Pebane or to drive off the invaders that still
controlled the area. I was reminded of Roland Barthes's quote from
Blanchot[2]:

There was something marvelous in that song, secret, simple, and everyday,
which had to be immediately recognized . . . a song from the abyss which, once
heard, opened an abyss in each word and lured one to vanish into it. (1985:256)

In Mozambique the streets of all the major cities are filled with
orphans whose parents have been killed or lost to them in the chaos of
the war. Streetwise, tough, and full of bravado, their songs are raw with
the reality of their lives. One song a group of street children I had be-
friended sang to me goes simply:

They got [killed] my mother,
They got my father,
But they won't get me.

What, then, can we say about violence?

Is it the sheer act of force? Of being forced to watch force? Of being
subjected to the many humiliating injustices that follow from one (random) act of violence? Of being exposed to homelessness, hopelessness,
helplessness, and inhumanity? Of not being able to perform the actions
necessary to combat the ongoing onslaught of violence; to reconstruct
humanity? Most of the Mozambicans I talked with said it is all of these,
and more.

Violence, then, is not some *thing* simply formulated in terms of historical conditions of conflict played out along a conflict trajectory to affect
the present. *Violence is culturally constitutive.* Its enactment forges, in fact
forces, new constructs of identity, new socio-cultural relationships, new
threats and injustices that reconfigure people's life-worlds, new patterns
of survival and resistance. These emerge in interaction as the idiosyncratic (the personal) and the immediate (the contextual) both shape and
are shaped by historical knowledge and forces. In this sense, violence

is generative. Allen Feldman, in his work on the conflict in Northern Ireland, argues against the idea that violence is simply a product of the historical evolution of (political) identities within relations of antagonism: "Modal violence detaches itself from initial contexts and becomes the condition of its own reproduction" (Feldman 1991:20). Violence is not a static "thing" or a passing "event," unchanging and monolithic, that is variously employed to achieve certain ends. It is a transformational cultural dynamic expressed and resisted within a changing and often contradictory social universe.

Chronic violence transforms material and experiential contexts and renders the relations between structure and event, text and context, consciousness and practice labile and unfixed. . . . Novel subject positions are constructed and construed by violent performances, and this mutation of agency renders formal ideological rationale and prior contextual motivation unstable and even secondary. (Feldman 1991:20)

Violence is also culturally deconstitutive

Violent interaction is not just a relationship among people struggling against a tangible force, but entails as well an interaction with a potentiality, a dread, a veil of possibility hanging over one's entire life. People's actions, interactions, and sense of self and conceptions of community are continuously reconstituted in the relationships linking potentiality and the harsh reality of violence. And, as we will see in the following pages, they are equally constituted in the potentialities and hopeful realities of defeating, not just troops, but the violence itself.

Creativity / ~~Violence~~

We local physicians [we curandeiros] we have had to set up new ways of treating people with this war. This war, it teaches people violence. A lot of soldiers come to me. Many of these boys never wanted to fight, they did not know what it meant to fight. Many were hauled into the military, taken far from their homes, and made to fight. It messes them up. You see, if you kill someone, their soul stays with you. The souls of the murdered follow these soldiers back to their homes and their families, back to their communities to cause problems. The soldier's life, his family, his community, begin to disintegrate from the strain of this. But it goes further than this. These soldiers have learned the way of war. It was not something they knew before. They have learned to use violence. Their own souls have been corrupted by what they have seen and done. They return home, but they carry the violence with them, they act it out in their daily lives, and this harms their families and communities. We have to take this violence out of these people, we have to teach them how to live nonviolent lives like they did before. The problem would be serious enough if it were only the soldiers, but it is not. When a woman is kidnapped, raped, and forced to work for soldiers, when a child is exposed to violence in an attack, when people are submitted to assaults and terrible injuries, this violence sticks to them. It is like the soldier carrying the souls of those he has killed back into his normal life, but here, the soul carries the violence. You can see this even with the young children here who have seen or been subjected to violence: they begin to act more violently. They lose respect, they begin to hit, they lose their bearings— and this violence tears at the order of the community. We can treat this, we have to. We literally take the violence out of the people, we teach them how to relearn healthy ways of thinking and acting. It is like with people who have been sent to prison. They go in maybe having stolen something, but they learn violence there. They learn it because they are subjected to violence. We treat this too, in war or in peace, violence is a dangerous illness. And the thing is, people want to learn peace. This violence, it tears them up inside, it destroys the world they care about. They want to return to a normal life like they had before. Most work hard with us to put this violence behind them. The leaders of the wars, those people who profit from the wars, they teach this violence to get what they want, without regard to the effect on people and communities. It is our job to thwart this violence, to take it out of the people and the communities. We are getting good at this, we have had a lot of practice.

How is it possible to speak of creativity and violence in the same breath? Is this an insidious way of glorifying violence, of reproducing its hegemony? If I had not seen how average Mozambicans redefined and reconfigured violence as an act of resistance *against* violence, I might have assumed this. But in taking control of the definitions of violence, in redefining them in a way that resisted the hegemony of politico-military control, Mozambicans demonstrated a creativity in conflict resolution as sophisticated as any resistance to political oppression I have seen in fifteen years of studying war. This response is perhaps one of the most sophisticated of techniques. Ultimately, the Mozambicans who forged systems of resistance to war remind the rest of us that violence is not a fixed entity, a "truth" to be dealt with, but instead it is a social, political, and cultural construction that noncombatants—the targets of most violence—can redefine to assert their own political will. In de-legitimizing violence, people reconstruct a new political culture, one that delegitimizes the politics of force. Such political reconstructions are a serious threat, for they simultaneously delegitimize the political systems that rely on force to maintain power. They remind us that violence crushes political will only if people *believe* in its ability to do so. When people take the definition of violence into their own hands, they *are* affecting political will.

The physician's statement shows how people set up healing networks to, quite literally, "take the violence out of people": redefining it as a fluid process that can be *un*constructed as well as constructed as political force. But what it does not convey is that *every* locale I visited or researched countrywide had set up systems to resist violence in this way. Everyone who had been exposed to violence was encouraged to receive physical and psychological care that included counseling towards peaceful responses. Every community had generated ad hoc conflict resolution mechanisms. All these resources were constructed at the local level, all were locally generated, none were institutionalized through governing bodies or formalized social services.

The physician's statement, however, only begins to convey the true extent of services people developed to combat war. It was my experience that one of the first responses Mozambicans instituted in the midst of abusive injustice was to teach people how to respond without perpetuating destructive systems of interaction. The examples are legion, as the following chapters will show. The passage at the beginning of this section conveys a viewpoint common to African doctors and healers throughout Mozambique: that everyone who has been physically harmed by violence has also been emotionally scarred, and that these problems can reverberate across lifetimes and communities long after the violence of war has subsided. They treated violence like any other disease. As one healer said to me: "Violence is like a rash on the soul—we must treat this to return the person to health. And we can, we heal this rash on the soul." Extending on this philosophy, a number of primary school teachers began classes in relieving traumatization, knowing children exposed to violence not only suffer its impact, but as well are prone to reproduce it. They taught children nonviolent ways of combating injustice.

Deslocados (the war-displaced) were helped to build a comfortable place to live. Ceremonies were held to remove the trauma of war. For example, one of the reconstructive ceremonies performed for people was "remaking the marriage bed." Even if the person's family was scattered and unaccounted for, the marriage bed symbolized the continuity and succor of family and tradition. In fact, one of the common complaints about military attacks was that "home" was destroyed, rendering the victims *brutos na mata*, animals in the bush. In "remaking the marriage bed," "home" was refashioned as a place of security. This was also a very tangible act: people were given a sense of place and belonging, they are reintegrated into the practices and values of daily living. Meaning is given form.

Afetados (the war-affected) were reintroduced into the rhythms of life and stable society. People assumed that the war-traumatized, especially those who had spent time as kidnap victims or as soldiers, had been severed from the foundations of nurturance, and nurturance is antithetical to violent abuse. Numerous ceremonies exist to assist those who have been exposed to war and violence. Most involved cleansing ceremonies, physical and emotional healing, and practices to reintegrate the person back into the community and a healthy lifestyle.

One ceremony I participated in involved a woman who had returned after having been kidnapped by soldiers and held at their base for months. She returned physically sick and emotionally traumatized. The ceremony actually began days before the time of the public gathering. Community members stopped by to bring food, medicines, words of encouragement, and friendship. They helped the woman piece together a bit of decent clothing to wear, and collected water for her to bathe with. They sat patiently and told her stories of other atrocities: a constant reminder that the woman was not alone, nor was she somehow responsible for her plight. On the day of the ceremony, food was prepared, musicians called in, and a dirt compound shaded by pleasant trees and plants swept and decorated with lanterns and cloth. The ceremony itself lasted throughout the night, a mosaic of support and healing practices. Several high points included the ritual bath the woman received at dusk. Numerous women picked up the patient, and carefully gave her a complete bath—a cleansing of the soul as well as the body. The bathing was accompanied with songs and stories about healing, about dealing with trauma, about reclaiming a new life and being welcomed into the community. The patient was then dressed in her new clothing, and fed a nutritious meal. Shortly thereafter, the musicians began a new rhythm of music, and all the women gathered about the patient to carry her inside the hut. There, they placed her in a ball on the floor and gathered round her, supporting her. The support was emotional as well as physical: they tended her wounds, they stroked her much like one would stroke a frightened child, and they quietly murmured encouragements and reassurances. After a while, the women began to rock the patient, and lift her up among them. They held her up with their arms, talking of rebirth in a healthy place, among people who cared for her, far from the traumas of war and the past. They carried her outside, where the community welcomed her as part of it. Everyone began to play music, the audience accompanying the musicians, and after a while, each member of the audience got up in front of the musicians and danced: for the patient, as part of the community, to reaffirm life. Slowly the formal structure of the ceremony gave way to the more natural patterns of community interaction, and the patient was drawn into these interactions. Throughout the ceremony, the woman was continually reassured with stories of ongoing support; of her need to place responsibility for her plight with war and not her own actions; and of her own responsibility to heal the war's wounds so she does not inflict the violence that she was subjected to on others. Respected traditions and nonviolent values are revitalized in story, song, and interaction. With this, community is rebuilt for, and with, the patient.

In the same way the ceremonies of healing and reintegration start long before the actual public gathering, they continue long after the musicians have put away their instruments and the community returned to their homes at sunrise. In the days and weeks that follow, the promises of support people made during the ceremony are acted on. Becoming self-sufficient is an important part of a person's reintegration into the community. This reintegration can be symbolic as well as literal. In the case of the woman described here, she actually reentered the community after having been kidnapped. But some who are exposed to severe violence during attacks may never leave their community physically, yet find their worlds so completely disrupted that in some cases they lose the very concept of normal daily life. Reintegration in this sense means helping a person reconstruct a viable life, a livable day. One powerful way of doing this in Mozambique is through farming. In an agricultural society, the rhythms of working the fields are at the core of healthy life. In agricultural work people are not only linked with the cycles of planting and harvesting, they are relinked with their ancestors and the traditions that keep society sound. Victims of violence were encouraged to begin farming plots of land. Often others in the community would work with them: giving solace, telling traditional stories, redirecting anger and vengeance into community building and positive political action, reminding scarred and battered limbs how to work.

I found it interesting that these resources were not restricted to the civilian victims of war. Demobilized soldiers were also carefully reintegrated into communities with similar sets of ceremonies and assistance. As people explained, "We have to take the war out of these soldiers." While community members often had suffered at the hands of soldiers, and maybe even from the ex-soldiers in their midst, they explained that to harbor revenge and anger would simply fan the flames of war and violence. If they were truly to defeat their opponents, they had to defeat the war, and that meant turning soldiers from warring to peaceful pursuits. If ex-soldiers were banished from communities—from the possibility of home, family, and a civil livelihood—they would continue to use violence to sustain themselves. One of the most fascinating acts of civil resistance I saw in Mozambique involved civilians kidnapping soldiers and taking them back to their villages to put them through ceremonies to remove them from the war—and to remove the war from them—and to reintegrate them into civilian life. People told me they were often successful; many "kidnapped" soldiers gave up the war and remained with the community, or returned to their own homes and families.

The coherence, the truly national extent of this system of resisting and resolving violence was a surprise to many in Mozambique. When I began this study, I was continually reminded by Mozambican colleagues that a great deal of difference characterized the country. With more than a dozen major languages and cultural affiliations, diversity, not homogeneity, was the key theme of the country. I was reminded that each language group, each part of the country, had its own experiences of the war, personal and cultural, and that these would diverge widely. In some very important ways, this is true. But, as my work here has consistently shown, a very nuanced and widely shared set of practices and cultural responses were transmitted from person to person, from province to province around the country along with the war.

The cultures of war and survival cross-cut ethnic and linguistic affiliations, making new alliances and channels of information exchange. From the south of Maputo to the north of Niassa, from urban centers to rural outposts, from refugee camps to burned-out villages, every place I visited hosted people who shared a similar view about dealing with violence. These views were coded in medical and healing traditions, religious traditions, and community values about power and sustenance. They were set into play through local dispute resolution councils and coded in precepts of justice and human rights. And, as I turn to discuss here, they spawned entire social movements.

I began this section by looking at individual perspectives on "taking the violence out of the society." In the same way, on a larger scale, entire social movements were generated around these principles. Manuel Antonio, introduced in the "cast of characters" in Chapter 2, demonstrated how peasant values can do battle with modern troops—quite literally, when this commander's troops liberated some 150,000 people in a year from Renamo troops with traditional "white" weapons (spears and knives) alone. Mungoi demonstrates a different kind of example: a fully pacific, and very successful, "war against war."

I did not have the pleasure of meeting Mungoi, who has been dead for decades and now speaks through his offspring, or of visiting his place of residence some seventy kilometers north of Xai Xai, the provincial capital of Gaza in southern Mozambique. But Mungoi captured the attention of the whole country, and a friend of mine, the Mozambican journalist Gil Lauriciano, made the trip to Gaza to meet him.[3]

In a land where virtually no road travel was possible because of landmines and rogue troops, people surrounding the area colloquially known as "the settlement of the spirit of Mungoi" were traveling freely. There were neither military attacks nor kidnapping of civilians by soldiers. The spirit Mungoi, angered by the war, not only protected the people who lived and traveled in his area from violence, he ensured that people kidnapped by Renamo were returned to their families. His area grew famous as a zone where people with violent intentions could not enter: it was an oasis in a sea of war.

When Gil made the trip to Mungoi's settlement, he noted that the area was awash with vast fields of corn and manioc—itself strong acclaim to Mungoi's powers in a country devastated by drought and troops who plunder crops. It was a strong contrast to the barren and razed fields that characterized all too much of Mozambique at that time. He joined a pilgrimage of scores of people who visited Mungoi's residence (on Tuesdays and Thursdays—Mungoi's workdays) to seek help from the famous spirit or to pick up family members who had been kidnapped by Renamo and returned under Mungoi's guidance.

Greeted by Mungoi's son and daughter (who sat under a mango tree and a cashew tree respectively), and a cadre of assistants, the supplicants were directed to a spot in the center of the settlement in the shade of fruit trees. Soon singing was heard from one of the huts, and, shortly thereafter, a woman—the *portadora* (the conveyor of the spirit) of the spirit Mungoi—emerged. She was dressed in a leopard skin draped over a navy blue coat, long white pants and a shirt, gray shoes, and a black hat. Mungoi began to talk:

> It is good, my children, that you have decided to come to the land of Mungoi. Mungoi died a long time ago and has no problems with anyone. The enemy came here with arms [the son explained this had been on 22 September 1987] and entered through the back of the house. When the enemy arrived, they found my children cooking. The enemy did not ask anything, they entered into the houses and pillaged everything they found. Others ate all the food that my daughter was preparing, with the pans placed on her legs. After eating, they threw the hot water in the face of my other daughter. (Lauriciano 1990a:9).

The various groups, Mungoi went on to explain, were pillaging, killing, and kidnapping people all over town. Finally they met in his house, where they put the looted goods in a big pile and began to choose the youngest of the kidnapped.

> My children. The enemy has done even more than this. He entered into the house where Mungoi is [the burial ground where his mortal remains are deposited], and they threw everything all over the place — even this wristwatch here [the portadora pulled up the sleeve of her jacket to show an old wristwatch with no hands] that they had taken. When they were on their way out they threw a baby against a tree (a mango tree) and carried off the children of Mungoi.

The spirit, speaking in a relaxed way, looked over the heads of the listeners, and once in a while looked at the wristwatch with no hands. Previously I have discussed the havoc terror plays with time — collapsing past, present, and future into a seamless now; revoking time, and with it the tradition of a meaningful past and a progression toward a hopeful future. The spirit's wristwatch is a classic statement on this irony of time and terror.

Mungoi went on to explain that, after the enemy left, he asked his son what was happening, and his son replied there was war. Mungoi then told his son he wanted to speak to Renamo. While waiting, the spirit explained, he got bored and went to the enemy's camp and began to "attack their heads" (*atacar os cabeças*: a double entendre meaning he caused misfortune and illness among Renamo, and attacked the leaders). Concerned, the spiritual advisors of Renamo sought to find out what the cause was, and finally discovered that it was Mungoi. Mungoi then had a conversation with the leaders of the attacking group, and explained to them that if they did not stop their attacks and return the kidnapped people and looted goods, misfortune would continue to befall them. A large ceremony was performed to appease Mungoi, and several days later a group from Renamo arrived at the settlement of Mungoi to return both people and goods that had been taken during the attack. The chief of the area told the leader of the group that Mungoi wanted to talk to him. After Mungoi explained his feeling about the war and the killing, the Renamo leader promised to stop all terrorist activity in the area.

Mungoi then explained to his son that he wanted to work, and that he was going to devote himself to the eradication of terrorism and war in his area. In the spirit's address, Mungoi explained how he wanted to work with the government but that the governor of Gaza did not have time for him: "he just orders people." Mungoi went on to explain that the local party officials attended a *missa* (traditional African mass) in his (the spirit's) honor. They were completely supportive of him, and, as one official said, "We have no alternative but to respect the people's belief in Mungoi" (Maier 1990a). But the FAM commander of the area called Mungoi a *Matsanga* (Renamo follower) and would have demolished him and his area, Mungoi noted, if a "high up person in our country" had not intervened. Word has it that it was the intervention of President Chissano himself that saved Mungoi (embodied in his offspring) from arrest by FAM Commander Sathana (colloquially known as Captain Satan). Mungoi was clearly reinforcing a strong belief among the local population: while local party members and presidents may support you, you can never fully trust the government or the military in this war; if you want to survive, you must trust your traditions and your communities.

The government's concern, as with Manuel Antonio and his peasant army Parama, was not as staunchly military as it was political. Both Mungoi and Antonio championed traditional African power and culture, and threw political will back onto people, their communities, and the chiefly traditions that governed these—as threatening to the scientific-Marxist government of Frelimo as it was to the Renamo rebels. Ken Wilson quotes the Professor of History at Eduardo Mondlane University in Maputo as arguing that Mungoi

is a "peasant intellectual" before he is a traditional medium; and is re-establishing, directly or indirectly, the fabric of the chiefdoms and rural-national monarchies and appears as the organizer and linkman of the social hegemony and political administration of this fabric. (1992:556)

And like that of Manuel Antonio, Mungoi's "magic" did work. In an area of over seventy square kilometers, people and vehicles, sporting Mungoi's flag with a blue cross on a white background, traveled safely, and attacks dwindled significantly. Looted goods and people were in fact returned to their homes. I spoke with several people who had successfully sought Mungoi's help in having a kidnapped family member returned home. One family told me:

We went to consult with Mungoi, to ask for the return of our son who had been kidnapped. We sat at his compound for several days, and then, one morning, our son, skinny and bedraggled, walked into the Mungoi settlement and up to us. He said he had been working under Renamo orders one day when suddenly, and without explanation, the Renamo leader came up to him and told him he was free to go. He dropped his work, and while fearing for his life, fearing they would shoot him in the back as he walked away, he turned and walked off. No one stopped him, and he found himself walking in this direction.

Hundreds of people told similar stories. Mungoi's settlement remained safe throughout the remainder of the war.

Mungoi's settlement is not unique in Mozambique, though it is perhaps one of the best known. Peace zones, guarded by chiefs, curandeiros, and spirits, exist throughout the country. In Chapter 3 I discussed the little-known peace zone of the province of Niassa in the north. More famous peace zones existed in areas of Renamo strongholds (Samantanje, in Casa Banana in Gorongasa, where a high Zimbabwean official mediated a peace between the reigning spirit and Mozambican authorities) and in areas of high disruption, like those at the Mozambican/South African border. Gil Lauriciano writes of his visit to the south of Mozambique, long before he visited Mungoi:

> The first time I felt myself close to the world of spirits in Mozambique was in 1986 in the region Mapulanguene close to the frontier border with South Africa. A young FAM captain was priding himself on the collaboration he maintained with *Nhamussoros* [curandeiros] of the area after a difficult period. Captain Sulemane said that he had lost one half of his battalion without even entering into combat with Renamo. In each patrol unit, according to him, the cobras took care of three out of five men. The mystery was clarified with the help of an old combatant from Cabo Delgado. . . . The cobras were sent by spirits revolted by, and revolting against, the actions of the authorities. (1990b:9)

By the time Gil arrived in the area, the problem had been resolved: there had been a change in the attitude of the authorities. Not only was the problem with cobras solved, the atrocities of war and power were addressed and in a number of instances resolved. It is a curious irony that Lauriciano, a Mozambican, first felt close to the world of spirits when he began reporting on the war. But maybe not too curious: in Mozambique spirits are entrusted with guarding the health and welfare of their lands.

Notes

1. A number of scholars in anthropology and the social sciences have made considerable inroads to challenging the "accepted wisdoms" of a static and reified notion of violence. One of the earlier contemporary attempts to decenter the concept of violence from its monolithic construct and its focus on physical force alone involved the concept of *structural violence* (Thee 1980). This is violence — personal, domestic, community, and societal — that is provoked by exploitative and unequal relations embedded within the social structure. Poverty, starvation, preventable disease, and relationships of antagonism whereby one does not have recourse to rectify the situation provide some of the more dramatic examples of structural violence. Some scholars (Thornton 1991) take odds with the notion of structural violence, seeing it as an offshoot of purely structuralist theory, one, as Thornton has said to me, that is mired in a static image of

an "architecture of relationships." Thornton (1991:218) opposes a structuralist approach because, to him, "violence itself, raw and unthought, is meaningless." He argues against accounts, however historically and culturally nuanced, that posit violence as instrumental to the processes of domination, hegemony, and resistance. Instead, he is concerned with how violence, in and of itself, constitutes social forms and meanings, and how it emerges as a form of social interaction. For Thornton, violence "is integral to the social processes that generate the symbols and values that provision the political process." A number of scholars, however, do not consider "structural" violence to constitute "structural" theory—noting instead that to see violence codified in institutions, hence social structures, is a constructivist (in the meaning of Bourdieu) approach. Feminist theory takes structural violence as a useful concept without implying a structuralist theory.

While the concept of structural violence has certainly been employed in the restrictive sense outlined by Thornton, others follow Bourdieu's (1989) approach that he labels "constructivist structuralism or structuralist constructivism." Bourdieu brings to the fore the category of *symbolic violence*, which is maintained in socio-economic relationships cast in less than conscious hegemonic constraints. The disenfranchised and the oppressed not only participate in, but actually reenact, relationships of inequality that perpetuate their own stigmatized status, but they do so unwittingly as actors in a larger system into which they were socialized. *Habitus* determines relationships of inequality and antagonism as much as, and possibly more than, self-reflective action. This is, in Bourdieu's (1977:191) words: "unrecognizable, socially recognized violence." Bourdieu's contribution challenges the more restricted definitions of violence. For example, Riches (1986:10–11), in a perceptive anthology on violence, nevertheless states that "everyone implicated in violence is very likely to recognize it as such," and "the practice of violence is highly visible to the senses." (To be fair to Riches, I must point out that his concern in this article is predominately with the fact that " 'violence' is very much a word of those who witness, or who are victims of certain acts, rather than of those who perform them.") Violence, as this book stresses, has an intangible as well as a tangible quality, and each quality can have a tremendous impact on both people and socio-cultural process. Yet Bourdieu's focus on the less than conscious reproduction of relationships of inequality leaves us to ponder the origins of resistance and change. Comaroff (1985, 1991) has refined Bourdieu's approach by asserting that distinctions between conscious and unconscious are more heuristic devices than representative, and notes that it is in the hazy arena of partial, socially and personally negotiated consciousness that the conflict of hegemonic force and the voices of resistance are most powerfully articulated.

2. From Maurice Blanchot's *Le livre à venir* (1959).

3. See Gil Lauriciano, "Espirito Mungoi: Um poder alternativo ou apenas mais um fenomeno da guerra?" Domingo, Maputo, 2 Setembro 1990.

Chapter 5

The Grotesque and the Terror-able: The Ultimate Defeat of War

In the Massacre of Namacurra

A burst of the machine-gun
and he fell in the truck
his back broke
the neighbor's frogs croaked
tickles in his blood
the first cry was
the pitiful song of the swan

The trees exalted
noises of the metals—Death
with its scythe continued the fight
sucking all his spilt blood
and took the cross of suffering from him
painfully from the common pit

The river of tears dried up
the wheel of life
the essence of his heart stopped
The dam holding his blood fell down
the candles diminished

Death came into his nest
and there, inside
became quiet and happy
laying its lark eggs
and the silent tomb of worms
at last

A praying mantis
was the first living creature
to land on his dead body
I watched! With the heart of a glow-worm.

—Enuerto

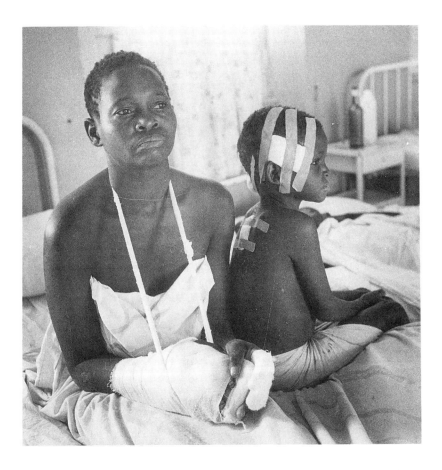

Victims of MNR bandits, Inhambane province, 1986. Photo by Anders Nilsson.

The grotesque . . . might more appropriately be called a play with the very indeterminacy of existence. (Henning 1981: 107)

Aristotle has said the dialectic of tragedy is built upon the two nodes of fear and pity. Tragedy is often a word associated with Mozambique, as evinced in Lina Magaia's book, *Dumba Nengue—Run for Your Life: Peasant Tales of Tragedy in Mozambique.* The chronicles of horror, deprivation, and suffering to which the population has been exposed are an anguished drama that instills both fear and pity in the primordial sense. But for Aristotle tragedy did not accrue to tales of good people who, for no reason of their own, fell into disaster. Nor did it apply to stories of bad people who made good. Instead, tragedy revolved around good people, who *through an error of judgment* were thrown into calamity.

Unarmed villagers who are tyrannized, not because of any actions on their part but because they unwittingly constitute tokens on a field of military endeavor, do not fit the description of good people who have made a fatal error in judgment. Instead, Mozambican civilians constitute people who, through no act of their own, have fallen into catastrophic circumstances. They do not embrace the Aristotelian tragic.

It is the grotesque, rather than the tragic, that most aptly portrays the unsettling ethos of the war in Mozambique. The grotesque, as this Chapter will show, is a double-edged sword: it is used by military and paramilitary forces to effect terror and thus control; and it is used by the citizenry as a way of defeating the holds of terror.

The grotesque, as Mikhail Bakhtin[1] demonstrates, constitutes at the same time an act of oppression and the means of resisting it. Stories of grotesque actions circulated among Mozambicans in a way that ridiculed, and thus stigmatized, those who relied on such barbarisms to effect political power. To give a moral voice to these stories was to take the sting—the terror—out of terror-warfare. "To give form to the unspeakable has always been a function of the grotesque" (McElroy 1989: 184). The personal as well as political significance of the grotesque, as site both of repression and resistance, is evident in the fact that, as Bernard McElroy (7) reminds us, "There is no such thing as an abstract grotesque."

Redefining, and thus controlling, the grotesque is an extension of the redefinitions of violence discussed in Chapter 4 and relies on using the metaphors of excess to delegitimize violence, whereby the victims become not the enemy but the *judges* of unjust war techniques. The grotesque is a dialogue of power and powerlessness and their representations. I am reminded of a conversation with one of the news journalists at Radio Mozambique at the height of the war. We were in her office, and she was preparing the afternoon news. She showed me one of the news items that had come in over the wires that day from a correspondent in Sofala province to the north. It was a quote from a woman interviewed after a recent attack in her village:

> The Bandidos Armados came into our town. They rounded all of us up who had not been killed in the initial attack, and brought us to the center of the village. They took my son, and they cut him up, they killed him, and they put pieces of him in a large pot and cooked him. Then they forced me to eat some of this. I did it, I did not know what else to do.

The journalist said in frustration,

> This is not news, this is the norm. I get a quote like this every day. It is this war; I'll read this and it will sound like what I read yesterday and the day before and the day before that.

And in her tone, conveyed as well in her news broadcasts, was a powerful rhetoric against the war. When she read this over the news, she was not horrified, and in defeating horror she denied terror-warfare its terror. Instead she was angry: the women's plight was changed from helpless terror to an inexcusable human rights abuse to a fellow human being. The war, not the victim, became delegitimized.

The grotesque, employed as a powerful political critique, extends back to the sixteenth century and Rabelais. Rabelais critiqued political power and its abuses through his larger-than-life characters whose bodies were so enormous that even as infants they killed their mothers in childbirth; whose features were so enlarged that protruding ears, eyes, tongues, and body parts began to define their very natures; who urinated on their enemies in battle to conquer them; and who suffered drought and catastrophe with mouths agape and tongues lolling out like those of dogs.

Rabelais at first appears to have little to do with either Mozambique or contemporary warfare. But, as Bakhtin (1984) stresses, he brings the grotesque into the center of life, and the grotesque, ultimately, is about terror and its defeat.[2] The grotesque of Rabelais is not confined to the battlefield, but can be found in all power abuses. His scenes of battle, however, resonate across centuries from the fictions of the 1500s to strangely salient comments on war today:

> Thus being hastily furnished, before they would set forward, they sent three hundred light horsemen under the conduct of Captain Swillwind, to discover the country, clear the avenues, and see whether there was any ambush laid for

them. But after they had made diligent search, they found all the land round about in peace and quiet, without any meeting or convention at all; which Picrochole understanding commanded that everyone should march speedily under his colours. Then immediately in all disorder, without keeping either rank or file, they took the fields one amongst another, wasting, spoiling, destroying and making havoc of all wherever they went, not sparing poor nor rich, privileged nor unprivileged places, church nor laity, drove away oxen and cows, bulls, calves, heifers, wethers, ewes, lambs, goats, kids, hens, capons, chickens, geese, ganders, goslings, hogs, swine, pigs and suchlike; beating down walnuts, plucking the grapes, tearing the hedges, shaking the fruit-trees, and committing such incomparable abuses, that the like abomination was never heard of. Nevertheless, they met with none to resist them, for everyone submitted to their mercy. (Rabelais 1933: 108–9)

The army is defeated by Friar:

He hurried, therefore, upon them so rudely, without crying gare or beware, that he overthrew them like hogs, tumbled them over like swine, striking athwart and alongst, and by one means or other laid so about him, after the old fashion of fencing, that to some he beat out their brains, to others he crushed their arms, battered their legs, and bethwacked their sides till their ribs cracked with it. To others again he unjointed the spondyles or knuckles of the neck, disfigured their chaps, gashed their faces, made their cheeks hang flapping on their chin, and so swinged and belammed them, that they fell down before him like hay before a mower. To some others he spoiled the frame of their kidneys, marred their backs, broke their thigh-bones, pushed in their noses, poached out their eyes, cleft their mandibules, tore their jaws, dash'd in their teeth into their throat, shook asunder their omoplates or shoulder blades, sphacelated their shins, mortified their shanks, inflamed their ankles, heaved off of the hinges their ishies, their sciatica or hip-gout, dislocated the joints of their knees, squattered into pieces the boughts of pestles of their thighs, and so thumped, mawled and belaboured them everywhere, that never was corn so thick and threefold thrashed upon by ploughmen's flails, as were the pitifully disjointed members of their mangled bodies, under the merciless baton of the cross. (113)

My choice of theater metaphors, from Aristotle's tragedy to Rabelais's grotesque, is intentional. Not only the grotesque, but the *spectacle*, came to characterize Mozambican violence. This distinguishes it from examples of terror-warfare that depend on secrecy and torture conducted behind the walls of prisons. In Mozambique the spectacle of violence is carried out in the center of society and the heart of the community for all to see. Perhaps this is the reason people speak of a "theater of war." But theater is not removed from life, it—like all human cultural action— is life. Theater, the grotesque, the spectacle, and living are a dialogue that spans the immediacy of the present to the historical past made immediate. The following sections discuss the immediacy of both past and present as they unfold through terror-warfare and fighting terror.

The Historical Past Made Immediate: Ancestors and the War

Bakhtin has said that (cosmic) terror—the abode of power abuses—is hidden in the ancestral body of mankind. This observation is literally true in Mozambique. Ancestors share the life-world of Mozambicans. They provide and protect; they punish when the living make mistakes; they counsel; they even eat, drink, and enjoy a good joke. And they suffer the fates of war as do their living descendants. Properly ministered to, ancestors share fruitfully in their offsprings' lives. Their demands are not excessive. A proper funeral and burial, and fealty and respect shown in ongoing ceremonies for them in their "home-land" are the things that constitute wealth and peace of mind for the ancestors. To disregard an ancestor's wish is stupidity; to desert one a sin. People cannot, in good faith, leave their ancestors unattended in a land ravaged by violence. But if they invite their ancestors to relocate with them, they generally ensure their ancestors' unhappiness. Severed from their homeland, subordinate to the lineage of those controlling the new destination, shorn of normal family supports, the ancestors can bring turmoil, misfortune, and even death to the living. The ancestors, quite literally, make life and death possible.

But what happens to the ancestors in war? What happens to those killed in an attack or in fleeing through the bush in no-man's-lands who cannot be given proper burial ceremonies? I discussed this with Mozambicans throughout the country, and three categories of answers emerged. All agreed that the spirits fall into the category of the unnatural: angry, restless, ungrounded, and vengeful.

Some say these spirits seek revenge on those who have wrought their death. As an old curandeiro told me:

> I walked across the site of an attack near here right after it occurred. I could feel the spirits of the people killed swarming around there, angry and full of vengeance. These people killed, they were not soldiers, they did not battle, they were simple unarmed villagers. They died for no reason, they died unnaturally, in violence. Now they stay with the blood, they seek revenge on those who spilled it. They will follow those who killed them—inflicting harm, madness, and death. These Renamo, they should fear these dead, they cannot escape them. I walk by that place now, and still I sense those spirits, restless with anger. The ground is hot with their blood. They will not rest until they have had their revenge.

At this point another curandeiro joined us, and added:

I know that spot you are talking about, and what you say is true, the spirits remain with the blood, causing all who pass by that way to sicken and die. We all know of that place, we respect the anger of the spirits, we know their power, and we give wide berth to the area. No one from here would walk that way. But the soldiers, those who continue to kill, they pass that way. They do not know or they do not care. And it is they who will fall because of those dead.

I do not want to leave the impression that these attitudes exist only in the rural areas, or pertain only to Renamo. I was sitting in the capital city of Maputo one day, and some friends brought up a problem people were concerned with, one that had been alluded to recently in the newspaper.

You know that bridge outside of town, the one that so many people use? The military that control that bridge have gotten greedy. They demand money or goods from some of the people crossing. If the people don't have anything to give, if they talk back, if the soldiers are angry, sometimes they kill the people and throw their bodies in the water. Just recently, people found a body riddled with bullet holes, and another all cut up, floating face down in the water. You are never safe crossing that bridge, you may have to pay with your life. Oh sure, the soldiers can say that these people were suspected Renamo, but we all know these people, we know what is going on. The soldiers grow rich on our troubles, they kill whom they please. You cross that bridge and you cross a place of death. Those bodies lying just out of sight know what has happened to them, they know the truth. They are full of anger, and those soldiers stand there all day long, standing over the blood and the bodies of the people they have killed. It will eat away at them, it will destroy them; those dead people will have their own back.

In partial contrast with those who think the wrongfully killed will take revenge on their attackers, others say the disembodied are released on the winds of violence, capable of roving the earth to afflict all with whom they come in contact. Never at peace themselves, they bring disharmony and misfortune in their stead.

We moved up here at the beginning of the war. The land was open, there was no claim on it. Where we lived before was parched, the land was not so good, and the conditions were harsh. The drought made it impossible. We are not far from our original site, we can look down the hill upon it, but the life here is better, we are not wanting. The war was not so bad then, it had not moved into our area. But as it got worse, people fled their own areas, and settled more and more in the land we had vacated. And as the war came closer still, the bandits came into the low lands and massacred people. Many innocents have been killed. The soldiers have not arrived here yet, but we worry. We worry not only about them coming into our homes, we worry about the spirits of all those who have been killed below, all those restless spirits unleashed. The air down there is heavy with their spirits, their outrage. Those kinds of spirits loosened on the winds bring havoc and illness. They can spoil the land and the health of the people. When the wind blows up the sides of the hills, we hear the screams of those who were killed, and we fear the winds will carry those anguished spirits to spoil our lands.

Finally, there are those who believe that the people cut down by war, spirits embittered and wrathful over a meaningless death, will return to inflict harm on their own families. Deprived of the support of a proper burial and its attendant ceremonies, deprived of a proper death, these phantoms turn to vent their anger on those who should have taken care of the death rituals, and could not. This lack is most acutely felt when no burial at all could be performed, when a body had to be left where it fell in fleeing an attack.

They came to attack our village one day. I was on the far end and could hear the gunshots, the screams. I grabbed my children and we ran. We decided to try to make it to the next town, where we thought we would be safe. But as we ran, we ran right into some more soldiers, and they shot my oldest boy. Shot and killed him. In the confusion, we ran on, and finally made our way here. There are so many of us here, all running from the violence. So many of us here have lost someone. This place is not a good one. It is more secure, that is true. But it is full of too many people, too little food, too much disease, too many people who have been spoiled by the violence they have seen. All these problems here, all the illness and sadness, are surely caused by the spirits of those we left behind. I could not bury my son properly, I do not even know what has happened to his body. His spirit is out there in the bush, alone and cold, uncared for. I have not seen my husband or most of my family since I ran, I do not know if they are dead or alive, if their bodies are lying somewhere unattended. I am sure this is why there is so much pain and sickness here—the spirits of those we left behind have come to show their displeasure. They will take some of us with them.

As I sat outside on the ground and talked with this woman, a number of her acquaintances joined us. All agreed with the conclusions of the speaker, and all added their own stories, fearing the wrath of the souls they could not care for. It reminded me of many such conversations with people in similar circumstances throughout Mozambique, and it struck me that I consistently heard fears of spiritual retribution on family members unable to care for murdered relatives from the people who themselves had been burned out of home and village, who had had to flee for their lives.

After that conversation, I did an informal survey, asking both *deslocados* and people who had stayed in their homelands if the spirits of those killed were vengeful about their deaths, and who suffered their rancor. Consistently, *deslocados* took the responsibility for the death on themselves and felt themselves to be the recipients of the spirit's anger. Their inability to conduct proper ceremonies, to return home and honor the dead in the respected ways, underlay their fears. Those who remained in their villages after an attack tended to think instead that, while the spirits of the innocents killed might harm their immediate family members, the bulk of their retributive anger would be directed toward those who had cut them down. And some, like the two old curandeiros I quoted at the beginning of this discussion, thought that the spirits turned their vengeance on those who continue the war, regardless of who they are, as a powerful warning for conflict cessation.

Aristotle's sense of tragedy resurfaces in this context. Tragedy, for too many people, begins to resemble his definition that the wholly good do not suffer the tragic end, but only the good who have fallen through some character flaw or fatal error in judgment. The victims who have managed to survive the war become somehow responsible for those who have not, and they feel they must pay the price. The people who have lost the most—family members, homes, and villages—pay the heaviest penalty: it is they who feel responsible for the deaths of their loved ones.

Not only with the ancestors does this Aristotelian sense of the tragic come to define people's war experience. All too often victims of violence are impugned with some essence of complicity by the society at large. There are always those who cast victims as responsible for what has befallen them. They were politicized, they were not politicized, they were collaborating with the other side, they refused to collaborate with anyone, they did not do enough to protect their communities—the critiques are legion. In Mozambique, one of the "tragedies" involves the confrontation between dialogues of responsibility: are deaths or mutilations senseless, ignoble, or somehow the product of one's actions?

The Immediacy of the Present: The Body-Politic

The ongoing dialogue of war's terror, of its enduring embodiment, became clear to me one day when I was walking home in Zambezia. Children made homeless by the war lived and slept on the streets in front of my home, and they usually greeted me and came for a talk when I returned at the end of the day. New children joined the ranks of the street dwellers weekly. This day, a child I had never seen before came up to me. As I greeted him, I realized that he had no pants on. A shirt but no pants. I had seldom seen a street kid without pants—they might be tattered rags that concealed nothing, but, as the children told me, "We are men, we wear pants."[3] The child spoke no Portuguese, and I did not recognize his dialect. He was not only painfully thin and scarred, he was erratic and disoriented. An adult I did not know came up to me to explain that the child was "crazy: It's the war, you know, it has taken the child's family and driven him mad." Soon a number of people passing by on the street stopped to talk, to discuss the war, its disastrous effects on people's lives, its vile actions that can turn a child to madness. People did not talk to the child, they talked about him. The child became a symbol of the atrocities of the war, a font of dialogue, a focal point of all the anger people held toward those who committed such violence on the communities of the innocent. He became a living reenactment of terror-warfare: a spectacle that brought the war daily into the streets and lives of everyone who saw him.

The mad child, the homeless, the wounded and war-deformed all are powerful actors in the drama that brings the truth of terror and resistance closer to the heart of society. Whether in Latin America or southern Africa, as Michael Taussig brings out,

It is in the world of the beggars that the culture of terror finds perfection. They are misfits, cripples, blind, idiots, dwarves, twisted, and deformed. They can neither talk nor walk nor see straight, and they exist in two critically important zones: huddled on the steps of the cathedrals in the main square opposite the presidential palace, or, like the idiot, splayed out on top of the city's garbage heap. Here indeed is the figure embodying the society as a whole: on account of his idiocy he has struck at a high-ranking officer, and therefore at the president himself. (1987:6)

The grotesque calls to the fore the fact that undermining the determinacy of existence (to which Sylvia Henning refers in the quote at the beginning of this Chapter) is a lethal play of power and politics aimed at alienating the individual from the society at large, and thus from a basis for political resistance and change. Enacting the grotesque plays on a

number of powerful themes: destroying wholeness, sabotaging compre-
hension, violating boundaries, and doing all these in the most excessive ways.

In the grotesque, writes Bakhtin (1984:316), "special attention is given
to . . . all that prolongs the body and links it to other bodies or to the
world outside." This linking of body to body, of human to human, and
of these to the greater world is fundamental to notions of the grotesque.
It is not the individual per se that is of interest to the grotesque, but that
which links people with people, humans with world systems. "The events
of the grotesque sphere are always developed on the boundary dividing
one body from the other and, as it were, at their points of intersection"
(Bakhtin 1984:322). Dis-*member*-ment becomes a double entendre that
separates person from membership: the latter a prerequisite for political community and action.

Clearly a great deal of political effort goes into making the connection between individuals and geopolitical communities, as exempli-
fied in Benedict Anderson's *Imagined Communities*. Severing the actual
boundaries of human bodies through maiming and torture can simultaneously serve to convey an assault on the boundaries of the body politic.[4] Without boundaries, human bodies, states, and communities are
all inherent paradoxes, each a conceptual as well as a geopolitical absurdity. We should not assume that there is any fundamental naturalness
to the association between individual bodies and political bodies. Like
all cultural phenomena, such relationships are socially constructed. As
Cynthia Enloe (1993) says, if these constructions were natural, we would
not find such a concerted effort to create and maintain them in societies. This linkage is clearly tied to the development of nationalism and
to the fetishizing of borders, ownership, and power that links human
characteristics to particular nondynamic notions of political space(s).
The grotesque spectacles point to the control of bodies as a crude de-
nominator between people and the pursuit of power. The grotesque is
not a wanton production, attacking any bodily protuberance, severing
parts from wholes in random excess.[5] When I visited the southern province of Gaza, a spate of male castrations were taking place, all with what
I call the same "signatures of terror," the same techniques. By following
the trajectories of the attacks, it appeared obvious that a group of Renamo had recently entered from South Africa and were working their
way north into the interior of Mozambique. If one plotted the castration episodes on a map, one could virtually follow the soldiers' path.

Because castration is not the most common form of mutilation in
Mozambique, it was not surprising that the soldiers had come from
(apartheid) South Africa. Influenced by foreign military trainers and

strategists (channeled largely through white South African military intelligence), the cultures of terror the foreigners employed in subjugating a population were transmitted to the Mozambican rebels. Throughout Mozambique, people told me that if a white foreigner was present during an attack the level of brutality was generally much worse. As one woman summed up:

> If Mozambicans attack, you might be raped and even beaten. But if a white man is among the attackers, you know it will be worse.

Thus troops coming straight from South Africa reproduced terror tactics more reflective of combat cultures of white South Africans and their western military peers than with Mozambique. Each spectacle follows a script. These cultural scripts, as emphasized in the opening chapters, are international and fluid in their construction.

Even in the specifics of the grotesque the theatrical world of Rabelais and the dirty war in modern Mozambique share graphic similarities. In his discussion of Rabelais, Bakhtin explains that the nose, mouth, and ears are the most important features of the human head in grotesque imagery. The eyes have no part in these images unless they protrude unnaturally. This is because, Bakhtin notes, eyes express an individual, self-sufficient human life, something outside the purview of the grotesque. The parallel with Mozambique is striking. Ears, noses, and lips were cut off by Renamo soldiers with some frequency. I do not think I ever heard of a person's eyes being purposely injured or removed. With these actions, the message is powerfully articulated not only to the victim, but to all who "see" the war: "you will not hear, you will not speak out against the violence. But you will see the spectacle." Yet this is a message devoid of content, and that is the intent. Both "senses" (in the literal meaning of sense organs) and "sense" (meaning intellectual understanding) are intentionally "cut off" by the violence. In discussing this sense-lessness with me, the novelist Tamara Jane said:

> I'm also struck by the notion that the dismembering and mutilating of a corpse steals the mutilated person from themselves—it makes them a non-individual. I can really only "conceptualize" this by imagining the "spectacle" of a whole murdered body—let's call him Bob—who, as evident to all, is Bob in death as he was in life. But if his mouth, lips, nose, ears, genitals are cut off, his signifiers (public, and to some degree private) of Bobness are also mutilated, he is more than murdered, he is obliterated in a sense, his entity lost amidst the genericification of his parts.

This is not mere disorder, for disorder is part of ontological order—a fact and a fiction appreciated in cultural lore. Worse: the world has been un-ordered. Human nature isn't. World process doesn't. Sense can't.

Part of the "un-ordering" caused by war lies in the fact that life cannot proceed by the normal rules of human interaction. People remain poised for flight; every action is destabilized by the worry, "Do I have to flee?" Heartfelt thought is tarnished by the dread "Where is my mother, brother, child, friend?"—whomever has disappeared into the gaping mouth of the war process. Trust, the foundation of communities, is undermined: "Who among my acquaintances might be a dangerous collaborator, a mercenary jackal selling information to the other side, a scout or a spy for enemy troops, a profiteer who will gain from my misfortune?" There is no home. The place of comfort, succor, reproduction, and rest has become a battlezone. Many stories of attacks related by Mozambicans take place at hearth and home. Everyone knows this, and even if they have not yet been attacked, people realize that to go "home" is to court danger, to have no home is to be safe. But to have no home is not to be human.

> I sneak home now only to do my work. Home is now my job. I leave home to be safe, I sleep in the bush with the animals, and I become like them. This war turns us into animals, one and all.

Working in tandem with dehumanization is the attempt to "animalize" the population. To be like an animal, Mozambicans lament, is to lose that which makes one human. One woman sat talking with me in her fields one day. She was tired, she said, tired of the war and what the war had made her become. She felt she could not wash the dirt and isolation off of her, the "dirt" not only of violence but of the *mata*, the bush, where the war now forced her to live out her life:

> They have made us inhuman. We sleep in the jungle like animals every night to avoid attack. We run from every sound like the animals we hunt, we scavenge for food in the countryside like animals because we cannot maintain our crops like humans. Our family is scattered on the wind—we don't know where our children and parents are, or even if they are alive. We can't even help and protect them—we are even worse than animals in this sense. Do you know what this does to a person, living like this?

Dehumanization, then, is employed not to end life but to end the humanness of the individual. Human will, coupled with the capacity of humans to produce themselves as actors in a reality of their own creating, becomes an intolerable threat, becomes the enemy to the few who seek to dominate the many. It is not people, but a will to resist, not individuals, but the existence of a counterhegemonic that challenges repressive forces. Camus's famous phrase, "I rebel, therefore I exist," seems to be heard in its inverse by the perpetrators of dirty war: "I exist, therefore I rebel." The response is to attack the fonts of humanity, sever person from personhood and individual from identity. Duly dehumanized, the population can then be domesticated like any other animal.

When the home is invaded, it is turned "inside out" the private becomes the public, and the public becomes a display for the whole community. The normal and the life sustaining become deadly weapons. Note the use of the mortar and, equally, the brother-in-law as instruments of death in the following story told to Lina Magaia:

On that night in October 1984, the bandits came to Julieta's house. They knocked brutally on the door. Julieta's husband, wearing only his trousers, opened the door. Julieta woke up and followed her husband. They were forced out of the house. Julieta's brother and her seven children were also forced to wake up and to leave their sleeping mats to go outside. There was a moon, so it was a bright night.

There were nine bandits and they were all equipped with guns, bayonets and knives. They searched the main house and found some boots. They took them outside, asking whose they were. Julieta's husband replied that they were his. They told him that since he had boots he must be a militiaman, which he denied. "So why do you have boots?" they wanted to know. "Because I work on the railway and they gave us boots there," he replied.

"So you're one of those who repair the line when we cut it?" yelled one of the bandits. Julieta began to be afraid. She was already big-bellied from pregnancy. She sat on the ground, crying. Her children clustered around her. The brother said nothing, watching anxiously and perhaps remembering some of the things he had heard about the bandits in his own area.

The bandit who seemed to be the chief looked around and saw the mortar that Julieta used to grind maize and groundnuts.

"You're going to pay today," said the bandit, grabbing the man by one arm.

The chief bandit then instructed Julieta's brother to put the mortar by the railwayman.

"Lie down here," he ordered.

Her husband lay down on the curve of the mortar. The bandit chief then ordered Julieta's brother to get an axe.

"Cut here," he ordered, pointing to Julieta's husband's throat.

Julieta's brother stared, but was incapable of making the stroke.

"I'm telling you to cut here," the bandit repeated. Julieta's brother could not make the cut. The bandit, calling another bandit, told him to bring the people who had been kidnapped in the area and were waiting under guard nearby. Julieta's husband remained stretched out with his head on the curve of the mortar.

When the people arrived at gunpoint, the bandit chief insisted again that Julieta's brother cut his brother-in-law's throat. The latter was silently weeping. And Julieta's brother could not cut his brother-in-law's throat.

The bandit chief muttered a command to one of his subordinates, who grabbed the axe from Julieta's brother's hands. Without blinking an eye, the bandit cut the throat of Julieta's husband. His cries of pain went to the depths of the hearts of Julieta and her children, who shielded their eyes with their hands. When the bandit chief noticed this he screamed at them to take their hands from their faces if they did not want to die. The people nearby lowered their eyes, and a silence heavier than death hung in the air. Julieta's husband was writhing. The bandit chief took out a knife and pointed it at Julieta's brother. He ordered that the brother be given the axe and use it to put an end to his brother-in-law's torment.

Julieta's husband was gripped by the legs by two bandits and his head was held in the curve carved on the wooden mortar. Her brother raised the axe and delivered the fatal blow. Her husband's neck was severed on the two sides of the mortar, and he died. . . . The bandit chief said to Julieta's brother, "Now you're one of us." (1988:32–34)

When the familiar and the everyday are turned into implements of torture and murder, the familiar everyday world is rendered grotesque —not merely by the fact of the present terror and repression, but by the enduring nature of associations. Will Julieta, her family, and the community that were present ever be able to see or use a simple mortar to pound grain without having the drama and the terror of Julieta's husband's murder flash into their minds? Although Julieta's brother killed her husband as an act of mercy, will anyone ever be able to disentangle this from the fact that he took part in the husband's murder, and was congratulated as a Renamo supporter for doing so? Will this community ever hear a footfall at night without startling because the world has suddenly become a dangerous place? Long after the soldiers have gone, their presence is invoked with each glance at a mortar. These associations can remain long after the war has come to a close; they can last a lifetime. With them lasts the *possibility* of terror and repression.

But, in a countering force, Lina Magaia's reproduction of this tale serves to stigmatize these military actions, to turn the onus of responsibility back on the offending soldiers. In *telling* the story, civilian to civilian, the technique of terror is undermined. The grotesque becomes a place of mourning and resistance in Magaia's (and the victim's) hands.

Past and Present Combined: (Un)Making the World and Reaching Toward the Future

The notion of the (grotesque) spectacle calls to the fore the distinction between the socio-political violence conducted just out of sight behind prison walls and that conducted intentionally in the center of people's lives and societies.

The unmaking of the world, as Elaine Scarry (1985) so skillfully demonstrates, is a core phenomenon to torture. But for those who are held in isolation in the military institutions or political prisons of Scarry's focus, the unmaking is an isolated process. It is the victim's world that is unmade. As the victim is separated from home and community by imprisonment and from consciousness and communication by pain, his or her isolation is doubly elevated to a form of torture in itself.

The torturer works to control the victim's entire world. In prison, this world extends to the boundaries of the room. "In torture," writes Scarry (1985:40), "the world is reduced to a single room or set of rooms." The torturer dominates this space, and with it the victim; the room becomes an instrument of torture, its objects those of the torturer's work. "The room, both in its structure and content, is converted into a weapon, deconverted, undone. Made to participate in the annihilation of the prisoners, made to demonstrate that everything is a weapon, the objects themselves, and with them the fact of civilization, are annihilated" (41). In ensuring the room is the victim's universe, the torturer's acts are totalizing.

But what if torture is not "reduced to a single room"? What if it is expanded to the world? In Mozambique, it is not the victim that is hauled off to an isolated room, but the torture that is hauled into the center of home and community. The room does not become the social universe of the victim, the social universe itself becomes the victim. It is not the room, but cultural process that becomes the staging ground for violence.

For those subjected to the spectacle—the public performance—of terror-warfare, the world is unmade for victims and spectators alike. In fact, the line between the two is intentionally erased. Not the victim, but the world, is separated from society. And the world is unmade a bit further each time a war story is told and retold, each time a war-mutilated person is seen or a crazy child wanders down the road, each time the dead are felt to walk the earth and harm its inhabitants because they enjoyed neither a normal death nor proper death ceremonies. Terror is concretized in the realm, as Taussig would say, of the "really real." The spectacle lives on by producing injurious specters.

Bringing violent spectacles into the heart of society and culture is intended to quash political will and social agency. Dirty-war assaults on a generalized, and unmobilized, population may well prove to be more devastating in certain ways than institutional repression. Consider the camaraderie of resistance Michel de Certeau discusses in his work on the "institution of rot" defining state repression:

Accounts by torture victims indicate the stage of breakdown at which their resistance intervenes. They "held up," they say, by maintaining (perhaps we should even say "enduring") the memory of comrades who, for their own part, were not "rotten"; by keeping in mind the struggle in which they were engaged, a struggle which survived their own "degradation" intact, and did not unburden them of it any more than it depended on it; by discerning still, through the din of their tortures, the silence of human anger and the genealogy of suffering that lay behind their birth, and from which they could no longer protect or expect anything; or by praying, in other words by assuming an otherness, God, from which neither aid nor justification was forthcoming, and to which they were of no use and could not offer their services. (1986:43)

The unmobilized civilian—targeted in terror-warfare precisely because of his or her politico-military ignorance and innocence—is bereft of the supports de Certeau identifies. Such a person has no fallen comrades, no cherished struggle, to sustain her or his faith and upon which to forge a resistant identity.

Two facts combine in situations of torture, however ironically, to produce a will of resistance in the face of all that is trying to crush it, whether the victim is held incommunicado in a prison cell or is attacked in the central plaza of a community. First, violence becomes a tool of power, and then comes to stand as a symbol of power itself:

Now, at least for the duration of this obscene and pathetic drama, it is not the pain but the regime that is incontestably real, not the pain but the regime that is total, not the pain but the regime that is able to eclipse all else, not the pain but the regime that is able to dissolve the world. (Scarry 1985:56)

But the second fact, as Scarry concludes, is that the torturer's claims to power are as fraudulent as they are merciless. The attributes of pain can in no real sense be translated into the cultural insignia of a regime. In fact, as Scarry (1985:332) notes, "it requires neither strength nor skill to inflict hurt on a *wholly defenseless* human body," something a weak child could do.

For Scarry, the obscene and pathetic drama of torture and power is relegated to the prisoner's cell. For Mozambicans, by virtue of its public enactment, this drama comes to define the world at large. Scarry worked with political prisoners and Amnesty International Reports—all of whom are cast in state-sponsored institutional settings. Isolation from family and society defines their plight. Had Scarry worked in places where torture is conducted as public ritual, had she followed torture victims back into the community and seen their impact on all those who have knowledge of them, she might not have concluded so readily that pain is incommunicable. I do agree with her that pain can destroy formal language, but there are many "truths" and many ways of communicating them. I am concerned here with another "truth": that terror-warfare is employed precisely because pain is communicated, that one victim can victimize a community at large. There are many "languages" in any social setting, some competing, even contradictory, but nonetheless true. Pain both undermines communication and communicates throughout a society at large. Because the infliction of pain creates an enemy, one rooted in a fraudulent claim to power, *torture creates resistance to the regime by its very enactment.*

I have attributed to terror-warfare two rather contradictory results. One is to "unmake" the world—to destroy the creative fonts of political will and identity—and the other is to promote resistance to oppression. The same is true of the grotesque, as Bakhtin points out. So far, I have discussed the grotesque as a weapon employed to render the knowable world impossible. But the ultimate intent of the grotesque, as Rabelais so aptly demonstrates, is to defeat terror by laughing in its face—not lightheartedly, but in resistance.

Mozambicans do not laugh lightheartedly at the violence of the war they live in, nor do they find it comic, but they do subvert terror by applying a Rabelaisian form of grotesque critique. Dramas and tales of the destructive forces in their lives abound, caricaturizing them as larger-than-life figures with larger-than-life comic features and foibles: figures so pathetically powerful they hasten their own demise, though deplorably they trample many in their downfall. The songs, the parables, the stories presented throughout this book represent examples of subverting the grotesque. The war exists not only in the physical battlefields, but in the application and subversion of violence—something that means far more than maimed and distorted bodies. It is a battle about personhood, will, identity, society, power, existence.

The war, its terror, and constructions of the grotesque are not "things" that happen to people as static, passive, generic victims. When spectacles of war's terror collapse time and individuality, people respond by dealing with these realities in a dynamic way. People negotiate their survival, they negotiate the *possible*, on a daily basis. They construct themselves in the face of terror and the grotesque, not solely in the here and now, but as an ongoing reality that extends into their future, that literally forges the future. Spectacles of war set "specters" into action that concretize the amorphous. People then struggle with these truths of war and oppression in order to overcome them. Absences are made present, terrors named, perpetrators identified. And in this, people construct themselves in resistance. Yet the truth of terror is interwoven into this resistance. Sending a loved one out to do a chore becomes something different, forever, after experiencing the threat of death in the midst of the everyday. For Julieta, using a mortar will never again be a simple domestic act of food preparation. But it may become a symbol of resistance.

If violence seeks to crush the possible, people, far from passive victims, re-create the possible as a tactic of survival and political agency. If the grotesque is used against people to repress them, then people identify these grotesque tactics to delegitimize the politics and the actions of the perpetrators. In illuminating the harsh realities of terror-warfare, its victims are demonstrating that those who employ the grotesque are, by definition, not fit to govern. The use of the grotesque negates its own claim to power.

Notes

1. Bakhtin points out that the concept of the grotesque has undergone a number of permutations, the most noteworthy being the essential differences between Romantic grotesque and medieval and Renaissance (folk) grotesque, especially in regard to terror:

> The world of Romantic grotesque is to a certain extent a terrifying world, alien to man. All that is ordinary, commonplace, belonging to everyday life, and recognized by all suddenly becomes meaningless, dubious and hostile. Our own world becomes an alien world. Something frightening is revealed in that which was habitual and secure. If a reconciliation with the world occurs, it takes place in a subjective, lyric, or even mystic sphere. On the other hand, the medieval and Renaissance folk culture was familiar with the element of terror only as represented by comic monsters, who were defeated by laughter. Terror was turned into something gay and comic. . . . The images of Romantic grotesque usually express fear of the world and seek to inspire their readers with this fear. On the contrary, the images of folk culture are absolutely fearless and communicate this fearlessness to all. (Bakhtin 1984:38–39)

In my discussion, the term grotesque is applied in its many guises: used by the (para)military as an instrument to create terror, and used in its ironic sense by the targets of that terror to defeat it.

2. If, as Clausewitz says, war is an extension of politics, then the extremes to which this can be carried in the name of power show how terror-warfare as the grotesque "stand[s] at a margin of consciousness between the known and the unknown, the perceived and the unperceived, calling into question the adequacy of our ways of organizing the world, of dividing the continuum of experience into knowable particles." (Harpham 1982:3)

3. Street children were almost always boys. Although boys and girls are equally subjected to the conditions that force children to live on the streets, girls are not as evident in the ranks of the homeless. Some say this is because it is easier for girls to move into the homes of relatives and sympathetic friends. However, many of the boys on the streets I talked to had seen their entire home villages destroyed. There was nothing left for the girls to move into. While the idea that

girls may find lodging more easily may be true in part, there is a more tragic side: girls are more easily forced into prostitution and child labor. During my stay there was one episode I knew of where foreigners were making porno-graphic films of young girls. It came to the attention of a few when a dog one girl was forced to have sexual relations with mauled and killed her. The plight of homeless girls is sadly captured by the stock phrase I heard when I tried to follow up what became of them: "We just do not know." While the *presence* of homeless boys on the streets is a constant reminder of the tragedy of war, the *absence* of the girls is another.

4. As body, family, and society resonate symbolically, the attack on any one constitutes an attack on all.

5. I am reminded of a 1988 Anthropological Association panel where Leith Mullings was critiquing Marcelo Suárez-Orozco's paper on the dirty war in Argentina. Suárez-Orozco had argued that the pathological focus on the torture of the genitals was in part an attack both on the site of masculinity, power, and identity for men and on reproductive nurturance for women. Mullings argued back that one could not privilege the genitals as symbolic sites for torture—they were targeted because they were so sensitive to pain. Having seen torture vic-tims on several continents, I have found that the body sites targeted for torture do vary from regime to regime, and in each case correlate with strong cultural themes. I have also found that every site—nose and lips, teeth, genitals, severed limbs—hurts equally. Torture, in my experience, indeed carries cultural meta-messages.

Chapter 6
Identity and Imagination

"Leave me in peace," said the young girl broken
        hearted. Her parents and friends left her
        and she continues without peace.

"Leave me in peace," said the mother inconsolable with
        the death of her child. Her friends left her, but
        she continues without peace.

"Leave us in peace," we say so many times
        when others hurt us, when
        we get fed up with something, when
        we get fed up with somebody. And rarely
        do we live in peace.

                Peace.

        The truth is crystalline.

Peace only exists when we feel good with ourselves
and with life even if life or someone
has hurt us.

        What is necessary is to compose ourselves.
        The peace you lost only returns
        to those who accept others into
        their lives.
        Loneliness in these moments softens.
                    —Germana

Children turn crashed plane into playground, Niassa province, Mozambique, 1990. Photo by Carolyn Nordstrom.

```
        . . . we cannot feel
    the old problem of ontological
insufficiency of having
                no answer to *Who am I?*
        no there there . . . (Scott 1988:17)
```

Of whom and of what indeed can I say: "I know that!" This heart within me I can feel, and I judge that it exists. This world I can touch, and I likewise judge that it exists. There ends all my knowledge, and the rest is construction. For if I try to seize this self of which I feel sure, if I try to define and to summarize it, it is nothing but water slipping through my fingers. I can sketch one by one all the aspects it is able to assume, all those likewise that have been attributed to it, this upbringing, this origin, this ardor or these silences, this nobility or this vileness. But aspects cannot be added up. This heart of mine will remain indefinable for me. (Camus 1955:14)

The first time a Mozambican said to me that the war had taken from them everything they had, including who they were, I realized that identity, self, and personhood were strategic targets of war. The casualties and fonts of resistance of this war thus include intangibles beyond the physicality of bodies and actions. Self, society, and culture comprise Being-in-the-world, and this, for many Mozambicans, was Being-in-a-world-of-war. And that included Being as a target of war.

Flavia's Story and the Curandeiro

To understand what is attacked in a dehumanizing war necessitates an understanding of what it is to be human. In discussions with Mozambicans, the idea(l) of humanness—that which makes living in the world special—involves, but is certainly not limited to, the following: Mozambicans are nurtured in the bosom of family, and this is grounded in the skills and behaviors that sustain life: working, cultivating, harvesting, consuming. As family members, they illuminate the nexus of a time/place continuum—the fecundity of the ancestors has been instilled in them and comes to fruition in the familiar landscape of home, hearth, and the land they were born to. They thrive as part of a community, and a pattern of friendships, obligations, and shared goals gives tangible substance to their sense of world. Mythological space landscapes geographical space: ritual, ceremony, and belief bring the universal home. The eternal, the social, and the collective are made apparent through the individual and the particular. Cultural process brings home the nature of reality through the physical form of the participant's everyday world. People sit in a gathering place in their community, just outside their homes, surrounded by their fields and animals and belongings, supported by their family and acquaintances, and they peer through ceremony's door into the mysteries of the universe until they have made sense of it, and it of them. Their community, mythical and physical, takes shape in relation to a landscape of cultivated and wild spaces, within a network of other communities that together follow patterns of exchange of everything from people and goods to aggressions and innovations.

In this discussion I specifically intertwine notions of land and person, for as Michael Watts (1992) has pointed out, landscapes are ways of seeing—of seeing not only outward to culturally constructed realities, but inward to ideas and ideals of self and identity. Quoting Stephen Daniels, Watts underscores the fact that "the place is inseparable from the consciousness of those who inhabit it" (1992:122). To dismantle the world as we know it, then, is to dismantle what defines who we are and what reality is. Is identity dismantled simultaneously? Is the unmaking of the world simultaneously the unmaking of the self? Surely this is the basic premise of terror-warfare. For an antagonistic military wishing to destroy, to control, or to subjugate a people, what more powerful "target" could be found than that of personhood and reality?

Consider what is destroyed in the daily life of an average Mozambican. The words of Flavia, a Mozambican womanfriend of mine, poignantly demonstrate the kind of destruction the war has brought to millions of her countrypeople:

> Epah, Carolyn, this war. My youngest son came of age not too long ago, and I felt obliged to take him back to the land of my people to perform the ceremonies that would ensure he grows into a strong and healthy member of our family. The journey was a heartstopping one— as you know the roads are so unsafe, and we had to walk a majority of the way to avoid landmines and rogue soldiers. I was so frightened I would lose my son before he could even come of age properly. But when we arrived in my birthhome, it was so very disappointing. I remember a house filled with the happy shouts of children, lush farmlands flowing out from its doors, vegetables to pick for food, and our animals dotting the hillsides. Always a fire with food cooking, always a story being told. A home bright and full of people.
>
> It is so awful to see it now. My mother is the only one there now: my father, as you know, was killed by soldiers, my grandparents just died of the war: not enough food, medicines, hope. My mother, she will never be the same after all the attacks she has lived through, after seeing her husband killed. The horror of the violence is etched on her face and her soul. The house is dark, decrepit, and empty—the soldiers and bandits have carried off everything they could in the innumerable times they have come through. The fields are destroyed, and my

mother refuses to replant them, for every time she does, the Bandidos come and raid and then burn the fields. The animals are long gone, killed by the soldiers. The neighbors are few and far between, killed off, run off, starved off. No more laughter, no more stories, no more children playing. No more home. Even worse, when we arrived there, I found it was going to be really difficult to hold the ceremonies we wanted to for our son. The noise and music of the ceremonies attracts the Bandidos, and they hear it and come to attack. We cannot even perform the ceremonies that make us human. We did a ceremony, yes, but a mere skeleton of that which tradition calls for. Skeleton, yes, that is a good word—we are living skeletons of the war.

Flavia was telling me this as we walked down the road to visit the cu-randeiro. She had made the long trek back to the city alone, leaving her son at her mother's. Every block or so she punctuated her words with a sigh about missing him, or looked out over the landscape in the di-rection of her mother's village and pondered his safety. As nervous as she was about leaving him in an area so full of soldiers and fighting, she was even more worried about her mother. Her mother had seemed to age a decade since she had last seen her, and only her son could coax hearty laughter from her. "She seemed," Flavia said, "bent under the weight of the war and her grief." She knew her son's indefatigable spirit would bring some life back to her mother, but in the meantime, Flavia grew thin worrying about attacks on a village she could only see in her mind's eye.

Her sighs were not directed solely toward her son. We were going to the curandeiro to solve a problem she was having with her husband. The year before, her husband's mother had been kidnapped by Renamo and carried off to their base. He had spent all his money and a great deal of time seeking her release. There were rogues who found the war a very profitable experience; you could always find someone who fought for no one, but moved with ease between competing troops to carry in-formation, goods, and the money of worried family members trying to gain the release of a loved one who had been kidnapped. They could extract exorbitant prices from people like Flavia's husband desperate to find lost family members. Her husband had heard his mother was being held in an area he had never been to, one where he did not speak the language. Eventually he had actually succeeded in getting his mother back, but the months-long ordeal had taken its toll. When he returned home, there was a distance between them she could not bridge, and over time he had taken up with another woman. Polygamy was practiced here, and Flavia would have accepted this other woman ("what option do I have?" she said with a choice Mozambican explicative). The problem was that her husband had not expanded his family, but had simply moved in with the other woman.

The curandeiro knew why Flavia was there; he had predicted problems from his previous conversations with her. As we sat amid his fragrant medicines while he put together a mixture to ensure the return of her husband, the curandeiro lamented the fact that he was overworked because of the war. "The bullet and machete wounds and the sexual diseases are bad enough, but all the young people like you Flavia," he said shaking his head. I asked him about what the war brought. "Everything," he replied:

> Physical illnesses and malnutrition and epidemics like cholera. Mental diseases, spiritual diseases of all kinds, ones I have never even seen before. Alcoholism, abuses of all kinds. People who become estranged, people who become violent or mean, families that fall apart from the stress: people so marked by the violence and the inhumanity they have seen and been subjected to. The list is too long.

The curandeiro had by this time taken me under his wing and, given my interest in African medicine, had decided I needed to be tutored in the basics of healing. If I could find a car to borrow, he would take me to the bush the following morning. This decision, he explained, was not made lightly. He had consulted his diagnostic tools and the spirits to find out who I was and why I was here. The inquiries, he said, confirmed that my intentions were good. "You just can't be sure in this war . . . people don't know who people really are like they used to. . . . I have to do these consultations all too often." His concern was well founded. Curandeiros, banned until 1989, were primary targets of both Renamo (who sought to enlist or control them) and Frelimo (who saw them as obscurantists and Renamo collaborators).

The Department of Health lent me one of their few cars, with the admonition that I was out of my mind, did I know I was going into an area thick with Renamo, and would I please try to bring myself and the car back safely. After a drive of an hour or so, the curandeiro directed me to a site in a forest some miles from a large relocation center for *deslocados*, a no-man's-land where roving predatory bands of soldiers—often teenagers in tattered clothes bearing AK-47s—launched raids on the *deslocados* who had already lost everything they had. As we left the car and set out on foot, I asked "What about Bandidos?" in a quiet voice. "No problem," boomed the curandeiro. "I performed a consultation that confirmed we will not run into any harm, and I prepared protective medicines. We are completely safe." He was good at such consultations: people could not altogether avoid travel in the war, but they would not go without protection, and most people stopped at a curandeiro's house on their way out of town. If the curandeiro cautioned them not to go, they followed the advice. They had heard too many sing the praises of a curandeiro who saved their lives by warning them about an attack "I would have been in the middle of had I not canceled my plans."

As I was tutored in the curandeiro's endlessly nuanced pharmaco-poeia, I was saddened to hear just how many of the remedies went to curing the ills of war—ills that struck at the heart of self and society. The *deslocados* we encountered were as well endlessly nuanced, each face and form etched with its own unique story of suffering and hope.

We came across a man dressed in a loincloth who was traveling with his young daughter foraging for food. They were either frightened to go to the relocation center or unable to find food there. We stopped to talk with them, but refrained from asking what had happened to them—we did not need to. The man seemed bowed with imponderable grief. Yet through the numbing weariness and painful anguish marking his every move, he maintained a gentle dignity with his daughter. His whole effort focused on providing what order and nourishment he could to what re-mained of his family. I doubt anything could have persuaded that child to leave her father's side. She followed him tirelessly and without com-plaint, her eyes held open just a little too wide as she stared, rarely blinking, at a world that had somehow become incomprehensible. The tragedy that had befallen them was almost palpable, and I realized that the quiet isolation of the forest provided some scant protection from the onslaught of a world whose webs of significance had been severed for them.

The second group we encountered actually found us. I was concen-trating on trying to chop small pieces of medicinal bark from a tree with a large ax when I heard approaching footfalls in the thick forest be-hind me. Instantly, every sense in my body became hyperattuned to the sounds. I knew it could be renegade soldiers or Renamo. When I saw the curandeiro was unconcerned, I relaxed, but my body felt like a bolt of electricity had gone through it. How do people live with constant hyper-vigilance, I wondered? Hypervigilance is a survival technique, but one that takes its toll. As well as alerting people to potential dangers, it is a constant reminder that the world people occupy is not a safe one. Onto-logical security, in its most basic sense, is undermined (Giddens 1991).

The curandeiro nudged me to return to the task at hand. The bark had to be cut according to exacting specifications. Like many remedies, this contained a palimpsest of meaning: the bark itself was medicinal, but behind the physical ailments it cured lay the existential problems that had brought on the illness. The shape of the cut bark and the way in which it fell to the ground answered questions about the underlying nature of the problem to be treated. Sometimes people simply came to the tree to ask a question, reading the answers in the fall of the bark.

Several young women and children emerged out of the thicket, chatting and laughing, baskets of foraged foliage on their heads. When they saw us, they ran up and said,

Oh, you are asking questions of the tree, we come here too. Tell us, uncle, what will we encounter?

I asked them what questions brought them to the tree.

Oh, you know, where is my mother, is she safe, will I see her again? Will we be attacked again? Will my brother get better from his wounds? Will the Bandidos leave our area so I can return home soon?

The women and children had seen the war first-hand and had lost family members to it, but they wore the scars of the war in far different ways from the man and his daughter we had encountered earlier. We met many other people that day, and the Curandeiro explained to me how to read the pain and troubles on their faces and souls. The little boy goatherd with one scrawny goat, so proud of having an animal in a countryside wiped clean of livestock by hungry troops with automatic weapons. The mad woman who sat under a tree and endlessly recounted the story of her life. The people selling bits of scavenged food and goods, and exchanging wry jokes and information with all who passed their way. The volunteer work groups in the refugee camps singing sad ballads as they built huts for new arrivals. Each was a testimony of war and of the endless complexities of the human spirit. Identities forged in like circumstances, yet adapting with individual proclivities. Identities so similar in what they had faced, so different in the ways they had responded.

The curandeiro was right—we did not encounter any soldiers that day. Many hours later, we returned to the car and drove back to our hometown, stopping to buy bits and pieces of scavenged foods and goods, and to collect bits and pieces of gossip about the war, lost friends, and other crucial topics from people along the road. The war makes compatriots of everyone.

The next day, Flavia stopped by my home. "There is someone I would like you to meet," she said. Her "little cousin" had arrived from a Renamo stronghold. Flavia explained that she and her brother had been kidnapped "some time ago"; somehow the little girl had escaped, but her brother had not been able to.

I don't know what to do. She is thin, sickly, and terribly depressed. But I cannot get her to eat, or to sleep. When I bring her food, she will eat nothing. All I can get her to eat are things like the most basic roots. And the little girl replies, "How can I eat when I know my brother is starving?" She will not sleep in a bed or on a mat, but curls up on the ground. And she looks at me with big sad eyes and says, "How can I sleep in comfort when I know my brother is sleeping on the cold hard ground?" And when I try to give her a bath, take her to the clinic, or tend to her in any way, she just pulls away and says, "How can I think of myself when I know how my brother is suffering?" When I try to talk to her about this, to tell her she must get better to help her brother when he comes home, she shakes her head sadly and says, "I know what he is going through, it is so bad you cannot imagine." But she will say nothing else.

War Identities

We have arrived here from all over, scattered victims of Renamo violence. Everyone has lost everything they had. Their homes were burned, their goods stolen, their crops destroyed, their family members slaughtered. Even those that managed to run often ran in different directions from the rest of their families, and today do not know if the rest are alive or dead. Many have been through this cycle more than once, having fled to a "safe area" only to be attacked again. Me, this is my third relocation. I do not know where most of my family is. Maybe we will be attacked yet again—we hear Renamo passing by here at night. It is difficult to find the will to plant crops and tend children when it may all be taken from us tonight, and maybe we will not survive this time. The worst of it is the way this attacks our spirits, our very selves. Everyone here thinks: "Before this I knew who I was, I farmed the land that my father farmed, and his ancestors before him, and this long line nurtured the living. I had my family that I fathered, and I had my house that I built, and the goods that I had worked for. I knew who I was because I had all of this around me. But now I have nothing, I have lost what makes me who I am. I am nothing here." (A middle-aged man in a beleaguered village of deslocados in the southern part of Mozambique)

What happens to people when the landscapes of their lives—personal, social, and cultural—are landmined, when the "maps of meaning" (Jackson 1989) that order people's lives are blown apart? What happens to people when what they believe makes them human—home, hearth, family, and tradition—has been wrenched from their grasp?

If *who* people *are* is determined by their relationships with and in their world, the new relationships thrust on war's victims (soldier and civilian alike) begin to define them as much as their lifelong ones did. The notion that a formed, self-sustaining, enduring self will feel and suffer the ravages of misfortune but will return home as basically the same person, to basically the same life, is an unrealistic legacy of Enlightenment logic.

Consider, for example, the woman or man whose village is attacked. They and their loved ones are victims of violence, their family is scattered, their possessions destroyed. Possibly they are kidnapped by the rebel forces and forced to endure a life of hardship, deprivation, and brutality. They may escape the clutches of the war and flee to a center for *deslocados*—a makeshift oasis promising at best an illusory security and a lifestyle far different from anything they have known before. At some point they are able to return home, and find it changed: new people, missing loved ones, different buildings and settlement patterns, farmlands refigured by war or usurped by the conniving and unscrupulous. The patterns of home, work, play, ceremony, friendship, and family no longer match pre-war traditions.

Is this woman, or this man, the same person as before the attack that set these events into play? If self is continuously constructed in thought and action, and identity forged through lived experience, then self-identity is defined by what one has lived through. Experience is not something that happens to the self, but *experience becomes the self*—it is that through which identity is forged. If cultural landscapes are layered on social and geographical landscapes to provide meaning to a person's life-world, a change in the former necessarily refashions the latter.

People exist in a continual process of re-formation. Even in locales far removed from war, people undergo constant, if often imperceptible, change. But in the vast dislocations that can mark war experiences, what can we say of the relationship between people as they were before exposure to violence, and as they are after they have weathered it? An irreversible alteration has taken place. Can we say that the person who existed before the war has, at least in some small way, been killed—a casualty of war? A veteran, bearing the scars of war, has returned to take up residence in a post-war world.

The impact of such change is nowhere more visible than with those who have been mutilated, who are doubly constructed by their war experience. Violence has changed not only the contours of their universe but of their bodies as well. The change endures in a vicious cycle: the war cannot be relegated to memories of the past, but is experienced afresh each time the mutilation intrudes into thought or action. These people cannot control the flow or form of change, for each person they encounter sees the drama of the war unfold before his or her eyes in the shape of the scars and deformations. And each person they meet interacts not with the unscarred individual of pre-war times but with the individual who carries the mutilations of the war into the present. The person is, quite literally, re-mutilated with every interaction. Their self-identity and their world are profoundly altered through these life experiences. These realities cannot be erased like the writing on a chalkboard.

Duirno's Sister-in-Law and the Processes of Self-Identity

The events that befell an acquaintance's sister-in-law have stood for me as a poignant summary of the connection between violence and identity. Duirno had told me the plight of his brother's wife, Jacanta. Their hometown had been attacked two years previously in a particularly vicious raid by Renamo. The family had scattered and run in different directions. Duirno made it to safety, walking several days through the bush to a relocation center, and had finally settled in the town where I lived to wait out Renamo's occupation of his hometown. The rest of his family were not as lucky: one was killed, and he never heard again from his sister-in-law, her mother, or his cousin. As weeks turned into months and no word came from them, he decided they must have been kidnapped by Renamo, for their bodies had never been found. Duirno's brother was disconsolate; Jacanta was a good wife: strong, healthy, stable.

One day Duirno came to visit brimming with good tidings: Jacanta and her mother had just come home. They had arrived sickly, bedraggled, and scarred, but alive. They had in fact been kidnapped by Renamo during the raid. Both had been forced to walk, portering the very goods looted from their town on their backs, well into the next province. What exactly had happened to Jacanta was a bit difficult to ascertain as she had completely lost the ability to speak Chuabo, her native language. The Renamo base was located in a different language zone, and the majority of the people there spoke a completely different dialect. She learned to speak a bit of this dialect, but no one in her family could understand it. Duirno sat down with a frown and said to me:

> You know, we have heard of this happening to others. Jacanta's mother told us some of the terrible things that happened to them during these last two years. They were raped, they were beaten, they saw others killed. They were forced to do difficult labor, and were given little to eat, and no medicines when they were sick. Jacanta's mother can still speak Chuabo, but she doesn't want to speak of the experiences

much—we really do not know all that happened to them. But this thing with Jacanta, I think the experiences were just too horrible, she did not want them to be a part of her real life, so she forgot Chuabo so that these things could not touch her life. There was that life, and then there is her real life. She can speak of that awful life in the other dialect, and none of us understand, but she cannot speak of them in Chuabo. We are hoping as her life comes back to her, so will her language.

Questions concerning the nature of identity for Duirno and his family are not abstract epistemological endeavors, they are a pressing reality. People do not talk about their identities; they live them, talk through them, or are silenced by them. Soldiers and battlefields may represent the focus of traditional political and military science, and the exposing of torture and massacres may provide a counterhegemonic influence— but self and identity constitute the hidden casualties of war, core experiences of war's violence that are as voiceless as Jacanta in war's discourse.

Clearly the evidence from Mozambique, like that from current social science, points out that we need to rethink our concepts of identity and selfhood. And what can we really say we know about these concepts with utter conviction? When we turn our analytical gaze to these issues, we find most of our convictions are cultural lore, slippery assemblages of belief and happenstance that rest on a foundation of assumptions sorely lacking in empirical bases. Sorting serious scholarship from personal conjecture and cultural supposition is difficult at best. Even serious scholarship is marked by contention and contradiction. We may never be able to answer with any confidence the questions surrounding the nature and culture of the self and its identity. These may prove to be, as Steven Lukes has said of power, essentially contested concepts, defying all attempts ultimately to define them.

There is a tradition in western social science to quote western theoretician-philosophers of the last several centuries—from Kant through Nietzsche to Taylor—in discussions of self and identity. A (western) hemisphere of wisdom lies in these works. But legacies of Enlightenment theories also run through some of these traditions. If we start from epistemologies crafted on other continents, a different way of engaging with questions of self and identity can emerge. For example, the entire debate about the dynamism of personhood and the Cartesian-generated notion that epistemology (the thinking self) stands separate from ontology (the experiencing being) is rendered moot in the following perspective. Interestingly, I found many Mozambicans held a view in resonance with that expressed by E. A. Ruch and K. C. Anyanwa:[1]

The African culture makes no sharp distinction between the ego and the world, African culture makes the self the centre of the world. . . . The world which is centered on the self is personal and alive. Self-experience is not separated from the experiencing self. The self vivifies or animates the world so that the soul, spirit or mind of the self is also that of the world. . . . What happens to the world happens to the self. Self disorder is a *metaphysical contagion* [italics in original] affecting the whole world." (1984:86–87)

It would appear to be equally valid to conclude, as many Mozambicans in fact do, that world disorder is a metaphysical contagion affecting the whole self. In creating solutions, both the tangble and the ineffable are equally privileged, and the self is defined by dynamism:

The African maintains that there can be no knowledge of reality if an individual detaches himself from it. Bear in mind that the African, a life-force, is not a passive spectator of the universe but an active participator of life-events. So, he operates with the logic of aesthetics which holds that the whole is real. Knowledge, therefore, comes from the co-operation of all human faculties and experiences. He sees, feels, imagines, reasons or thinks and intuits all at the same time. (94)

The knowledge presented in this perspective is not simply of the here and now, or of the personal alone. It is a knowledge imbued with a history and a society, as creative as it is reflective: "The African makes use of the concepts by inspection, imagination, and intuition, but all these have aesthetic qualities. The meanings of these concepts are derived from personal and immediate experience, from the social and historical experience of the people. The Africans do not only think about such concepts, they live and feel their realities" (95).

Another legacy of Enlightenment philosophy that is under challenge is the idea that the self is set and stable through life. William James was one of the first contemporary western theoreticians to lay to rest the ideal of a fixed identity: "Properly speaking, a man has as many social selves as there are individuals who recognize him and carry an image of him in their mind" (1890:295). And he continues with a line that could not speak more directly to the Mozambican experience: "To wound any one of these images is to wound him."

The richly nuanced complexity of self has recently come to stand as one if its defining characteristics in contemporary philosophy. Like the stories people fashion to survive the war, self is a continually emergent phenomenon: crafted, enhanced, re-sculpted. The process is a *creative* one.

What is essential about that self is not found primarily in its differences from others but in its freedom to pursue a story line, a life plot, a drama carved out of all the possibilities every society provides. . . . Our true authenticity, in this view, is not what we find when we try to *peel away* influences in search of a monolithic, distinctive identity. Rather it is the one we find when we *celebrate* addition of self to self, in an act of self-fashioning that culminates not in an in-dividual at all but in—and here we have to choose whatever metaphor seems best to rival Mill's bumps and grinds of atomized units—a kind of *society*; a *field* of forces; a *colony*; a *chorus* of not necessarily harmonious voices; a manifold *project*; a *polyglossia* that is as much in us as in the world outside us. (Booth 1993:89; italics in original)

Self-identity thus emerges as a complex fluid *process*. Identity is, ultimately, "a way of endowing ourselves with significance" (West 1992:21). It extends beyond sheer personal significance, providing people with a way in which "you can be held together in the face of the terrors of nature, the cruelties of fate, and the need for some compensation for unjustified suffering: what the theologians used to call the problem of evil" (21).

It is interesting that questions of identity often arise, as Cornel West has observed, in the face of terror (warfare) and cruelty. It is perhaps here that people meet the most significant challenges to their sense of self and humanity. "Violence," as Allen Feldman (1991:5) has noted, "itself both reflects and accelerates the experience of society as an incomplete project, as something to be made." A person's own experience of self is much like breathing air. Under normal circumstances we take it for granted; it is only when our supply, our existence, is threatened that we take notice. Gasping, people seek new sources of survival; they seek to understand what it is they need, and how it is they are to go about getting it. This is perhaps why, as unsettling as the topic of violence is, it is often one that leads us to core aspects of human nature and culture.

Re-Creation and the Imagination

Self, culture, and reality are regenerative. If people are defined by the world they inhabit, and the world is socially and culturally constructed by the people who consider themselves a part of it, people ultimately control the production of reality and their place in it. They produce themselves. As much as terror-warfare tries to dismantle the viable person, people fight back. They create themselves in resistance.

In turning to the question of how people build worlds anew, I find the theories on the cultural construction of reality[2] relevant but inadequate. They start from the basis of an operating culture which imparts knowledge through interpersonal interaction. These theories were produced by western philosophers whose understandings may have come from the fact that they found their worlds internally shattered, but they were not forced to produce their theories in a world that was as well externally shattered. What happens when very little of social and cultural relevance is left intact? Worlds cannot simply be created, they must be created anew.

The dilemma is clear: between the world as it was, the world as it should be, and the now of a world destroyed lies an abyss, a discontinuity, a need to define the one by the other, and the impossibility of doing so. Identity hinges on bridging this gap.

The solution, Mozambicans taught me, lies, in part, with the imagination.[3] When people look out over a land that should resonate with meaning and life but that now stares blankly back with incomprehensible images of barren fields, broken communities, tortured bodies, and shattered realities, they are left with the choice of accepting a deadened world or creating a livable one. It is the imagination—creativity—that bridges the abyss, if not to reconstruct the past, to make the present livable.

Elaine Scarry (1985:163) has argued that pain unmakes the world, and imagining makes it. Together "pain and imagining are the 'framing events' within whose boundaries all other perceptual, somatic, and emotional events occur; thus, between the two extremes can be mapped the whole terrain of the human psyche." She invokes Sartre in exploring the idea that absence provokes an imagining of a special sort:

> Sartre, for example, draws conclusions from the fact that his imagined Pierre is so impoverished by comparison with his real friend Pierre, that his imagined Annie has none of the vibrancy, spontaneity, and limitless depth of presence of the real Annie. But, of course, had he compared his imagined friends not to his real-friends-when-present but to his wholly absent friends, his conclusions would have been supplemented by other, very different conclusions. That is, the imagined Pierre is shadowy, dry, and barely present compared to the real Pierre, but is much more vibrantly present than the absent Pierre. (163)

In like fashion, it is the destruction of the world that prompts such vivid powers of imagining in victims of war and violence. But unlike Scarry's view, some Mozambicans are able to imagine their real friend, their real home, their real society and culture as vibrantly as the "real thing." We can afford to leave underdeveloped our ability to imagine our real friend Pierre in a reasonably stable world. But when Pierre is dead, disappeared, or maimed, and when the world that held him is so hopelessly destroyed that, left in such a state, it can only ring a death toll for the society affected, people must create. To do so, they must first imagine what it is they are going to create. People cannot simply re-create what has been before. If they refashion their lives as they knew them, they create conditions as vulnerable to attack as existed previously. But worse, much of what occupied their previous world is gone: communi-

ties ruined by attacks; family members and friends lost or killed; possessions looted or destroyed; rituals rendered ineffective.

Identity, too, is reforged to withstand the assaults of chaos and violence. When not only Pierre is lost, but also everything a person holds
dear, the person is lost as well. People must imagine themselves in
new and vital ways. To do so rests on the fundamental question of who
we are. The answer to this explains why terror-warfare does not suc-
ceed in neutralizing a population into domesticated acquiescence. It
would appear that this form of warfare starts from the Enlightenment
assumption that "self" is a set and concrete substance. But as I have
discussed above, self is better viewed as a complex process of constant
self-production. People are the sum total of the reflections (ontic) of
the world on them as they interact with it, and their reflections (epi-
stemic) on these experiences. Continually engaged in the process of
experiencing and being, people are constantly increasing their repertoire of thinking, self-reflexivity, and being-in-the-world. The sum total
of humans' understanding of both self and world is far greater than
human experience in the world. People have reflected on one experience from various vantage points offered by other experiences. They
have viewed time, place, and event in the world as physical attributes,
as symbolic ones, as mythological ones, as spiritual ones, as imaginary
ones. People do this continuously as experience carries them through
work, narrative, ritual, play; and as self-rumination personalizes being-
in-the-world. The fact that everyone brings his or her own personalized
universe to bear in self-creation explains the tremendous variation we
see in people's responses, from the isolation and anguish of the father
and his daughter in the bush to the wry humor of the young women
scouting for food outside refugee camps, from the rogue traders in flesh
that benefit from the dislocations of war to the storytellers who try to
teach people how to resist oppressors.

For Scarry (1992), imagining is grounded in perceptual mimesis. For
the Mozambicans contemplating their ruined villages and contentious
political imbroglios, there is little to mime, and imagining becomes an
act of pure creativity.

Not all Mozambicans have such developed powers of creative imagining. Not unusually, the creative members of the culture—healers, vision-
aries, performers—have developed these skills to a fine art. Their talents
lie not only with their abilities to imagine, but to convey these images
to others so that they too may share in the reconstruction of their symbolic and social universes. I visited a number of communities that had
been recently decimated by the war. One of the most powerful experiences I had at these times was sitting with people amid the fragments of
their homes and communities, listening and watching the imagining—

the creation of identity, home, and resistance afresh. I choose the word watching as well as listening purposefully: as the Mozambicans talked about what had happened and what will happen, and as they discussed this in the context of human nature and the meaning of life, I found I could not only understand, but "see" the world they were creating. Apparently so did the others present. New identities of suffering and resistance were forged, home was reinvented, the world was revitalized with significance, people survived.

Self, identity, world, culture, and being are inseparably interwoven. They are mutually defining, and they are experienced as a composite whole. To attack any of these is to attack them all. And to attack them is to instigate the creative process. Susan Langer (1942) has said that the mind can tolerate anything but chaos. Yet it appears that the human mind's revulsion with chaos ultimately manifests itself in the urge to repair it—to supply it with comprehensibility and order. This is not to say that this order is necessarily a positive one for all: sadistic soldiers, jackals preying on the victims of war, lonely refugees, resistance fighters, and poets seeking to subvert the hold of violence all produce themselves in the midst of chaos in a way that somehow makes sense to them.

For Sartre and Scarry, it appears as if the landscapes of our social and physical world carry a weight that impresses itself on our imaginations; however, the landscapes of the mind are equally vibrant, rich, and nuanced—and they are endlessly creative. They extend beyond the horizons of the physical, the temporal, and the social world to delve into the potential and the possible—as expansive as our sleeping and waking thoughts and dreams. The landscapes of the mind and of the world resonate within the other. The vitality of the former easily matches the latter and, if need be, can create it, and ourselves within it. This process is not easy to capture in words, but in turning to the subject of creativity I will explore some of the ways in which this autopoiesis is produced in practice.

Notes

1. See Masolo (1983), Oruka (1983); Jackson (1989); and Okot p'Bitek (1983) for similar analyses of African epistemology. I do not mean to imply by these quotes that any single "African epistemology" can be universalized. Certainly these texts referencing African philosophy are no more a generalization than Kant's, Nietzsche's or Taylor's discussions of "the self."

2. For the early definitive works on the social construction of reality, see James (1976, 1978), Schutz (1962, 1964), and Berger and Luckmann (1967).

3. I do not use imagination here in quite the same way as Castoriadis (1987). Although for Castoriadis the imagination is a central force in the creation and perpetuation of society and culture, he is more concerned with social level con-

structions. For him, imagination is not something that accrues to specific individuals and consciousnesses, but unfolds as a socio-cultural process. It is the dynamic between action, institution, and change that stirs the imagination into its creative processes. There is much of value in what Castoriadis writes, but I am concerned here as well with a creativity that is equally immediate, individual, interpersonal, and world forming. It includes the interactive daily events that Ueland (1992:105) writes about when she says that in the profound current of listening and talking people are constantly being recreated. "And it is this little creative fountain inside us that begins to spring and cast up new thoughts and unexpected laughter and wisdom." For Ueland, this creative fountain exists within all of us: "It is the spirit, or the intelligence, or the imagination."

Chapter 7
Mundus Imaginalis:
The Creation of Self and World

Moçambique

Moçambique, the time has come
to awaken
The time has come to look
for your children
hungry, with swollen bellies
for the skeletal mothers
for the elderly without
ears, or arms.
The time has come to clean
the ashes and to awaken
To awaken for peace.

—Maria

Center of Displaced People, Gorongosa district, Sofala
province, 1988. Photo by Anders Nilsson.

Sculpting Creativity and Resistance

I no longer ask whether the creation of self and world is a possibility. From the broken bodies and the ashes of burned towns in Mozambique, I have seen people forge themselves and their worlds in new and vital ways. Yet scholars have few tools for explaining these phenomena. In a world where most people interact in a relatively coherent social universe, we seldom see people building wholly new universes of meaning and action. We seldom see sheer creativity.

In a relatively stable society, creativity is largely emergent, as Renato Rosaldo, Smadar Lavie, and Kirin Narayan (1993:5) write: "Members of a society's younger generations always select from, elaborate upon, and transform the traditions they inherit." It is perhaps this fact that has led these authors to conclude, in agreement with Edward Sapir, that "Invention takes place within a field of culturally available possibilities, rather than being without precedent. It is as much a process of selection and recombination as one of thinking anew. Creativity emerges from past traditions and moves beyond them; the creative persona reshapes traditional forms (Sapir 1924:418, quoted in Rosaldo et al. 1993:5)." For most times and places, I agree with these conclusions. But what happens when young and old alike inherit a world undermined by the chaos violence has wrought, a world where the traditions themselves are strategic targets in a very dirty war? Until I witnessed some of the ways in which people struggle with devastating chaos in Mozambique, I never questioned the assumptions that cast creativity as a more or less coherent process of transformation that built upon "the old" in achieving a "newer," if not a "new."

I have begun to accept that, at special times, a true spark of creativity is possible, a spark that defies the logic of tradition and the bounds of the culturally possible to forge the wholly new. Yet this spark of creativity is not a light in an otherwise darkened horizon. It is attended by the minutia of daily acts that take place within a field of cultural possibilities; it works amid processes of cultural selection and recombination that hone the day-to-day manifestations of the creative process. In this sense, Rosaldo, Lavie, and Narayan (1993:5) are right when they say that "mundane everyday activities become as much the locus of cultural creativity as the arduous ruminations of the lone artist or scientist." Every society is replete with artists and scientists, many of whom have never seen the inside of a school.

I am reminded of walking down a road in a town in the northern province of Cabo Delgado and chancing upon several men sitting under a tree fashioning wooden sculptures. This area of Mozambique is famous for its sculptures, sophisticated figures that in their poetry of shape and form capture a raw essence of life and politics. Many of the sculptures are of bodies, parts of bodies, or collectivities of bodies that are artistically, and often tragically, misshapen: cavernous mouths calling out, grotesquely large hands reaching out, impossibly ponderous breasts bereft of nursing infants, all featured on bodies grotesquely emaciated in places. Yet the poetry and fluidity of the movement of the bodies and their messages, the intertwining of people and their motifs, speak to a collective spirit of resource and resistance. The art represents the *povo*, the people.

I stopped to talk with the men and look at their work. One piece in particular caught my attention. It was a cross between a mask and a sculpture of a face. It was as large as a human head, but had a curious ripple effect as if it were seen refracted through water. The eyes, nose, and mouth were inhumanely expanded to dominate the face: the eyes wide open and staring through distended pupils, the nose swooping across the face in a slant that placed the nostrils below the right eye, the mouth open and swinging from one side of the face to the other. One tooth glinted on the right side in lips drawn up in what might have been a smirk or a smile. Inside the mouth on the other side was the figure of a man: the head emerging between the teeth and lips, the arm holding onto the lip itself, the torso extending out from behind the inside of the mouth.

Enamored by the strange and poignant sculpture, I asked the artist to explain the story behind it. He set down his tool, leaned back against a tree, picked up the mask-head, and looked at it as if he were about to engage it in conversation.

In our history, there lives among us a very evil person, a demon. This is a powerful being, a being who craved ever more power, who craved things, those in his grasp and those beyond his reach. And he cared nothing for others, they were food fueling his evil intentions, filling his belly. None of us could be said to be truly safe from his appetites. He ate people, he chewed them up and swallowed them down into his big belly. But these people, they do not chew so easily; no, we do not chew and die just like that. These people, you see, they began to stir in his belly, to climb up out of his stomach and into his mouth, across his tongue, past his teeth to the freedom beyond his lips. He tried to chew these people up and swallow them again, and he bit down on them with a ferocious force. But when he chomped down on these people, he broke his teeth on them—the more he bit and chewed, the angrier he got, the more he broke his teeth. These people he ate, they could not be kept in his stomach. They could not be bit off or ground down with his teeth. They just kept climbing up and out as he raged and bit down and spit out pieces of his teeth. This person you see here, he is defeating this demon, he has emerged out of his stomach, alive, to the light of day.

When he finished the story, the sculptor dropped his narrative tone and fixed me with a serious look: Did I understand? I looked around me at the hungry, thin child in the yard across the way; at the dilapidated houses of impoverished refugees crowding through the town; at the imported truck rumbling down the road, a possession rare enough to serve as a constant reminder that a privileged few managed to maintain, or gain, fortunes through war. I looked back at the man and the carved face he had propped on his knee and nodded that I thought I understood. He handed me the carving and settled back into his working position. In a quiet voice reinfused with the tone of a storyteller, he added, as much to the piece of wood he had picked up as to me: "It is an old story, but it is still our story."

As the sculptor's account shifted back and forth from past to present tense, the carving seemed to cast a long shadow from the present back through history. From colonialists to slavers, from usurious marketeers to warmongers, the grinding of the demon's teeth as he bit down on his prey was still all too audible.

The Problem of Hobbes — World-Making and the Imagination

Also grinding down on people in the last century has been the Hobbesian-esque notion that social order depends on established and smoothly functioning social and political institutions. Like political alliances, blackmarketeers, and the networks of military supplies and personnel that link zones of contention around the world, this Hobbesian notion is international in its construction and impact. It has been forged across political institutions, nation-states, and military treatises. The perspective is not restricted to occidental or modernist thought. The Chinese philosopher Hsün-tzu (298–338 BCE) developed a similar analysis of human nature and politics (see Nishida 1990). This view posits that elites—those who build and maintain social institutions—create order from the inherent chaos that is the raw state of humanity. The corollary of this notion is that when the social institutions governing society break down, the world and the people in it revert to a "dog-eat-dog" mentality—that chaos prevails as self-interest and personal gain override a concern with the good of humanity. This notion is clearly tied to the dynamics of power: if order is established through social institutions, then top-down hierarchies of control through political, military, religious, and educational structures are legitimated as necessary. These institutions keep in check the chaotic dog-eat-dog urges growling and snapping at the edges of civilized society. But is this scholarship? Philosophy and not politics? How often do the scholars that propound these theories see or study worlds destroyed?

Creativity as world-making has been obscured by this Hobbesian-esque line of reasoning in occidental thought. If social institutions determine order, the founders and elites of social institutions are then the locus of forging order from chaos. Creativity is relegated to the individual, the elite, and the institutionally bounded. Thus, while individual acts of creativity have been empirically explored to some extent, the generation of wholly new universes of meaning—the dynamics of meaningful world-making—remains largely unexplored in academia, more relegated to poetics than to scholarship. This Hobbesian legacy ripples through a number of epistemological traditions from traditional political science to the Bladerunner-esque forms of post-modernism. Such a "worldview" is not simply apocalyptic, it is a call for some form of hegemony. In traditional science it is cast in terms of the need for informed political elites to wrest order from the anarchy of the masses; in more progressive social and literary sciences it is presented as a need for informed intellectuals who can see through the vicissitudes of hegemonically induced despair in postmodern existentialism. Yet the true realm of the day-to-day experience of creating self and world by those who populate the world is largely ignored in these scholarly assumptions. And in a curious irony, while contemporary scholars acknowledge that reality is culturally constructed, this Hobbesian-esque view supports the idea that there is something essential to culture—something enduring, something given—the culture-nature of the "political animal."

Hobbes aside, the whole question of the cultural constitution of reality, while central to much of contemporary theory, remains largely unexplored. When theoreticians speak of the cultural construction of reality, they are mostly speaking of the cultural reconstruction of reality: how individuals are introduced into a larger meaningful universe, and navigate the rules and realities they are confronted with given the tools their culture(s) provide. In this sense, to create is to "add to," to go beyond what is given. But the given is "always already"; it is a foundation of culture, self, and identity through which creativity emerges. People are not expected first to create themselves, then their worlds, and then their actions. Yet they do. But how?

Mundus imaginalis. The term is used by Henry Corbin (1969, 1972) to refer to a very precise order of reality, which corresponds to a very precise order of perception. It refers to the creative imaginary.[1]

We realize immediately that we are no longer confined to the dilemma of thought and extension, to the schema of a cosmology and a gnoseology restricted to the empirical world and the world of abstract intellect. Between them there is a world that is both intermediary and intermediate, described by our authors as the . . . world of the image, the *mundus imaginalis*: a world that is ontologically as real as the world of the senses and that of the intellect. This world requires its own faculty of perception, namely, imaginative power, a faculty with a cognitive function, a *noetic* value which is as real as that of sense perception or intellectual intuition. (Corbin 1972:7)

Fundamentally and perceptually real, yet a place outside of all places— "outside of *where*" (1972:7), the realm of the imagination mediates between sense and intellect, matter and mind, inside (self) and outside (self-in-world), the given and the possible.[2]

It is important to hold in mind that for Corbin the imagination is a noetic, cognitive power, "an organ of true knowledge" (1972:13). Beyond being perfectly real, its reality is more irrefutable and coherent than that of the empirical world, where reality is perceived by the senses.[3] Western epistemology tends to locate the creative in special individuals and their specific acts; it is a singular, personal, individual productiveness. Corbin discards the idea that one mind can stand as the sole substratum for the creative. *Mundus imaginalis* is a metaphysical necessity: the imagination is the cognitive function of this world. Building on Corbin, Jadran Mimica (1991:36) adds: *the imagination is the main source of autopoiesis.*

How do we navigate the theoretical shoals and empirical reefs of researching the creation of self and world *in* the everyday world among real people? When scholars come to theorize self's potential for creativity, they encounter a series of dilemmas. Primary among these is that the Enlightenment left western theoreticians with a legacy that accepts that there *is* some "truth" we can speak about the creation of knowledge. In one of the most profound ironies of postmodernism—a set of theories that eschews paramount explanations and established truths— many theoreticians posit "truths of perception and knowledge." We find scholars variously arguing that perception is primary, that language conditions cognition, that proto-conscious symbols exist to inform action. Closer to the topic at hand, we find scholars debating if imagination is spoken before seen (Ricoeur), flimsy recollections of reality (Sartre), generative of reality (Castoriadis), or moral (Heller). The modern and post-modern alike in this sense try to "fix" a starting point of reality, be it semiotic, perceptual, moral, performative. It is an attempt to try to fashion a "truth" of being.[4]

It seems to me these various theories do not constitute a discussion about any transcendent way of "knowing," but are a reflection of the fact that we all know differently. This notion applies equally to Mozambicans on the frontlines and academics in their offices. The possibilities of relationships to knowing and the creation of knowledge are as vast as the possibilities people as a whole are capable of employing. As I sit here at my computer writing about the angst of war and the hope of creative transcendence, dancers are dancing this same set of themes, painters are painting it, singers are singing it, poets are crafting poetry about it, victims are feeling it, children are learning it—all in the ways their own individual capacities and talents lead them. None is more powerful, more accurate, or more moral than the others. We cannot privilege one form of presentation over others.

Scholars live and work in a world of words written and spoken. They do not dance or sing or paint their observations; they think and speak and write them. Thus there is a tendency among academics and writers to privilege not only the written, but the fundamental role of language as an ontic reality. Western theories are replete with assumptions positing reason as semiotically founded, consciousness as irrevocably language linked, and being as discursively founded. It is not surprising that images and imagining have either been relegated to a sideline or subsumed under a larger "discursive truth"—they are not language-bound. Yet many nonacademics agree that there is much to the creation and expression of knowledge that is non-language based. Language is one of many capacities available to humans; it is like one of many senses which together reveal our realities.

This discussion is a preface to a core piece of my ethnographic data. I have "seen" (a western phrase elevating sight to knowing) Mozambicans create worlds from the voids of burning embers that were once home, family, and accepted reality. The problem I face is not with the knowing or understanding of this, but with translating it into words, words incapable of fully communicating this experience, this creativity. Possibly this dearth of explanatory tools relates back to the simple fact that writers depend on language. How can we write of that which does not partake of language? How can we communicate what the printed word cannot convey? Yet in the same way that the lack of knowledge of the circular nature of the earth or the circulatory system of the human body once thwarted, but did not arrest, scientific understanding, I do not think our inability to transcribe some of life's larger realities should obscure the fact that we theorize in an academic world limited by a language not yet capable of encompassing the vicissitudes and depths of existence.

Creating Linkages, Creating Society: Symbologues and the Complexities of Creative Resistance

While the description of the sheer font of the creative act—the forging of *mundus imaginalis* into *mundus literalis,* of imagined worlds into literal ones—may defy the scope of the written word at present, the ways in which world-making is sustained as part of daily living is easier to explain. In this book, I have talked about how people in Mozambique used parables, myths, songs, stories, poetry, theater, and a host of other creative tools to forge and circulate knowledge about surviving and resistance, about world-making and self-affirmation. I have termed these *symbologues*: dialogue through symbols. These constitute much more than a conversation. They are creative blueprints for "making" the world and imbuing it with vitality. Symbologues are active forms of resistance and fonts of social identity. I will add a few additional examples in the context of following creativity from inception to realization by returning to the theme of sculpture introduced above.

Monkeys

The mask story that opened this chapter reminds me of another set of intriguing figures. Like the mask, the following example of sculpture is a story of resistance that circulates from person to person across linguistic and tribal divisions. When I first went to Mozambique in 1988, the war economy was such that few market goods of any kind were available. I was always interested in the fact that one of the things that could be found with some regularity was a set of three little carved monkeys: see no evil, hear no evil, speak no evil. This seemed especially telling considering the Renamo tactics of severing people's ears and lips. One day I was sitting on the curb talking with a street vendor acquaintance with whom I frequently discussed the war which had taken his legs, his family, his home, and better days. During a lull in the conversation, with a sly twinkle in his eye, he pulled out a set of three monkeys to show me. The first monkey had one hand over his mouth and the other over one eye, but the second eye peered out wide open and both ears were uncovered and listening. The second monkey had one hand over one eye and the other hand over one ear—this time the mouth uncovered and opening to speak, and still one eye watching and one ear listening. The last monkey sat with a cynical grin on its face: eyes, ears, and mouth open and cognizant, with both hands covering its groin. The subversive message of the monkeys—that we will watch, listen, and speak, but we will "cover our tails" in doing so—circulates along war's paths across the country. The first part of the message conveys resistance, the second laces it with wry humor. The two together have given many hope and the will to survive a very dirty war.

In warzones it can be physically dangerous to speak directly about the war. So "symbologues" (dialogues based on symbolic representations) like the monkeys and masks, the songs and parables and jokes, circulate—each a palimpsest of meaning where "mythical" or "imaginary" villains, heroes, murderers, and traitors implicate contemporary actors in the war drama. Everyone in the know "knows" what is being conveyed about whom: who to trust, fear, avoid. And in this, people are creating a world of increasing safety and knowledge for themselves and their communities to defy chaos and oppression.

Vem Amor, Vem

Some of the antiwar efforts that took place in Mozambique were far from subtle. One of my favorite examples was the play *Vem Amor, Vem* (Come Love, Come) put on in the capital city of Maputo by the theatrical group Mutumbela Go-Go. The play was a loose adaptation of the Greek play *Lysistrata* set in war-torn Mozambique. *Vem Amor, Vem* was written during the time the government was negotiating with Renamo for a peace accord. The negotiations were taking place in Rome, and the newspapers were full of stories about the fine accommodations and luxurious conditions the negotiators were enjoying. The negotiations, however, did not put a stop to the killing in Mozambique, and during the time the papers were reporting the talks in Rome they were also carrying stories of the many people killed daily in Mozambique as the war raged on.[5]

The play opens with an attack in the suburbs of Maputo, one of the many frequent attacks people in the country faced during this time. One market woman killed during the attack is transformed into a spirit, and she works to find a solution to the war. She decides that the war is made by men, and women should be able to divise a way to stop it. She determines that they should stop making love to men until the killing ceases. The spirit starts to mobilize the women in the markets to make deals with their boyfriends and husbands to find a way to end the war. The market women point out that if they enact a sex strike at home their men will simply go to the prostitutes in the area, so the spirit and the market women go to the prostitutes to seek their help and mobilize them to stop the war. The prostitutes point out that, although the market women can give up sex and still make money to feed their families, for them to give up sex is to give up their means to feed their families. So the market women strike a deal to support the prostitutes during the sex strike. The play shows not only the process of mobilizing the women, but the problems they have with government representatives. In one scene, a representative of the government (a play on the prime minister) approaches the women on a skateboard to try to get them to stop the strike because it is so "uncomfortable." The government representatives keep making excuses: "The peace process is difficult, it can't be solved so easily; these are delicate negotiations, you women don't understand." The women respond that while these men are making war and not solving it, women and children are the ones being killed. Some of the men physically threaten the women if they continue their strike. In the face of the intimidation and the frustration from lack of sex, some of the women begin to have nightmares and worry that they may betray their compatriots. When one woman weakens and is about to make love to her husband, the spirit of the murdered market woman appears to her to give support and strength to continue with the strike. The play ends on a successful note: the peace accords are signed, the war ends, and in the last scene, the women say *vem Amor, vem.*

The play was a powerful and public message to the government that during the long protracted peace accords, during the "battles" around the negotiating table in Rome over words and phrases in the treaty, attack after attack was taking place, and taking lives, in Mozambique. The negotiations were doing nothing to alleviate suffering. Only the end of the war could do that. Such political frankness is an act of courage in a warzone. It is also a very effective act. Governments and their wars can continue only so long without popular support. These groundswell actions for peace, often deleted from traditional political and military science treatises on war, are potent mechanisms in bringing violence to a halt.

Teachers and Traders

There were many ways people worked to subvert terror and destruction and to reconstruct a purposeful social universe. Creating social linkages across no-man's-lands and among tribal groups was an important means of doing this. Average civilians on the frontlines set up remarkable resources. These actions were self-generated: they depended on no established social institutions or political infrastructures. People established services to find lost and kidnapped family members, find homes for orphans, and care for the wounded and maimed. They instituted healing ceremonies, and even classes in primary schools, for the war-traumatized. They organized informal food exchange programs, markets, and resource centers. They set up dispute resolution committees and informal mechanisms to take care of the dislocated and impoverished. They initiated communication networks to inform people about attacks, troop movements, political developments, and safe zones. They created a warzone society with functioning social institutions.

Often people provided community services on the frontlines at considerable danger to themselves. Teachers are only one example of many. People who worked to build community services for one political party were the primary targets of the other throughout Mozambique. Teachers, health care professionals, and administrators were sought out for persecution and execution by both Frelimo and Renamo. Worse, a teacher or nurse could be taken by one side and forced to provide services, and then shot by the other side for doing so. I remember arriving at a town that had been completely burned out and looted. Nothing of value, from crops to building materials, was left, including school materials (and the school, from which everything of value had been taken or destroyed). The war rolled over towns time and again in Mozambique; most people in battlezones lived their day-to-day lives preparing for another attack. One would think in this climate, activities like schooling would be relegated to second-place nonessentials, but when I walked into town I was greeted by a group of children sitting under a tree "in class." A teacher from the community had elected not to flee the area even though it was commonly known that soldiers targeted educators. And, completely on this teacher's initiative, classes for the children of the community had been set up—under a tree, for the schoolhouse was no more. The teacher worked without texts, writing materials, or supplies. Children were taught to master writing and do school lessons by writing in the dirt under the tree with sticks. The classes were well attended. Such stories were legion throughout Mozambique.

Not all people who worked to reforge a viable social universe did so in traditional institutional settings. Traders provide a telling example. Traders often walked hundreds of miles across embattled zones with goods that could bring little financial compensation. Why make such a trip? As I listened to such traders talk, I realized that through their journeys they performed invaluable services far exceeding the scope of transmitting goods. They carried messages for families and friends separated by the fighting; conveyed details on deployments and dangers; and transmitted critical economic, crop, trade, and political news, not to mention gossip and irreverent stories, between communities severed from one another by the war. They linked different ethnic and language groups in a statement that the war was not about local rivalries, and could not be if they were to survive. They forged trade and social networks through the disordered landscapes of violence. And, by walking through lethal frontlines, they simply defied the war in a way that everyone they passed could enjoy and draw strength from. They were, literally, constructing social order out of chaos.

Kids Creating

Children as well as adults create systems of knowledge and survival. Orphaned street children stand as one of the more poignant examples for me. I mentioned earlier that my lodgings in Zambezia were located on a street that "housed" a significant number of homeless children. Most days, coming home from work, I sat and talked with the children and gave them some help in finding food and clothing. In an irony evident to most fieldworkers, these children often had the most current and detailed information on attacks, troops movements, zones of safety and danger, and resources. They established an organization on the streets where they helped care for the younger children and newer arrivals, helping them find safe places to sleep, food to eat, and a bit of clothing to wear. Knowledge was a resource, and its circulation a primary activity. One of the most surprising foci of information was that dealing with education. Many of the homeless children were concerned with going to school. Information on what schools might accept them, what resources they needed to attend school, and how they could obtain these resources was a common topic of conversation. Education was viewed as a means to get off the streets, as a valuable survival tool. Information on education circulated like a commodity: a symbol of hope for the future.

Jackals

Of course, creativity is not solely relegated to those things concerned with the ultimate good for a society. People create dangerous systems of oppression and exploitation as well. Thus battlezones demonstrate a constant tension between those profiting from violence and its dislocations, and those working to refashion a stable, peaceful existence. Each trader, teacher, healer, or civilian engaged in establishing social order dealt with the harsh truths that there existed among them those who exploited networks of violence for self-gain. Arms merchants, mercenaries, modern-day slavers, thieves, murderers, and other jackals also set up self-generated social institutions.

People readily distinguished between jackals who profited from the war but also ensured that their countrypeople profited somehow and those jackals who harmed others in their profit-seeking. People falling into the first category were those who, like the man Flavia's husband paid to find his kidnapped mother, took money to find missing relatives or get them released from military bondage. These people did provide a service, and desperate people were reunited with lost family members. The placing of a monetary sum—and often an extravagant one at that—on matters of honor and the heart was what rankled most people.

There were, however, those who profited from the war by incurring even greater brutality and suffering. I am reminded of a riot that broke out one day in the capital city of Maputo. Cars were stopped, overturned, and burned, their occupants beaten. The riots were reported in the papers, but not the reason for the rioting. After some investigation, I discovered locals were trying to put a stop to an international network that sold Mozambican children—mostly disenfranchised war orphans—into domestic and sexual labor in what was at that time apartheid South Africa. The United Nations has sent up an alarm about the worldwide rise in this kind of racketeering, calling it modern-day slaving (Nordstrom 1996b).

Healers

What is of interest is that *most* people did *not* create abusive systems of self-gain and power. One of the most prevalent examples of creativity in Mozambique, grounded in the concepts of African medicine, demonstrates this well. Most ground-level actions to create meaning in the face of destruction involved the principles of Mozambican/African medicine. In fact, every healer I talked with in Mozambique (and this numbered in the hundreds) had developed methods to help people survive the war in a humane fashion, and to institute peacebuilding processes in doing so. And in all my conversations with Mozambicans during my stay in the country, I found only one person who did not consult with Curandeiros when their problems become pressing. Curandeiros helped people reconstitute their worlds in the most profound of ways. The success was in part due to the fact that traditional healing combines individual and collective resources—cultural wisdom applied by individuals to meet specific circumstances, flexible, fluid, enduring—a tradition dedicated to healing, protection, and re-creation at all levels of socio-cultural life. In a world where war profiteers do exist, this example shows that they do not predominate. It reminds us that under the most extreme circumstances, most people work to re-create a viable society, not demolish it.

The healing conceptualized in Mozambican/African medicine viewed violence as a pathology that needed to be cured like any other illness or misfortune. Hundreds of conversations I had with Mozambicans reflected their preoccupation with defusing the cultures of violence the war had wrought. It is a violence, they stress, that can last far beyond formal military cease-fires. People constantly reminded themselves and others about the insidious nature of violence to reproduce itself, and to destroy worlds and lives in this process. In doing so they set into motion a cultural dynamic that continually challenges the entrenchment of cultures of violence. The following is from a conversation with several older women in a village that had seen a great deal of devastation and lay largely in ruins. We were talking about the war's impact on people's lives:

> When people come back to our community after having been kidnapped and spending time with the Bandidos [Renamo], after having been harmed by [Frelimo] soldiers, or after their community has been destroyed by the war, there are a lot of things they need. They require food and clothing, they need a place to live, they need medical attention. But one of the most important things they need is calm—to have the violence taken out of them. We ask that everyone who arrives here be taken to a Curandeira or Curandeiro for treatment. The importance of the Curandeiro lies not only in her or his ability to treat the diseases and physical ravages of war, but in their ability to take the violence out of a person and to reintegrate them back into a healthy lifestyle. You see, people who have been exposed to the war, well, some of this violence can affect them, stick with them, like a rash on the soul. They carry this violence with them back to their communities and their homes and their lives, and they begin to act in ways they have never acted before. They bring the war back home with them—they become more confused, more violent, more dangerous, and so too does the whole community. We need to protect against this. The Curandeiros make consultations and patiently talk to the person, they give medicinal treatments, they perform ceremonies, they work with the whole family, they include the community. They cut the person off from any holds the war has on him or her, they scrape off the violence from their spirit, they make them forget what they have seen and felt and experienced in the war, they make them alive again, alive and part of the community. They do this with soldiers too. If someone finds a soldier wandering alone, we take him and bring him to a Curandeiro. Most people do not really want to fight, these soldiers have done terrible things, but many of them were kidnapped and forced to fight. They dream of their home and family and machambas [farms], of being far away from any war. The Curandeiros take the war out of them, they uneducate their war education. They remind the person how to be a part of their family, to work their machamba, to get along, to be a part of the community. They cure the violence that others have taught.

In the midst of war, the treatments of healers are not set prescriptions faithfully reproduced but creative acts in the most fundamental sense. Worlds are destroyed in war, so they must be recreated. Not just worlds of home, family, community, and economy—but worlds of definition, both personal and cultural.

The Peace Process

At a macro level in 1990 and 1991 while I was doing this research, the official political peace process was going through cycles of meetings and stalls, cease-fires and broken accords, diplomatic promises and withdrawals. Peace accords were being hammered out in various capital cities in the world, brokered by political elites from around the world. They took place far from the frontlines that continued to take untold lives. In fact, the war was never more lethal and destructive than during this time as each side tried to gain political advantage by demonstrating military strength. The civilians bore the brunt of these political exercises (Minter 1994).

International public support in these years went not to ensuring a defeat of one side by the other—as was the norm in Cold War relations—but to instituting multiparty elections with all formal political contenders represented in a government wherein all formal militaries were integrated. With the Cold War over Frelimo was diplomatically pressured to accept Renamo's demands for a multiparty democracy. In fairness to Frelimo, in these last years of war, they agreed to meet the majority of these demands. The peace process dragged out because Frelimo, within these constraints, sought to maximize its political position, and Renamo stalled to try to manipulate better political advantage. For example, when Manuel Antonio and his unarmed peasant army so successfully rooted Renamo in Zambezia and Nampula in 1990 and 1991, Renamo felt they had lost bargaining power in the eyes of Frelimo and the world. So they stalled the peace talks and mounted a large military attack to regain both territory and "military face." As a consequence, thousands died during this time and thousands more were forced to endure flight, starvation, and brutality.

The accounts I have given throughout this book, and in this chapter in particular, constitute key ways the population at large sought to affect the peace process in a political world where civilians and low-level military are locked out of formal political process for the most part. No peasants from the frontlines and no privates from either army were invited to Rome to help broker the accords.

As the talks resumed and failed, resumed yet again and broke down another time, the country as a whole was sustained largely by the work

and efforts of the average civilians discussed here. Few researchers follow illiterate traders, rural schoolteachers, and local healers as they
move around their communities and country forging both the principles
and the means to create and sustain peace and to heal the wounds of
war. Few have documented the sophisticated countrywide peacebuilding system these people forged day by day, from the ground up. Yet
without these people's work, the peace accord that was finally reached
in 1992 would never have been possible.

Mundus Imaginalis Moralis, **or Hobbes Appears to Be Mistaken**

Postulating a Humane Imagination

To postulate a creative imaginary does not, alone, do justice to the process of world-making, especially that undertaken in conditions of extreme violence. Although there is no doubt the usurious, the abusive,
the sadistic, and the untrustworthy create mechanisms to achieve their
own goals, such self-concern does not point to the conclusion that creativity is a process outside the bounds of positive and negative cultural
consequences. It is not Darwin's amoral adaptation to survival. I reached
this conclusion through a very simple observation. *Most* people I encounter in warzones work to create a healthy society. While the usurious
and abusive do exist, they do not predominate. In a society bereft of the
normal institutions that supposedly regulate society and moral norms,
people, for the most part, engage in humane world-building. In challenging the Hobbesian notion of chaos, I reiterate the level of destruction in which people in Mozambique struggled: one million out of 16
million died in the war. One-fourth were dislocated from their homes,
and fully one-half of the entire population were directly affected by
the war. One-third of all educational and health care institutions were
rendered inoperative, trade routes were devastated, and government
infrastructure was often rendered nonexistent. It is important to hold
in mind that a maximum of 60,000 troops (both Frelimo and Renamo)
out of 16 million people perpetuated this devastation. No police force,
no legal framework, no powerful traditional authority retained sufficient hold on the society to regulate behavior across Mozambique. Yet
I never encountered a community that succumbed to chaos, inertia, or
destructiveness. Certain individuals, yes; but they were in the minority.
Hobbes appears mistaken.

The creative imagination, then, would appear to contain a humane
or moral component, a fundamental ethics. In discussing this topic

one day with the Australian feminist political scientist Jan Pettman, she noted that her work had led her to postulate a "moral imagination." In her view, it entails a moral clarity concerning political realities; an ethical stance that, in John Rawls's view, allows people to empathize with the plight of others (see Pettman 1996). It is imbued with a political justice. It is not a valueless self-perpetuation for survival at all costs, but a world-building with an ethical foundation.

I realize positing a humane imagination takes reseachers into contested waters. This can be reminiscent of universalistic Enlightenment notions of moral reasoning. In fact, I do not agree with such moral essentializing. It has been used to create hierarchies of right and wrong that are more abusive than scholarly, usually placing the culture of the theorizer at the summit of moral reasoning. My stance is different: why, in the midst of a violent breakdown of order, do *most* people *not* respond with disorder and discord, but with vibrant ways of re-creation? Central to this position is Seyla Benhabib's (1992a, 1992b) view that ethics and morals are not abstract generalized universals, but concrete embodied realities. Ethics and morals are lived. They are lived by and through specific people living in specific circumstances with specific needs. There is, in essence, an embodied experiential ethics. Linking closely with the discussion of the creative production of self in Chapter 6, Benhabib (1992b:284) writes, "The self is not a thing, a substrate, but a protagonist of a life's tale." Self and action emerge in a universe of possibilities made meaningful through value judgments and moral discernments. There is no a priori value-free self.

I stand with Benhabib in arguing against Kant that any one moral position can be applied to all people and all times. Moral reasoning and ethical practice are cultural phenomena: culturally constructed, flexible, changing. Thus, while some may argue that it is ethical in their view to pillage their communities in times of stress, most recognize such behaviors, if applied across the board, are ultimately self-destructive. That the majority hold this view, and can agree on the fundamentals of moral foundations, results in the actuality of shared world-building. From the ashes of burned-out villages and broken families emerge new, shared communities. Communities that work. People do not blithely forget the traumas that necessitated such re-creation. If moral imaginations are forged with political clarity, as Pettman argues, they are created with the knowledge of the dangers of greed and sadism. But, for the most part, they are forged *against* such abusive realities. I give one caveat here, however. As with this whole book, my focus is with average civilians. It is clear that abusive political systems do emerge: political systems that are forged on greed and sadism. My interest here is with the people and communities that struggle in the midst of oppressive violence they seldom started and rarely support. Unlike Hobbes, it is here I found the foundations of self-creation and world-building.

This argument is not an exercise in blind idealism. To say people's creativity is endowed with an ethical imagination is not to say that people create worlds free of abuse and contestation. This harks back to the story of Lobster Boy introduced in Chapter 1. Lobster Boy, who brought the truth of pathos home to those who met him, beat his wife. People could not understand how a man who so profoundly felt the abuses of injustice could reproduce those injustices in his own family. There is no reason to conclude that, while people created new communities in war-torn Mozambique, they created communities free from injustice. Certainly theft, murder, oppression, domestic violence, sexual abuse, incest, and interpersonal aggression existed in the communities being rebuilt in Mozambique during the war. People might rail against the horrors of military abuse while beating family members. But what is of interest is that every community I visited recognized the potential of violence to reproduce itself, especially in conditions of severe war. Every community (and here I mean civil community) generated systems and institutions for dealing with exactly these problems. As discussed earlier, throughout Mozambique people recognized that war was reproduced on all levels of social life. Virtually every Mozambican I spoke with agreed with the healer who told me:

> People have just seen too much war, too much violence—they have gotten the war in them. We treat this, we have to—if we don't take the war out of the people, it will just continue on and on, past Renamo, past the end of the war, into the communities, into the families, to ruin us.

Responsibility and Moral Dilemmas

The sense of responsibility people held toward solving the cycles of violence confronting them often extended beyond a concern solely with the personal. This sense of responsibility was often born of moral imbroglios. I have discussed the belief many Mozambicans hold that the violence people commit follows them to disrupt the rest of their lives. If a person takes another's life, the soul of the murdered individual will cause harm to not only the murderer, but to the murderer's family and community as well. In the words of one of the respected elders in a community in the southern province of Gaza:

People involved in the war—especially soldiers—when they go back to their home, they carry the souls of those they have killed with them . . . these souls "stick" to them. They follow them into their homes and families. They can cause serious problems for the whole family, even the community. Remember, these are not just people that have been killed. They are someone's family, and now they are someone's ancestors.

Revenge ensures continuing cycles of violence, both revenge by the dead—restless because of the violent death—and revenge by the family and friends of the person killed. War or not, death is a personal issue. But personal does not translate into individual: responsibility for injustice is not solely an individual concern. Responsibility is a social issue. Some of the families of soldiers elected to perform peacebuilding acts on their own to try to mitigate the impact of these ongoing waves of violence. Families and communities who counted soldiers among their kindred often performed ceremonies to placate the dead. These ceremonies are not justifications of war, but attempts to stop violence altogether. In a number of cases, a family or community chose to pay a compensation to the family or community of those killed. During the war, it was not uncommon to hear of people from another community showing up in an embattled village to offer cows, goats, and other valuable resources. The message was clear. Nothing justifies this violence, even the actions of our own kin. This war is not about villagers, and we will do what is in our power to stop it. Even if the families and communities of soldiers did not participate in killing, they took responsibility for solving it.

In some cases the sacrifices made to stop ongoing cycles of violence were considerable. For example, in some cases, if a woman was killed before she had borne a child, a young girl of the family whose member was responsible for the killing would be given to the bereaved family to replace the loss. This demonstrates the lengths Mozambicans were at times willing to go in trying to stop the violence marring not only their lives, but the lives of everyone in the country. In a discussion of this with a curandeira one day, she said to me:

The winds and the water can carry the trauma of a battlefield to far reaches to affect innocent people. The spirits of the dead are restless, and walk about the country to affect everyone in their path. They increase the trauma of war. Bereaved people are susceptible to all kinds of illnesses: physical, emotional, spiritual. The violence that blows across the country is an illness. We have no protective vaccination against this contamination of war. We cure many of the ills such malaise brings about, but we cannot protect against it. These offerings people make to the beleaguered, they are taking responsibility for protecting their country from these ravages. They are doing what is in their own power to stop the horrors of war and killing.

Local/International: Locating the Font of Creativity

World-creating, then, involved the creation of systems to combat destructive behaviors in all arenas of life. While these could not stop all interpersonal abuses, the fact that these systems, and not ones that supported political and personal oppression, were created and set into motion at the civil level lends credence to the idea that the creative imaginary is more inclined toward creating viable rather than destructive worlds. In stressing my focus mainly on civil society, it was interesting for me to note that in Mozambique during the war, many transnational organizations did not support these local endeavors. Although money poured into health care, it was channeled to constructing clinics and hospitals, not to assisting African healers who were struggling to educate people away from a war mentality. Although millions of dollars were granted for educational redevelopment, almost nothing went to local and national programs to assist war-traumatized children at the primary school level. Although there was much concern with redrafting a legal system, almost no research was conducted on community systems of justice that developed to mitigate the abuses of war. The list of examples continues, and each attests to the fact that, while at the community level people institute remarkable systems of recovery and justice, they received little support from the more elite-controlled and powerful socio-political institutions operating in the world, perhaps because these institutions have a vested interest in the Hobbesian notion that formal social and political institutions are necessary to ensure political order and social morality. Community-generated solutions are often quite different, even contradictory to, those enforced through formal socio-political institutions. Ethical realities are forged in the complex dynamic of relations between these levels of social and political will. They are negotiated across the possible and the real.

Unmaking Violence

Creative world-building extends beyond the forging of social institutions to involve creating conceptual realms of meaning and action. One of the most profound examples is Mozambicans' commitment to "unmaking" violence. This idea stands in direct contrast to occidental views of violence. In the west, violence is subtly but powerfully presented as "thing-like." This is evident in the linguistic habits surrounding violence. The following phrases are common currency in the west: violence is avoided; violence is controlled; violence is surmounted; violence is turned inward or outward in anger; violence is released in cathartic mock-aggression; violence is held in check. These habitual responses to violence support the conclusion that violence is a fixed phenomenon. As a fixed phenomenon it becomes a manifest *thing*: set, enduring, concrete. Violence *exists*. This is in part a result of a tendency in traditional western epistemology to posit a fundamental naturalness to violence. Ten years of teaching peace and conflict studies have demonstrated to me that the majority of both popular and scholarly tracts on violence attribute some biological or natural foundation to violence. If violence is natural or biological in any sense, it is "determined"—that is to say, it has a specific *given* nature. Violence *is*. There is a dangerous aspect to this view of violence: if violence is a given, then there is nothing people can do other than to endure it, or protect against it.[6]

Most of the Mozambicans I spoke with, and especially those in civil society, hold a very different conceptualization of violence. In their view, violence is a fluid cultural construct. Violence is crafted into action by those seeking to control others. It is *made*. When it is employed by the abusive, it has serious repercussions for everyone. Those exposed to violence learn violence: and thus are capable of perpetuating it, as is evident in the many quotes given throughout this text that attest to the fact that people who have been brutalized by a military often return home more abusive themselves, more likely to employ violence to solve their own domestic and interpersonal dilemmas.

But people in Mozambique stress that if violence is made, it can be *unmade* as well.[7] In fact, it is not only an option, but an obligation of civil society to put into motion actions that unmake violence when it is employed against a society. If people *learn* violence, then they can *unlearn* it.

Sure, when people come here who have been exposed to violence in any way, we take care of them immediately. Their physical problems are a first priority, as so many are close to death with disease, beatings, starvation, who knows what. But their mental state is as important, and we make sure they see a healer as soon as they are able to calm their mental state. With what these people have seen and been through, their minds need as much attention as their bodies. But this is not the end of it all. We ask everyone who arrives to see a specialist in healing the war. These people, they've seen so much violence, it can destroy them, and worse, those around them—because people have learned violence, and they continue to act it. So these specialists, they treat people, they teach them how to live without this violence; they take the violence out of them. It is a strength, this learning how to stand up to the violence and defeat it. The whole community is expected to help: the healer teaches the person how to be reintegrated into a healthy community life, but we have to be sure that reintegration works. You can tell someone to go out and work a plot of land, but if they are battle-scarred, they may just not be able to move. We walk with them, talk with them, reach into the earth with them, coax a seed into food with them. We encourage them to do the ceremonies that protect them and their families and lands, appease their ancestors, make our community healthy and safe. You walk someone through these daily acts, with the help of the healers, they learn what words can never convey. We don't fight one side or the other in this war—we fight the war itself this way. We resolve the war in this way. And we heal its wounds in this way.

The reason peacebuilding in the midst of war was so successful in Mozambique was that the vast majority of people refused to restrict cultures of survival along community, language, tribal, class or gender lines. War was the enemy, and anyone fighting this enemy was a compatriot. Although I met a number of Mozambicans in government and military positions who elevated tribal loyalties to political causes, the majority of average civilians told me that to perpetuate tribal distinctions in the war was to perpetuate the war. Violence could only be defeated by refusing to be swayed by such divisions.

A related aspect of peacebuilding also helps to explain its success: one of the core values operating in Mozambique was that those who were helped then used this knowledge to help others. I discovered both the inter-community networks of support and the obligation to continue the tradition of helping one day when I was talking to four curandeiras about healing the wounds of war. In the midst of the conversation, a woman nearby began moaning loudly. I asked the curandeiras what the woman was suffering from. They explained that fighting was taking place outside of the town area, and the woman had stumbled into town that week and collapsed. She had a combination of physical and emotional war-induced problems they had not seen before, and they were baffled as to how to treat her. Because she was only partly coherent, and spoke their language only brokenly, they did not even know where the woman was from, or what had befallen her. They had ascertained that her family had all been killed and her village destroyed. They put out a call throughout the area, carried by word of mouth through healers, traders, and other travelers to find out if anyone could identify and treat her problems. They received a message from an old curandeiro well over a hundred kilometers away. He knew the problem, and had treated it successfully. He was now en route, traveling by foot. To reach them, he would have to walk through several areas of heavy fighting. When he arrived, he would spend sufficient time to treat the woman, and then to teach her how to cure others with these same problems. He knew, given the patterns of war, that others would suffer a similar fate, and someone in the area would need to know how to treat them. He also knew the four curandeiras hosting him had observed and treated war casualties that he had not yet seen, and that he would learn treatments to take back to his community when he returned. In accordance with the tenets of African healing, a person who has suffered an illness is more adept at treating others with the same problem. The nameless patient who had stumbled into town would be welcomed into this new community as a healer in her own right when she recovered; she would be given a home and respect. As her family and village were lost to her, this new location and the need for her skills would provide her with a foundation to re-build a life. The curandeiras, the patient, and the curandeiro who was coming to treat the woman were all of different language groups. The war severed people from their lives and communities, and people re-sponded by rebuilding these linkages across Mozambique.

There are no cultural canons, no legal doctrines, no religious texts in a society that specify how to treat these wounds of war and how, exactly, to rebuild in the face of destruction. Like the woman who stumbled into the village and collapsed with symptoms the medical personnel there had not seen before, wars continuously engender new kinds of violence and innovative responses to it. No one war can prepare people for the lived intricacies of another war or another day of war. What worked yesterday may not work today. One act of resistance is counteracted by a new form of violence and oppression. And new forms of resistance are forged in the face of these. Violence is constructed as a tool of re-pression. Creative responses are then set into play by the population to unmake the power and the potential of violence.

When these kinds of sensibilities and responsibilities become as widely reproduced as I found them to be in Mozambique—woven, as this book has demonstrated, through medicine, justice systems, art, education, religion, and daily stories, and across diverse language and cultural groups—they coalesce into a political movement. For ultimately, from medicine to art, these cultural precepts about violence and peacebuild-ing are about power, the abuse of power, dignity, and the truth of sur-vival. This is a political movement unaddressed in traditional political and military science treatises: there is no leader, no institutional bases, no strategic texts. It cannot be pinned down to any person, place, or ac-tivity. Perhaps that is why this "war against violence" ultimately proved to be so successful. I am convinced this is what paved the way for peace, and for an *enduring* peace. When a culture against war grows to the proportions it did in Mozambique, it becomes very difficult to sustain a war effort.

What is so powerful and innovative about this social process is that it is predicated on redefining violence in a nonviolent way. Fundamental to this sensibility is the idea that people choose to fight, not against one side or another, but against war itself. People choose to fight precisely by *not* employing violence as it has been used against them. This is in fact a potent solution. When people choose sides in a war, when they use the same kind of violence against others that has been used against them, they reproduce the political system and all of its justifications. Here, just the opposite took place: people delegitimized the political use of violence, both as a global process and a local reality. Rather than leaving the definition of community and security to the politico-military bodies, average Mozambican citizens took it upon themselves to reconstitute community, the body politic, security.

When average citizens met violence not with violence but by rebuilding town and citizenry, they were in effect saying that they did not need political institutions to forge community structure and keep social order. In doing this, they took political agency on themselves and away from formal governing institutions and military bodies. Unlike Hobbes, this was not a war of all against all, but the peacefulness of the many standing against the violence of the few. This position is in many ways heretical: if average citizenry in the midst of devastating social disorder and failed governing institutions are themselves capable of re-creating viable social and governing systems, how necessary are extensive controls of formal governing institutions? And even in the asking of this question, the necessity of these institutions is called into question—and hence their basis of power and privilege.

In Mozambique, the vast networks of creative resistance to violence, and the commitment to the unmaking of violence, preceded the peace accords. The Hobbesian legacy would have us believe that elite-brokered peace accords restore order to a disordered society. In forging political and military solutions to war, peace is brokered and violence reigned in and controlled. I found the inverse to be true: civil society crafted sophisticated institutions to stop violence and to heal the wounds war left in its wake. Average civilians unmade the possibility and the power of violence, and in doing so they set the stage for peace. They, in fact, created the conditions of peace. They made war an impossibility. And it was on this work that the peace accords were built.

Notes

1. *Mundus imaginalis* is a term Corbin uses in exploring the ontic significance of Arabic and Persian religious texts. He explains that the theosophers of Islam depict three interrelated worlds. There is the physical sensible, and its mode is that of the senses. There is the supersensible world—that of the imagination. And there is the world of the intelligences—that of the mind.

2. Corbin returns to the Latin phrasing of *mundus imaginalis* to capture this arena of creativity, lamenting the fact that modern western languages only allow for vague and misleading equivalents. Though it is tangential to the purpose of my presentation here, we may well ask why it is so difficult to speak of creativity as self-forging and world-making at all in the contemporary west. Corbin explains that the word "imaginary" does not provide an adequate translation, for today it has come to refer to the *unreal*; or, as with Sartre, a flimsy recollection of something experienced, not a creative act. Corbin calls this the westerner's "agnostic reflex"—responsible for the divorce of *thinking* and *being*.

3. This conceptualization of *mundus imaginalis* has close parallels with the processes of self-creation and world-building critical to Mozambicans' survival. Yet I found one difference. Corbin writes that in the Persian and Arabic texts ontologically the imagination ranks higher than the world of senses and lower than the purely intellectual world. This hierarchicalization appears to resonate through a number of major texts of the Middle Ages, as much as it is absent from Mozambican epistemology. Elaine Scarry (1994), whose work on pain, terror, and imagination has been groundbreaking, also returned to a medieval text to explore the realm of creativity and ontology: that of the philosopher-theosophist Boethius and his *Consolation of Philosophy*. Boethius too presents an ontological hierarchy in pursuing his question of "What is man? What is knowledge?" This hierarchy begins with the world of Senses (the material and particular), moves to the Imagination (the immaterial particular, the realm of animals), reaches Reason (the immaterial universal) with humans, and achieves the ultimate and simultaneous unity of God-Knowledge with Insight. While Insight is a unified immediate totality of knowing in the Simple Idea that integrates all the lower forms of knowing, it is the final step on a progressive path that distinguished different kinds of ontic-knowing. The fact that these hierarchical philosophies are influential from Persian and Arabic textual traditions to medieval European ones suggests an intellectual legacy sufficiently broad and powerful to lend an aura of "given-ness," of reality, to these ideas. Corbin and Scarry do not contest these hierarchies, but such hierarchical divisions do not penetrate to all philosophical systems.

Hierarchies are not universal. Judging from the experience of Mozambicans, I would posit instead that the world of the senses, the imagination, and the mind is fundamentally, irreducibly interrelated in the act and the fact of living—a triad of interdependent equalities rather than a hierarchy of possibilities.

In my more playful moments, based on my conversations with Mozambicans concerned with the ontological facets of life, I imagine the following conversation might not be too far off the mark if I were to ask them about these philosophies. "Dividing the processes of living is unrealistic," they might say. "But why place Insight at the top of the hierarchy? Why not Outsight as well? Or why not In-hear or In-taste or In-feel, or Out-hear and Out-feel as well?" The point being that in our traditions of knowledge we demonstrate our own preoccupations with hierarchies of sensing as well as senses—sight being privileged in western traditions. And, of course, playing further on the whole notion of sense, we might ask why we distinguish five senses, and then speak colloquially of "sense" as the realm of intellect and also of intuition. Maybe our patterns of speech attest to something our formal philosophies have missed: that senses and sense cannot be distinguished so readily or neatly. Maybe the world of the five senses is an intellectual realm; the intellect a "sense(ing)" in some capacity.

4. Allen Feldman once said to me that we all write our own autobiographies in our work. I take this to be a profound fact of scholarship. We "find" what we "know." We study what we are interested in. I would expand on this insight to say that we also theorize our own biographies. Elaine Scarry noted in discussing her work on imagination that psychological schools were divided by whether or not they thought people could "see" images. Some argued they could see images in their mind as clearly as they could see the person in front of them. Others simply did not understand this, and did not "see" images in their mind's eye. Rather than take this to be a result of different personal capacities, schools of psychology battled over whether it was possible to "see" images. People forged their theories according to their own personal abilities. Some see images, some speak images, some rely on image as reasoning. No theory positing the paramount importance of the visual imagination will hold for those who conceptualize differently. No theory that denies the creative power of the visual image will hold for those who depend on this faculty. We need a much more pluralistically nuanced set of theories to explain humans' relationships to knowing and being.

5. I would like to express my thanks here to Antonio Francesco for his discussions with me on this play.

6. Western legal, judicial, and political systems are largely set up along these premises.

7. This of course resonates with Elaine Scarry's work (1985) on the making and unmaking of the world in situations of extreme violence.

Epilogue
Unmaking Violence

Reality

There is a dam
behind my eyes
a dam containing water
that if I touch or blink
will make me cry

And that which is called Reality
will fall over me
covering me with a wave of terror
and the horrors of war

In between the dream and the waking up
I anxiously await
for that beautiful morning
to enter joyfully through my window
to tell me that
Reality is peace.

—Juleca

Election day, 1994. Photo by Carolyn Nordstrom.

As I write this in 1997, Mozambique's 1992 Peace Accord is still holding. Elections were held in 1994, the first ever in Mozambique. Frelimo won, but by a very narrow margin. Renamo held a close second. I was an election observer, and many Mozambicans told me it was not so much a vote for one side over another, but a vote for peace. While Renamo was not content with the election results, they did not go back to war. I think the dedicated culture of peace I have described has quite a bit to do with this. I saw it in action the opening day of the elections in October 1994.

I was a provincial coordinator for the election monitoring group, Association for Western European Parliamentarians with UN and Christian Council for Mozambique counterparts. I was asked to go to the northern province of Niassa because I knew the province and spoke Portuguese.

Even before the elections, however, it was evident that "taking the war out of the people" had been at least partially successful: Mozambique was unable to fill the quota set by the United Nations of a joint Frelimo/Renamo military. The UN protocols stating that an integrated army of 30,000 was to be in place by the elections had to be overlooked: fewer than half the positions were filled. Many soldiers simply refused to enter into further military service. Although against UN regulations, the election officials had no choice but to open the polling stations with far fewer security forces protecting them than stipulated in the conventions of the peace accord.

An even more powerful indication of people's commitment to ending violence became apparent the morning the elections opened. Early that day, one of the members of my team, a man from Malawi, called my attention to the BBC broadcast on his world receiver radio. It was still dark, hours before the elections were to start. The broadcast said that the presidential contender Dhlakama, the head of Renamo, had pulled out of the elections and called a general boycott. That was it. There was no news as to what was behind this, or if it signaled a return to war. All Mozambican news services had a complete blackout of information on this. There was no word to us from any of the governmental, nongovernmental, or election monitoring agencies at all about what was going on or what to do.

Most of my team had already left the day before for province-wide locations. We could communicate only by the gracious assistance of a Mozambican Red Cross radio operator, with a backup of the police radio for emergencies. If we in the provincial capital were ignorant as to what was taking place, clearly no one else on my team out in the province did. The rest of us decided to leave for our posts. Because I was a provincial coordinator, I was not limited to one polling station, but could travel freely and visit any.

The image etched in my mind when I arrived at the first polling station at dawn will likely remain with me throughout my lifetime. Hundreds of people were lined up waiting quietly for the station to open. On their faces were looks I had seen before: fear that war would break out around them at any moment, steeled with determination to stand up for their rights. One look at their faces and I had no need to ask if they had heard about Dhlakama's withdrawal. There was no electricity at this hour in Niassa, and few people had the resources to buy radios, much less batteries. World receivers could cost more than a year's salary, and only the BBC was broadcasting any news about the disruptions at the elections. Yet everyone knew. As there was no formal government announcement as to what was taking place, no one knew if the elections were being canceled, if war was resuming, if they were in danger for going to the polling stations. Person to person, as each individual elected to walk the distance to the polling station, Mozambicans coalesced into a movement that stood up for what people perceived to be their political right.

Long before they voted on the ballots, people voted, as they say, with their feet by showing up in the hundreds and thousands at every polling station across the country hours before the polls even opened. With this act, they voted for a peaceful resolution; they voted against the intimidation of war. Mothers walked the many kilometers to the polling stations with children on their backs; the maimed and elderly were carried. This was no small act of courage. After a war that had taken over a million lives, people had no idea how great the dangers of going to the polling stations were. More than 90 percent of the population voted during the elections.

When I entered the first polling station, the fear and determination were magnified—this time on the faces of the Renamo representatives. Election rules stated that every polling station was to have representatives of the main political parties to ensure free and fair elections. None of the Renamo representatives there knew if Dhlakama's boycott meant a return to war. None knew if they would be threatened or killed for defying the boycott. None knew what was happening in other provinces and polling stations. For all any of us knew, war could already have broken out in other locations. But they defied the boycott, and came to the polling stations.

The polling stations were orderly and quiet. People were cautious, courteous, and efficient. It was the same quiet that I have seen before in places expecting an attack, a bomb drop, the deadly unexpected. I asked several representatives what they thought of what was going on, wording my questions in the most general terms, not knowing how much anyone knew of what, or how much could be said of it. One Renamo representative summed up many people's sentiments, "Dhlakama can go back out in the bush and fight by himself if he wants war so bad."

The election rules were followed explicitly. The polls opened on time. One of the first people I saw vote sums up the spirit of the election for me. She was an elderly woman with gray hair, bowed over with age. She was a village woman, dressed in an inexpensive cloth wrap. She could neither read nor write. The impartial voter assistant showed her the election form, which had pictures of the contenders and parties as well as their names, and explained how to mark it. She walked with a limp to the voting booth, marked her choices with a thumbprint, and emerged to deposit her ballot into the ballot box. Then she straightened, looked at all of us in the room, gave a smile of great dignity, made a hand gesture like a personal salute of victory, and exited.

That day, Dhlakama announced he was back in the election. In Maputo, a contingent of high-level diplomats from around the world had converged on Dhlakama the minute he had declared a boycott the night before the elections. They pressured him with the conventions of diplomacy to reenter the election. When he decided some hours after the polls opened to give up the boycott, the ambassadors declared a diplomatic victory.

But no one recognized the true victory of the people at the polling stations. If the people had been intimidated by the threat of war and stayed home, the elections would not have taken place. If the Renamo representatives had followed the call to boycott, the elections would not have been possible. If they had responded by arming, a return to war would likely have been inevitable. No matter what diplomatic coups were declared, if the Mozambican people had not defied fear and intimidation and walked those dangerous miles to the polling stations, Mozambique might still be at war today. If people had responded to Dhlakama's call for election boycott, Dhlakama would not have rejoined the elections. He did not submit to diplomatic pressure so much as to the recognition that it is impossible to launch a boycott and a war without followers.

There is a concept of political might in the west that cannot conceive of resistance except in military terms. People fight back by fighting, literally. Not fighting with force is seen as passivity. The Mozambican example, evident both during the war and at the elections, soundly challenges this notion. Although it is impossible to speak of a whole nation as if it were a single entity, a culture of resisting violence and of peacebuilding did develop in Mozambique. But it was not one based on military or paramilitary might. Many Mozambican citizens fought, not one side or the other, not the governments or militaries, but violence itself.[1] They fought the harsh reality that people could control others through intimidation and the use of force. Not accepting that reality, creating a new one, is a powerful weapon, perhaps the most powerful in war's armory.

For a number of years after the war in Mozambique, I was left to wonder how special were the cultural resources average people constructed across the length and breadth of the country, how crucial to the peace process. Sri Lanka, where I had worked since 1981, was still undergoing wave after wave of political violence. Angola, Mozambique's colonial twin, had reverted to devastating war after the 1992 elections. Mozambique, struggling against considerable political tensions and economic deprivation, continued to maintain peace.

As I wrote in the Prologue, many of the questions that guided my research in Mozambique started while I was studying Sri Lanka's political violence. In this same way, comparative research expanding beyond the borders of Mozambique at the war's end provided me with further answers. One of the core questions the studies in this book prompted, but could not answer, is how special Mozambique's peacebuilding accomplishments are. Research I carried out in Angola in 1996 helped shed light on this question. Angola shares many characteristics with Mozambique. The country was colonized by the Portuguese. Because Angola, like Mozambique, is resource rich, colonization followed the same kinds of exploitations. A United Nations Development Program senior economist told me in 1996 that, according to their indices, Angola is one of the most resource-rich countries in the world. Excellent land and timber, low population density, a long coastline, and tremendous oil, precious gems, and mineral wealth are basic to Angola. Angola achieved independence in 1975, like Mozambique, and, similarly, was embroiled in war within the year. Angola achieved peace in the early 1990s, again like Mozambique. There are also several major differences. First, Unita rebel forces had more internal support than did Renamo. Second, the extensive gem mines and other precious resources meant militaries were not beholden to outside powers for support and direction. As many have said of Angola, "If you have mines, you can do what you want." Finally, war erupted again after the elections in 1992, and the fighting was the most severe since independence. In 1993, an estimated 1,000 people were dying each day. While at present a precarious cease-fire is in effect and peace accords are on record, no one trusts either, and few are willing to say the war is over. There are parts of the country, especially the contested areas around the gem mines, where a blackout of information and travel is in place. How severe the fighting is there is a guess at best. Cabinda, the province rich in oil, is still embroiled in a battle for independence (Maier 1996; Minter 1994).

The conventional wisdom bantered about by various international concerns in Angola is that the gems and oil explain Angola's continuing war. Simply, the untold wealth is too attractive to let the uncertainties of rule by multiparty elections prevail. There is no doubt truth to this, but it is not the whole truth.

When I traveled through Angola, I looked for the same rich cultural resources I have documented for Mozambique. Here I found a final significant difference between Mozambique and Angola. All the creative responses I documented in Mozambique existed in Angola, but only in circumscribed locations and groups. These had not coalesced into an inter-language and cross-cultural—nationwide—set of linked practices. Angolans have developed a wealth of cultural resources to withstand devastating war, many as sophisticated as anywhere in the world. But I am interested here in cultures of peace, in why Mozambique has achieved and sustained a peace accord and a reduction of societal violence when other countries continue to suffer cycles of political violence.

As this book has demonstrated, African medicine was one of the major creative fonts of Mozambican society during the war. In Angola, some healers have instituted practices similar to those found in Mozambique to "take the war out" of the people and the country—to unmake violence—while others remain embroiled in conflict ideologies. Some of the population go to Curandeiros after suffering war's violences, while others feel only the passage of time will ease the traumas and the tendency toward reproducing violence. As one leader of a war-devastated community responded when I asked if African medicine entailed conflict resolution practices that were applied to all war victims:

> No, it is not like Mozambique here, yet. Maybe a doctor knows these things, but maybe he has a son fighting and he has taken sides, and he doesn't want to help the others. Or maybe the government forces do not want him to be working against the war, maybe he can disappear if he does this kind of work. These divisions, these sides, they keep the war going, and until we get past these we won't get the war out of our society. We need to develop these solutions.

Possibly one of the more poignant examples I heard in Angola involved a local Angolan NGO working with children. This NGO recorded some children's antiwar songs devoted to peace and rebuilding society and arranged to have the songs played on the radio. But the broadcasts did not go on long: they were shut down by the military. The threat was clear.

These examples run the length and range of Angolan society. But the key point is that the cultures of creative resistance *to violence* did *not* run the length and breadth of the country.

Two things emerge as special about Mozambique. (1) The antiwar/peacebuilding sentiments were encoded throughout social life—from parables to medicine; from song and theater to land tenure settlements; from the crafts of street vendors to the classes of primary school teachers. (2) These many arenas were extensively linked. Children sang protest songs that teachers listened to in recognizing the need for conflict resolution education in the classes, and turned to the tenets of African medicine for assistance in this. People formed theater to warn politicians to end the war, based on international literature and Mozambican everyday market society—and these contained clear references to spiritual resistance fighters like Manuel Antonio and Parama. And from refugees to traders, the massive flux of humanity that characterizes a warzone carried these stories from village to village, province to province, across the many language and cultural groups of the country. Of course, as these stories circulated, new teachers adopted conflict resolution classroom practices; new songs and theater emerged to add to the cry for peace and dignity; new dispute resolution councils developed at the local level—all based on these shared models. The most remarkable example of this is the extensive data I collected on the healing/conflict resolution practices of African medicine that I found in *every* community I visited countrywide during the war—and I traveled extensively—no matter how devastated or remote. Practices that developed spontaneously at the local level—completely outside the formal purview of government, NGO, or regulatory officials of any kind. Practices instituted by average civilians, by themselves. Practices that drew on and fueled these extensive linkages forming a nationwide culture of creative resistance to war.

What I realized in comparing Mozambique's experiences with Angola's is that these arenas of conflict management in Mozambique—from local medicine, traders, and teachers to song, parable, and theater—formed a space of thought and action free from party politics. In Angola, this space is largely militarized. Political discourse is often strongly coded in conflict ideologies. To speak politically is deemed to be a statement for or against one side, one military, one ideology, one action over another. To speak at all is to take sides. Not to speak, equally, is to take sides. "Taking sides," with everything this entails, is a strong war tradition in Angola at present. An Angolan journalist I was speaking to about cycles of violence in his country—he lived in one of the more war-torn provinces—summed up the situation in a paragraph:

> When I walk down the street, I am always looking over my shoulder, wondering if someone will be coming up behind me to take revenge on me, if the war will continue on with these kind of hatreds. I was taken by the military and forced to join some years back. Now, years later, I wonder who remembers; who holds me responsible for what

happened to them because of the war. Or who is just consumed with the need for revenge. This may have nothing to do with my military background, but none of us can get away from these political hatreds, these political identities. Even if we dedicated ourselves to just the opposite: to refusing to buy into these political identities, these factional hatreds, even if we work toward solving this damn war, we aren't allowed to. For example, when I walk down the street, I know where I can and cannot walk. If I walk through certain neighborhoods, people will shout out at me: "Hey, MPLA/UNITA scum, get out of this neighborhood, we are UNITA/MPLA. We know you, your father (mother, brother, sister, aunt, uncle) voted for those dogs. Get out of here before we kill you."

This ethic of revenge certainly exists in Mozambique, but it was not nearly as developed or widespread as in Angola. It was common, in my experience across the length and breadth of Mozambique, for someone in a group to temper the tendencies to revenge. For example, if someone was talking of wanting to take revenge for a violence done, often a listener would calmly say:

We all know how you feel, we all sympathize. But taking revenge, killing someone else, that will just continue this war, it will certainly lead to more killing and violence and hatreds. And then they will take revenge, and you may lose yet another loved one in the future. Keeping our living protected is more critical than avenging the dead. This war is killing everyone, it is this violence we have to stop. It costs more than anything.

To return to the Angolan journalist's observations on the aggressions in his country: at present, the conflict is the defining principle of interpersonal and political relations. Thus, in this context, even talk, any kind of talk, of conflict resolution is deemed political, benefiting one side over the other. People live and die in warzones by these politics.

Without a space *outside* these politics, people cannot critique them. Without such a space, how do people create a place to fight against political violence and excess itself? If the politics in Angola is such that the citizens cannot forge a space of action outside lethal political scenarios, power politics is reproduced in every action, no matter how mundane and everyday. While citizens in this country put their lives on the (front)lines to create arenas of conflict resolution and cultures of peace, they have been actively discouraged by the brokers of conflict. These tenuous peacebuilding actions remain oases in a sea of animosity manipulated by political factions who stand to gain from the chaos and instabilities of war. But discourses change over time: they are forged, manipulated, resisted, reshaped across time and space. People create their discourses, and people are infinitely creative over time.

One can assume that Mozambicans are unique in what they created in the midst of war. Or, following the tenets of contemporary theory, we can assume culture is dynamic, that anyone can benefit from the examples of those who defeat oppressive violence. I prefer the latter view. A doctor in Angola summed this up to me when he said: "I understand this culture of resisting political violence, of peacebuilding. Now, how do we do this here?" People in violence-torn communities in the United States have made the same remarks to me.

In Chapter 1 I noted that the whole theoretical model of center and periphery, of elites, philosophers, and leaders, was more egoism than science. At that time I pointed out the dangers of assuming that what takes place in Europe, Moscow, or Beijing is fundamentally more important than what occurs in Sri Lanka, Mozambique, Guatemala, or Georgia. I would like to take that observation one step further: it is equally dangerous to assume that the solutions to the world's problems are more likely to arise in the so-called cosmopolitan centers of the world. To me, the days of salvage research, where scholars documented other cultures for a kind of textual zoo to be kept in libraries, has been put to rest. When I travel to Mozambique, I am not interested in documenting an "Other." I am interested in looking for solutions to the very pressing problems facing the world as a whole. Political violence, to me, is among the most pressing. If Mozambique provides solutions to these lethal matters, then that is where research should lead.

Note

1. People there told me that to take up arms against one side or the other was to play into the very hands they fought against. They would then be reproducing the same violent politics that oppressed them. Even the militaries they fought against won if they took up arms: for they followed the model of power those militaries had set into motion. Violence would continue to define their lives. To truly defeat someone, they said, is not to act by the oppressor's rules, but to institute another set of rules altogether.

Bibliography

Abu-Lughod, Lila
    1991   Writing Against Culture. In *Recapturing Anthropology: Working in the Present,* ed. Richard G. Fox. Santa Fe, N.M.: School of American Research Press.
    1993   *Writing Women's Worlds: Bedouin Stories.* Berkeley: University of California Press.

Anderson, Benedict
    1983   *Imagined Communities: Reflections on the Origin and Spread of Nationalism.* London: Verso.

Anzaldúa, Gloria
    1990   *Making Face, Making Soul: Haciendo Caras.* San Francisco: Aunt Lutes Books.

Appadurai, Arjun
    1990   Disjuncture and Difference in the Global Cultural Economy. *Public Culture* 2(2):1–24.
    1991   Global Ethnoscapes: Notes and Queries for a Transnational Anthropology. In *Recapturing Anthropology: Working in the Present,* ed. Richard G. Fox. Santa Fe, N.M.: School of American Research Press.

Arendt, Hannah
    1971   *The Life of the Mind.* New York: Harcourt Brace Jovanovich.

Ayisi, Ruth
    1991   Back to the Stone Age. *Africa Report* (January-February): 37–39.

Bacon, Francis
    1960   *The New Organon and Related Writings.* New York: Liberal Arts Press.

Bakhtin, Mikhail
    1984   *Rabelais and His World.* Translated by Helene Iswolsky. Bloomington: Indiana University Press.

Balandier, Georges
    1986   An Anthropology of Violence and War. *International Social Science Journal* 110:499–511.

Barthes, Roland
    1985   *The Responsibility of Forms.* Trans. Richard Howard. New York: Hill and Wang.

Benhabib, Seyla
    1992a   *Situating the Self: Gender, Community and Postmodernism in Contemporary Ethics.* New York: Routledge.

1992b   The Generalized and the Concrete Other. In *Ethics: A Feminist Reader*, ed. Elizabeth Frazer, Jennifer Hornsby, and Sabina Lovibond. Oxford: Blackwell.

Benjamin, Walter
1969   *Illuminations*. Ed. Hannah Arendt, Trans. Harry Zohn. New York: Schocken.

Berger, John
1972   *Ways of Seeing*. London: British Broadcasting Corporation.

Berger, Peter L. and Thomas Luckmann
1967   *The Social Construction of Reality*. New York: Anchor Books.

Berk, Richard A.
1972   The Controversy Surrounding Analyses of Collective Violence: Some Methodological Notes. In *Collective Violence*, ed. James F. Short, Jr. and Marvin E. Wolfgang, pp. 112–18. Chicago: Aldine-Atherton.

Bhabha, Homi
1994   *The Location of Culture*. New York: Routledge.

Blanchot, Maurice
1959   *Le livre à venir*. Paris: Gallimard.

Booth, Wayne
1993   Individualism and the Mystery of the Social Self; or, Does Amnesty Have a Leg to Stand On? In *Freedom and Interpretation: The Oxford Amnesty Lectures 1992*, ed. Barbara Johnson. New York: Basic Books.

Boothby, Neil, Abubacar Sultan, and Peter Upton
1991   *Children of Mozambique: The Cost of Survival*. Washington D.C.: U.S. Committee for Refugees.

Bourdieu, Pierre
1977   *Outline of a Theory of Practice*. Cambridge: Cambridge University Press.
1989   Social Space and Symbolic Power. *Sociological Theory* 7(1):14–25.

Bourgois, Philippe
1989   *Ethnicity at Work: Divided Labor on a Central American Banana Plantation*. Baltimore: Johns Hopkins University Press.

Brooks, Peter
1984   *Reading for the Plot: Design and Intention in Narrative*. New York: Random House.

Calvin, William
1988   Simulations of Reality: Deciding What to Do Next. In *Speculations: The Reality Club*, ed. John Brockman. New York: Prentice-Hall.

Camus, Albert
1955   *The Myth of Sisyphus, and Other Essays*. Trans. Justin O'Brien. New York: Vintage Books.
1956   *The Rebel: An Essay on Man in Revolt*. Trans. Anthony Bower. New York: Alfred A. Knopf.

Casimiro, Isabel, Ana Loforte, and Ana Pessoa
1990   *A mulher em Moçambique*. Maputo: CEA/NORAD.

Castoriadis, Cornelius
1987   *The Imaginary Institution of Society*. Cambridge, Mass.: MIT Press.
1994   Radical Imagination and the Social Instituting Imaginary. In *Rethinking Imagination: Culture and Creativity*, ed. Gillian Robinson and John Rundell. New York: Routledge.

Centre of African Studies, University of Edinburgh
  1978   Mozambique. *Proceedings of a Seminar.* December.
Cliff, Julie and A. R. Noormahomed
  1988   Health as a Target: South Africa's Destabilisation of Mozambique. *Social Science and Medicine* 27:717–22.
Comaroff, Jean
  1985   *Body of Power, Spirit of Resistance.* Chicago: University of Chicago Press.
  1991   Paper presented in Discussion of the panel "Inscriptions of Power on the Body," American Anthropological Association meetings, Chicago. November 20–24.
Comaroff, Jean and John Comaroff
  1991   *Of Revelation and Revolution: Christianity, Colonialism, and Consciousness in South Africa.* Vol. 1. Chicago: University of Chicago Press.
Corbin, Henry
  1969   *Creative Imagination in the Sufism of Ibn Arabi.* Princeton, N.J.: Princeton University Press.
  1972   Mundus Imaginalis, or the Imaginary and the Imaginal. *Spring: An Annual of Archtypal Psychology and Jungian Thought:* 1–19.
Couto, Mia
  1990   *Voices Made Night.* Trans. David Brookshaw. Oxford: Heinemann. First published in Portuguese as *Voces ancitecidas.* Lisboa: Editorial Caminho, 1986.
Crapanzano, Vincent
  1990   Afterword. In *Modernist Anthropology: From Fieldwork to Text,* ed. Marc Manganaro. Princeton, N.J.: Princeton University Press.
  1992   *Hermes' Dilemma and Hamlet's Desire: On the Epistemology of Interpretation.* Cambridge, Mass.: Harvard University Press.
Cruz Vermelha de Mocambique
  1994   *Projecto Brincar Curando: Consultoria para investigação das formas tradicionais de atendimenta à crianca vítima da guerra.* Maputo: Cruz Vermelha de Mocambique.
Daniel, E. Valentine
  1994   The Individual in Terror. In *Embodiment and Experience: The Existential Ground of Culture and Self,* ed. Thomas J. Csordas. Cambridge: Cambridge University Press.
Daniels, Stephen
  1985   Arguments for a Humanistic Geography. In *The Future of Geography,* ed. R. L. Johnson . London: Methuen.
Darch, Colin
  1989   Are There Warlords in Provincial Mozambique? Questions of the Social Base of MNR Bandrity. *Review of African Political Economy* 45/46:34–49.
Das, Veena
  1985   Anthropological Knowledge and Collective Violence. *Anthropology Today* 1(3):4–6.
  1990   Our Work to Cry: Your Work to Listen. In *Mirrors of Violence: Communities, Riots, and Survivors in South Asia,* ed. Das, 345–98. Delhi: Oxford University Press.

de Certeau, Michel
> 1986   *Heterologies: Discourse on the Other.* Trans. Brian Massumi. Minneapolis: University of Minnesota Press.

Dilthey, Wilhelm
> 1954   *The Essence of Philosophy.* Trans. S. A. Emery and W. T. Emery. Chapel Hill: University of North Carolina Press.

Dis, Adriaan van
> 1991   *In Afrika.* Amsterdam: Meulenhoff.

Domingo Newsjournal
> 1991   Barama: Uma Força Liberadora. Maputo, 5 May.

Dumont, Jean-Paul
> 1992   Ideas on Philippine Violence: Assertions, Negations, and Narrations. In *The Paths to Domination, Resistance, and Terror,* ed. Carolyn Nordstrom and Jo-Ann Martin, pp. 133–53. Berkeley: University of California Press.

Enloe, Cynthia
> 1993   *The Morning After: Sexual Politics at the End of the Cold War.* Berkeley: University of California Press.

Enzensberger, Hans Magnus
> 1990   *Civil Wars: From L.A. to Bosnia.* New York: New Press.

Fardon, Richard, ed.
> 1995   *Counterworks: Managing the Diversity of Knowledge.* New York: Routledge.

Fauvet, Paul
> 1984   The Roots of Counter-Revolution: The Mozambican National Resistance. *Review of African Political Economy* 29:108–21.

Feldman, Allen
> 1991   *Formations of Violence.* Chicago: University of Chicago Press.
> 1994   Writing the Inhuman: Aesthetic Control and Iconic Transgression in the Depiction of Violence. Paper presented at the American Anthropological Association meetings, Atlanta. November 30-December 4.
> 1995   Ethnographic States of Emergency: Connecting Confusions. In *Fieldwork Under Fire: Contemporary Studies of Violence and Survival,* ed. Carolyn Nordstrom and Antonius C. G. M. Robben. Berkeley: University of California Press.

Fetherston, A. B. and Carolyn Nordstrom
> 1995   Overcoming *Habitus* in Conflict Management: UN Peacekeeping and Warzone Ethnography. *Peace and Change* 20(1): 94–119.

Finnegan, William
> 1992   *A Complicated War: The Harrowing of Mozambique.* Berkeley: University of California Press.

Foster, Mary Lecron and Robert A. Rubenstein, eds.
> 1986   *Peace and War: Cross-Cultural Perspectives.* New Brunswick, N.J.: Transaction Books.

Foucault, Michel
> 1972   *Power/Knowledge.* New York: Pantheon Books.
> 1982   The Subject and Power. In *Michel Foucault: Beyond Structuralism and Hermeneutics,* ed. Hubert L. Dreyfus and Paul Rabinow, pp. 208–26. Chicago: University of Chicago Press.

Frelick, Bill
 1989   Renamo: The Khmer Rouge of Africa; Mozambique, Its Killing
           Fields. Testimony before the House Subcommittee on Foreign
           Operations, Washington D.C., February 8.
Galtung, Johann
 1992   Conflict Resolution as Conflict Transformation: The First Law of
           Thermodynamics Revisited. Paper presented at the International
           Peace Research Association meetings, Kyoto, 27–31 July.
Geffray, Christian
 1990   *La cause des armes au Mozambique: anthropologie d'une guerre civile.*
           Paris: Editions Karthala.
Geffray, Christian and Morgens Pederson
 1986   Sobre a guerra na provincia de Nampula: elementos de analise
           e hipoteses sobre as determinacoes e consequencias socio-econo-
           micas locais. *Revista Internacional de Estudos Africanos* 4/5 (Janeiro-
           Dezembro):303–18.
Gersony, Robert
 1988   Summary of Mozambican Refugee Accounts of Principally Con-
           flict-Related Experience in Mozambique. Report submitted to Am-
           bassador Jonathon Moore, Director, Bureau for Refugees Program
           and Dr. Chester Crocker, Assistant Secretary of African Affairs.
           Washington, D.C., April.
Giddens, Anthony
 1991   *Modernity and Self-Identity: Self and Society in the Late Modern Age.* Stan-
           ford, Calif.: Stanford University Press.
Goodman, Nelson
 1978   *Ways of Worldmaking.* Indianapolis: Hackett Publishing.
Green, Linda
 1994   Fear as a Way of Life. *Cultural Anthropology* 9(2):227–56.
Guenon, René
 1984   *The Multiple States of Being.* Trans. Joscelyn Godwin. Burdett, N.Y.:
           Larson Publications.
Gupta, Akhil and James Ferguson
 1992   Beyond "Culture": Space, Identity, and the Politics of Difference.
           Cultural Anthropology 7(1): 6–23.
Handelman, Don
 1985   Charisma, Liminality, and Symbolic Types. In *Comparative Social Dy-
           namics: Essays in Honor of S. N. Eisenstadt.* Ed. Eric Cohen, Moshe Lis-
           sak, and Uri Almagor, pp. 346–59. Boulder, Colo.: Westview Press.
 1990   *Models and Mirrors: Towards an Anthropology of Public Events.* Cam-
           bridge: Cambridge University Press.
Hanlon, Joseph
 1984   *Mozambique: The Revolution Under Fire.* London: Zed Books.
 1991   *Mozambique: Who Calls the Shots?* Bloomington: Indiana University
           Press.
Harpham, Geoffrey Galt
 1982   *On the Grotesque.* Princeton, N.J.: Princeton University Press.
Hayles, N. Katherine
 1990   *Chaos Bound: Orderly Disorder in Contemporary Literature and Science.*
           Ithaca, N.Y.: Cornell University Press.

Heidegger, Martin
 1962 *Being and Time.* Oxford: Blackwell.
Heller, Agnes
 1994 The Elementary Ethics of Everyday Life. In *Rethinking Imagination: Culture and Creativity,* ed. Gillian Robinson and John Rundell New York: Routledge.
Henning, Sylvia
 1981 La Forme in-formante: A Reconsideration of the Grotesque. *Mosaic* 14:107–21.
Henriksen, Thomas H.
 1978 *Mozambique: A History.* London: Rex Collins.
 1983 *Revolution and Counterrevolution: Mozambique's War of Independence, 1964–1974.* Westport, Conn.: Greenwood Press.
Hilsdon, Anne-Marie
 1995 *Madonnas and Martyrs: Sexual Violence in the Philippines.* Sydney: Allen and Unwin.
Himmelfarb, Gertrude
 1994 *On Looking into the Abyss.* New York: Alfred A. Knopf.
Hoffman, Piotr
 1986 *Doubt, Time, Violence.* Chicago: University of Chicago Press.
Honwana, Luis Bernardo
 1969 *We Killed Mangy Dog: and Other Mozambican Stories.* Trans. Dorothy Guedes. Harare: Zimbabwe Publishing House.
Husserl, Edmund
 1962 *Ideas: General Introduction to Pure Phenomenology.* New York: Collier Macmillan.
International Defence and Aid Fund
 1973 Terror in Tete: A Documentary Report of Portuguese Atrocities in Tete District, Mozambique, 1971–1972. Special report no. 2. London.
Isaacman, Allen (in collaboration with Barbara Isaacman)
 1976 *The Tradition of Resistance in Mozambique: The Zambezi Valley, 1850–1921.* Berkeley: University of California Press
Isaacman, Allen and Arlindo Chilundo
 1995 Peasants at Work: Forced Cotton Cultivation in Northern Mozambique. In *Cotton, Colonialism, and Social Hisotry in Sub-Saharan Africa,* ed. Allen Isaacman and Richard Roberts. Portsmouth, N.H.: Heinemann.
Isaacman, Allen and Barbara Issacman
 1983 *Mozambique: From Colonialism to Revolution, 1900–1982.* Hampshire: Gower.
Jackson, Michael
 1989 *Paths Toward a Clearing.* Bloomington: Indiana University Press.
Jackson, Peter
 1989 *Maps of Meaning.* London: Unwin Hyman.
James, William
 1890 *Principles of Psychology.* Vol. 1. New York: Henry Holt.
 1976 *Essays in Radical Empiricism.* Cambridge, Mass.: Harvard University Press.
 1978 *Essays in Philosophy: The Work of William James.* Ed. Fredson Bowers

and Ignas K. Skrupskelis. Cambridge, Mass.: Harvard University Press.

Jeichande, Ivette Illas
1990   *Mulheres deslocadas em Maputo, Zambezia e Inhambane (mulher em situação difícil).* Maputo: OMM-UNICEF.

Johnson, Phyllis and David Martin
1986   *Destructive Engagement.* Harare: Zimbabwe Publishing House.

Johnson, Barbara, ed.
1992   *Freedom and Interpretation.* Oxford Amnesty Lectures. New York: Basic Books.

Kahler, Erich
1957   *The Tower and the Abyss: An Inquiry into the Transformation of the Individual.* New York: George Braziller.

Kapferer, Bruce
1988   *Legends of People, Myths of State.* Washington, D.C.: Smithsonian Institution Press.

Kriger, Norma
1992   *Zimbabwe's Guerrilla War.* New York: Cambridge University Press.

Laclau, Ernesto and Chanal Mouffe
1985   *Hegemony and Socialist Strategy.* New York: Verso.

Lan, David
1985   *Guns and Rain: Guerrillas and Spirit Mediums in Zimbabwe.* Harare: Zimbabwe Publishing House.

Langer, Susanne K.
1942   *Philosophy in a New Key.* Cambridge, Mass.: Harvard University Press.

Lauriciano, Gil
1990a   Espirito Mungoi: Um poder alternativo ou apenas mais um fenomeno da guerra? *Domingo,* Maputo, 2 Setembro.
1990b   Uma outra Revolução no campo. *Domingo,* Maputo, 9 Setembro, p. 9.

Lavie, Smadar, Kirin Narayan, and Renato Resaldo, eds.
1993   *Creativity/Anthropology.* Ithaca, N.Y.: Cornell University Press.

Le Guin, Ursula
1989   *Dancing at the Edge of the World.* New York: Harper and Row.

Legum, Colim, ed.
1988   Mozambique: Facing Up to Desperate Hardships in Post-Machel Era. *Africa Contemporary Record* 19 (1986–87): B681-B701. New York: Africana Publishing Co.

Lopes, José Mota
1986   A Renamo não existe: e uma ficção ão servico da politica sul-Africana. *Diario Popular,* Lisbon, 13 May.

Magaia, Lina
1988   *Dumba Nengue—Run for Your Life: Peasant Tales of Tragedy in Mozambique.* Trenton, N.J.: Africa World Press, Inc.
1989   *Duplo massacre em Mocambique: historias tragicas do banditismo—II.* Maputo: Coleção Depoimentos 5.

Maier, Karl
1990a   Guarded by the Spirit of Mungoi: Lost Horizon Could Have Happened Here. *Independent,* London, February 25.
1990b   Healer in Mozambique Leads Attacks on Rebels. *Washington Post,* 8 August.

1991   A Traditional Revival. *Africa Report* (July-August).
1996   *Angola: Promises and Lies*. Rivonia: William Waterman Publications.
Masolo, D. A.
1983   Philosophy and Culture: A Critique. In *Philosophy and Cultures*.
             Edited by H. Odero Oruka and D. A. Masolo. Nairobi: Bookwise
             Limited.
McElroy, Bernard
1989   *Fiction of the Modern Grotesque*. London: Macmillan.
McIntyre, Martha
1993   The Sexualization of Warfare. Paper presented at the Human
             Rights and Gender Politics Conference, University of Melbourne,
             Australia, August.
McKusick, Tom and Mike Tronnes
1992   Pathetic Aesthetic. *Utne Reader* (November/December).
Mead, Margaret
1968   Warfare is Only an Invention—Not a Biological Necessity. In *War:*
             Studies from Psychology, Sociology, Anthropology, ed. Leon Bramson
             and George W. Goethals. New York: Basic Books.
Mimica, Jadran
1991   The Incest Passions: An Outline of the Logic of Iqwaye Social
             Organization. *Oceania* 62(1):34–58.
Ministerio da Saude/UNICEF
1988   Analise da situação da saude. Maputo, Septembro.
Ministry of Cooperation/UNICEF
1989   The Situation of Children and Women in Mozambique. Produced
             in cooperation with the Organization for Mozambican Women
             (OMM). Maputo.
Minter, William
1989   The Mozambican National Resistance (Renamo) as Described by
             Ex-participants. Research Report submitted to Ford Foundation
             and Swedish International Development Agency, March.
1994   *Apartheid's Contras: An Inquiry into the Roots of War in Angola and*
             Mozambique. London: Zed Books.
Mudimbe, V. Y.
1988   *The Invention of Africa: Gnosis, Philosophy, and the Order of Knowledge*.
             Bloomington: Indiana University Press.
Munslow, Barry
1983   *Mozambique: The Revolution and Its Origins*. London: Longman.
Nicholson, Linda
1990   *Feminism/Postmodernism*. New York: Routledge.
Nichter, Mark
1981   Idioms of Distress: Alternatives in the Expression of Psychosocial
             Distress, a Case Study from South India. *Culture, Medicine, and Psy-*
             chiatry 5:379–408.
Nishida, Kitaro
1990   *An Inquiry into the Good*. Trans. Masão Abe and Christopher Ives.
             New Haven, Conn.: Yale University Press.
Nordstrom, Carolyn
1990–91   African Health Care Systems and the War in Mozambique. Six part
             series. Maputo: Ministry of Health. In English and Portuguese.

1991   Women and War: Observations from the Field. *Minerva: Quarterly Report on Women and the Military* 9(1):1–15.
1992a   The Backyard Front. In *The Paths to Domination, Resistance, and Terror*, ed. Nordstrom and Jo-Ann Martin. Berkeley: University of California Press.
1992b   The Dirty War: Civilian Experience of Conflict in Mozambique and Sri Lanka. In *Internal Conflict and Governance*, ed. Kumar Rupesinghe, pp. 27–43. New York: St. Martin's Press.
1993   Treating the Wounds of War. *Cultural Survival* (Summer):28–30.
1994   Warzones: Cultures of Violence, Militarisation and Peace. Working Paper 145. Peace Research Centre, Australian National University, Canberra.
1995a   Creativity and Chaos: War on the Frontlines. In *Fieldwork Under Fire: Contemporary Studies in Violence and Survival*, ed. Nordstrom and Antonius C. G. M. Robben. Berkeley: University of California Press.
1995b   Contested Identities, Essentially Contested Powers. In *Conflict Transformation*, ed. Kumar Rupesinghe. New York: St. Martin's Press.
1996a   Girls Behind the (Front) Lines. *Peace Review* 8(3): 403–9.
1996b   Rape: Politics and Theory in War and Peace. *Australian Feminist Studies* 11(23):147–62.
1997   The Eye of the Storm: From War to Peace. In *Cultural Variations in Conflict Resolution: Alternatives to Violence*. Ed. D. Fry and Kaj Bjorkqvist. Mahwah, N.J.: Lawrence Erlbaum.

Nordstrom, Carolyn and Jo-Ann Martin
1992   The Culture of Conflict: Field Reality and Theory. In *The Paths to Domination, Resistance, and Terror*, ed. Nordstrom and Martin. Berkeley: University of California Press.

Nordstrom, Carolyn and Jo-Ann Martin, eds.
1992a   *The Paths to Domination, Resistance, and Terror.* Berkeley: University of California Press.

Nordstrom, Carolyn and Antonius C. G. M. Robben, eds.
1995   *Fieldwork Under Fire: Contemporary Studies of Violence and Survival.* Berkeley: University of California Press.

Nunes, Jovito
1990   Pilot Study to Investigate the Problems of Social Organization Within Displaced Communities. Preliminary Report. Unpublished Manuscript, Maputo.

O'Brien, Tim
1990   *The Things They Carried.* Boston: Houghton Mifflin/Seymour Lawrence.

Olujic, Maria
1995   Coming Home: The Croatian War Experience. In *Fieldwork Under Fire: Contemporary Studies in Violence and Survival.* Edited by Carolyn Nordstrom and Antonius C. G. M. Robben. Berkeley: University of California Press.

Oruka, H. Odera
1983   Ideology and Culture (The African Experience). In *Philosophy and Cultures*, ed. Oruka and D. A. Masolo. Nairobi: Bookwise Limited.

p'Bitek, Okot
1983   On Culture, Man and Freedom. In *Philosophy and Cultures*, ed. H. Odera Oruka and D. A. Masolo. Nairobi: Bookwise Limited.

Penvenne, Jeanne
1979   Attitudes Toward Race and Work in Mozambique: Lourenco Marques, 1900–1974. Working Paper 16. Boston: African Studies Center, Boston University.

Pettman, Jan Jindy
1996   *Worlding Women: A Feminist International Politics*. London: Routledge.

Price, Richard
1990   *Alabi's World*. Baltimore: Johns Hopkins University Press.

Rabelais, François
1933   *The Complete Works of Doctor François Rabelais*. Vol. I. New York: Boni and Liveright.

Rabinow, Paul
1986   Representations Are Social Facts: Modernity and Post-Modernity in Anthropology. In *Writing Culture: The Poetics and Politics of Ethnography*, ed. James Clifford and George E. Marcus, pp. 234–61. Berkeley: University of California Press.

Ranger, Terrance
1982   The Death of Chaminuka: Spirit Mediums, Nationalism, and the Guerrilla War in Zimbabwe. *African Affairs* 81(324):349–69.

1985   *Peasant Consciousness and Guerrilla War in Zimbabwe*. London: James Currey.

Reynolds, Pamela
1990   Children of Tribulation: The Need to Heal and the Means to Heal War Trauma. *Africa* 60(1):1–38.

Riches, David, ed.
1986   *The Anthropology of Violence*. New York: Blackwell.

Richman, Naomi, Anabela Ratilal, and Aires Aly
1990   The Effects of War on Teachers in Mozambique: Preliminary Findings. Maputo: Ministry of Education.

nd.   The Psychological Effects of War on Mozambican Children. Maputo: Ministry of Education.

Ricoeur, Paul
1994   Imagination in Discourse and Action. In *Rethinking Imagination: Culture and Creativity*, ed. Gillian Robinson and John Rundell. New York: Routledge.

Rivabella, Omar
1986   *Requiem for a Woman's Soul*. Trans. Paul Riviera and Omar Rivabella. New York: Random House.

Robarchek, Clayton
1989   Hobbesian and Rousseauan Images of Man: Autonomy and Individualism in a Peaceful Society. In *Societies at Peace: Anthropological Perspectives*, ed. Signe Howell and Roy Willis. London: Routledge.

Robben, Antonius C. G. M.
1995   The Politics of Truth and Emotion Among Victims and Perpetuators of Violence. In *Fieldwork Under Fire: Contemporary Studies in Violence and Survival*, ed. Carolyn Nordstrom and Robben. Berkeley: University of California Press.

Robben, Antonius C. G. M. and Carolyn Nordstrom
   1995   The Anthropology and Ethnography of Violence and Socio-Political Conflict. In *Fieldwork Under Fire: Contemporary Studies in Violence and Survival*, ed. Nordstrom and Robben. Berkeley: University of California Press.

Roesch, Otto
   1990   Renamo and the Peasantry: A View from Gaza. *Southern Africa Report* (December):21–25.

Rosaldo, Renato, Smadar Lavie, and Kirin Narayan
   1993   Introduction: Creativity in Anthropology. In *Creativity/Anthropology*, ed. Lavie, Narayan, and Resaldo. Ithaca, N.Y.: Cornell University Press.

Ruch, E. A. and K. C. Anyanwu
   1984   *African Philosophy: An Introduction to the Main Philosophical Trends in Contemporary Africa*. Rome:Catholic Book Agency.

Rupesinghe, Kumar
   1992a   *Internal Conflict and Governance*. New York: St. Martin's Press.
   1992b   *Early Warning and Conflict Resolution*. New York: St. Martin's Press.
   1994   *Conflict Transformation*. Basingstoke: Macmillan.

Rupesinghe, Kumar and Marcial Rubio C.
   1994   *Culture of Violence*. Toyko/New York: United Nations University Press.

Sartre, Jean-Paul
   1948   *The Psychology of Imagination*. New York: Philosophical Library.
   1957   *Being and Nothingness: An Essay on Phenomenological Ontology*. London: Methuen.

Saussure, Ferdinand de
   1959   *Course in General Linguistics*. Edited by C. Bally and A Sechehaye. Trans. and intro. Wade Baskin. New York: McGraw-Hill.

Scarry, Elaine
   1985   *The Body in Pain: The Making and Unmaking of the World*. Oxford: Oxford University Press.
   1994   *Resisting Representation*. Oxford: Oxford University Press.

Scheper-Hughes, Nancy
   1992   *Death Without Weeping: The Violence of Everyday Life in Northeast Brazil*. Berkeley: University of California Press.

Schutz, Alfred
   1962   *Collected Papers I: The Problem of Social Reality*. Ed. Maurice Natanson. The Hague: Martinus Nijhoff.
   1964   *Collected Papers II: Studies in Social Theory*. Edited by Maurice Natanson. The Hague: Martinus Nijhoff.

Schutz, Alfred and Thomas Luckmann
   1973   *The Structures of the Life-World*. Evanston, Ill.: Northwestern University Press.

Scott, Peter Dale
   1988   *Coming to Jakarta: A Poem About Terror*. New York: New Directions.

Simmel, Georg
   1950   *The Sociology of Georg Simmel*. Trans. and ed. K. H. Wolff. New York: Free Press.

Simons, Anna
   1995   Rumor: The Beginning of the End. In *Fieldwork Under Fire: Contem-*

porary Studies in Violence and Survival, ed. Carolyn Nordstrom and Antonius C. G. M. Robben. Berkeley: University of California Press.

Sivard, Ruth Leger
1993   *World Military and Social Expenditures.* Leesburg, Va.: World Priorities.

Sluka, Jeff.
1988   Loyal Citizens of the Republic. In *The Social Dynamics of Peace and Conflict*, ed. Robert A. Rubinstein and Mary LeCron Foster, pp. 107–25. Boulder, Colo.: Westview Press.

Spivak, Gayatri Chakravorty
1988   Can the Subaltern Speak? In *Marxism and the Interpretation of Culture.* Ed. Cary Nelson and Lawrence Grossberg, pp 271–313. Urbana: University of Illinois Press.

Starn, Orin
1992   Politics in Anthropology Since the Sixties. Paper presented at the American Anthropological Association meetings, San Francisco, December 2–6.

Strathern, Marilyn, ed.
1995   *Shifting Contexts: Transformations in Anthropological Knowledge.* London: Routledge.

Suárez-Orozco, Marcelo
1987   The Treatment of Children in the "Dirty War": Ideology, State Terrorism, and the Abuse of Children in Argentina. In *Child Survival: Anthropological Perspectives on the Treatment and Maltreatment of Children*, ed. Nancy Scheper-Hughes, pp. 227–46. Boston: Reidel.
1992   A Grammer of Terror: Psychological Responses to State Terrorism in Dirty War and Post-Dirty War Argentina. In *The Paths to Domination, Resistance, and Terror*, ed. Carolyn Nordstrom and Jo-Ann Martin. Berkeley: University of California Press.

Swedish International Peace Research Institute (SIPRI)
1993   *SIPRI Yearbook 1993: World Armanents and Disarmament.* Oxford: Oxford University Press.

Taussig, Michael
1987   *Shamanism, Colonialism, and the Wild Man.* Chicago: University of Chicago Press.

Tedlock, Barbara, ed.
1987   *Dreaming: Anthropological and Psychological Interpretations.* Cambridge: Cambridge University Press.

Thee, Marek
1980   The Scope and Priorities in Peace Research. Paper prepared for Consultations on Peace Research, United Nations University, Tokyo, 8–13 December.

Thornton, Robert
1991   The Shooting at Uitenhage, South Africa, 1985. *American Ethnologist* 17(2):217–36.

Trinh, T. Minh-ha
1989   *Woman, Native, Other.* Bloomington: University of Indiana Press.

Turner, Victor
1985   *On the Edge of the Bush: Anthropology as Experience.* Tucson: University of Arizona Press.

Ueland, Brenda
    1992   Tell Me More. *Utne Reader* (November/December): 104–9.
UNICEF
    1989   Children on the Frontline, 1989 Update. Geneva: UNICEF.
    1990   Annual Report. Maputo.
UNICEF/Ministry of Cooperation
    1990   The Situation of Women and Children in Mozambique. Maputo.
United States Commerce Department
    1980   Foreign Economic Trends and Their Implications for the United
              States. 80–026—Mozambique. Prepared by the U.S. Embassy, Ma-
              puto, April.
Urdang, Stephanie
    1989   *And Still They Dance.* London: Earthscan.
Vail, Leroy and Landeg White
    1980   *Capitalism and Colonialism in Mozambique.* London: Heinemann.
Vines, Alex
    1991   *Renamo: Terrorism in Mozambique.* Bloomington: Indiana University
              Press.
Warren, Kay
    1993   *The Violence Within: Cultural and Political Opposition in Divided Nations.*
              Boulder, Colo.: Westview Press.
Watts, Michael
    1992   Space for Everything (A Commentary). *Cultural Anthropology* 7(1):
              115–29.
West, Cornel
    1992   A Matter of Life and Death. *October* 61 (Summer): 20–23.
White, Eduardo
    nd.   Vozes do sangue: a Criança e a guerra em Moçambique. Maputo:
              ASDI/UNICEF.
Wilson, Ken
    1992   Cults of Violence and Counter-Violence in Mozambique. *Journal of
              Southern African Studies* 18(3):527–82.
World Health Organization
    1990   WHO/Mozambique Cooperation. Organização Mundial da Saude
              Representação em Mocambique, Maputo, March.
Wright, Sam
    1978   *Crowds and Riots.* Beverly Hills, Calif.: Sage Publications.
Zulaika, Joseba
    1991   *Basque Violence: Metaphor and Sacrament.* Reno: University of Nevada
              Press.

    1995   The Anthropologist as Terrorist. In *Fieldwork Under Fire: Contem-
              porary Studies in Violence and Survival,* ed. Carolyn Nordstrom and
              Antonius C. G. M. Robben. Berkeley: University of California Press.

Index